THE
THERAPEUTIC
NARRATIVE

THE
THERAPEUTIC
NARRATIVE

Fictional Relationships
and the Process
of Psychological Change

Barbara Almond
and
Richard Almond

Westport, Connecticut
London

Library of Congress Cataloging-in-Publication Data

Almond, Barbara.
 The therapeutic narrative : fictional relationships and the
process of psychological change / Barbara Almond, Richard Almond.
  p. cm.
 Includes bibliographical references and index.
 ISBN 0–275–95362–9. — ISBN 0–275–95579–6 (pbk.)
 1. Psychoanalysis and literature. 2. Literature—Psychological
aspects. I. Almond, Richard. II. Title.
PN56.P92A47 1996
809.3′9353—dc20   96–550

British Library Cataloguing in Publication Data is available.

Library of Congress Catalog Card Number: 96–550
ISBN: 0–275–95362–9
  0–275–95579–6 (pbk.)

First published in 1996

Praeger Publishers, 88 Post Road West, Westport, CT 06881
An imprint of Greenwood Publishing Group, Inc.

Printed in the United States of America

The paper used in this book complies with the
Permanent Paper Standard issued by the National
Information Standards Organization (Z39.48–1984).

10 9 8 7 6 5 4 3 2 1

To our children

David, Michael, and Steven Almond

and the memory of

Anne and Irving Rosenthal

CONTENTS

PREFACE

Literature and psychoanalysis have had a long association. Freud used myth, drama, novel, art, and sculpture as subjects and sources. Similarly, novelists before and after Freud have been observers of the complexity of the human psyche. The psychoanalyst is a student of the human imagination, the novelist an observer of the human condition. Recently, these two disciplines have been linked by their recognition of the important role of narrative in individual and group life. Literature has always provided stories, but the concept of narrative is now being applied to understanding how individuals structure their experiences and self-concepts. Someone who views himself or herself as a victim will emphasize those aspects of personal history that support a picture of victimization, and will interpret new experiences as exploitative. Narratives are also part of cultural life; a given social group defines itself through a particular set of narratives that have special importance.

In this volume we are seeking to demonstrate the presence of what we call the *therapeutic* narrative in both psychotherapy and literature. We argue that psychotherapy is a "special case" of a kind of relationship that may occur more widely, in real relationships and in fiction. We suggest that the therapeutic narrative is one of the powerful stories that novelists in the nineteenth and twentieth centuries use to engage their readers.

This study developed out of the combined interests of its two authors: a love of literature and curiosity about what makes it psychologically appealing, and an interest in the process of change in therapeutic situations. While immersed in trying to understand the mechanisms of change in psychoanalytic treatment, Richard Almond reread

Pride and Prejudice, a favorite novel; as he did so, he began to think about the relationship between Elizabeth and Darcy in a new way—in terms of developmental processes and changes in character propelled by transference-like involvements between two people. At the same time, Barbara Almond came to understand her puzzling affinity for a contemporary novel, Margaret Drabble's *The Needle's Eye.* On one level, this novel depicted the fate of an eccentric and masochistic heroine—a woman who, in the psychiatric office, would fill one with clinical concern. An alternate reading revealed how a *second* character in the novel was able—through his interactions with this woman—to make changes leading to the reinvestment of his personal ideals and the relief of his chronic depression. This reading explained the emotional appeal of the story much more satisfactorily. These two examples of "healing" in novels provided an impetus for us to look at many other works with the idea that some sort of cure takes place through the agency of a meaningful relationship.

These first two "case studies" came to us serendipitously, but led to a search for other literary instances. We found ourselves discovering new examples as we read, talked to friends, watched television, and went to movies. Excellent BBC productions of *Silas Marner* and *Jane Eyre,* and the film version of *The Accidental Tourist,* for instance, brought home the interaction patterns of the original novels. Memories of childhood favorites led us to reread a number of these books with the discovery of several fascinating cases and variants. Colleagues and friends brought other examples to our attention. We finally settled on nine novels, all familiar classics or recent, relatively well known novels, which were chosen because the curative element plays a significant role in the central action of the story. This book explores the idea that such literary transformations bear a resemblance to the process of change in psychoanalytic therapy, and that the study of these resemblances is illuminating from both the literary and psychoanalytic standpoint.

We should clarify at the outset that we are not looking at books about psychotherapy like *August* (Judith Rossner) or *I Never Promised You a Rose Garden* (Hannah Green), or the nonfictional *Love's Executioner* (Irvin Yalom). Rather, we are looking at novels that deal with the development of personality and the working out of certain psychological problems. Although biography, drama, and cinema would certainly provide rich examples, we have chosen to limit our study to novels alone. This avoids the difficulty of comparing different media.

We are aware that the novels we discuss are all from the delimited cultural sphere of Western, nineteenth- and twentieth-century letters and are almost all written in English. Furthermore, the characters in these novels are white and largely middle class. Naturally, thorough and abundant examples of therapeutic outcomes can be found in the literature of other cultures, or in the depiction of other classes—*The Magic Mountain* (Thomas Mann), *War and Peace* (Leo Tolstoy), and Zora Neale Hurston's *Their Eyes Were Watching God*, for instance. These nine novels were chosen because they illustrate the central phenomenon we wish to demonstrate—how change can come about through an interactive process. Many novels deal with change, sometimes for the better—in which case we call them comedies or romances—and sometimes for the worse—in which case we call them tragedies. But this change does not always come about through the medium of a relationship between characters. Life experiences of all sorts can create the conditions for change, too. Furthermore, even when characters are clearly affected by each other, it may not be possible to discover, within the novel's narrative, *how* that change occurs. With this in mind, the novels we have chosen for study have these characteristics: the central characters become involved in a relationship with each other, and this relationship leads to change in one or more of them through a process that can be discovered and described from the text of the novel.

ACKNOWLEDGMENTS

We have had guidance, editorial help, encouragement, and inspiration from many friends and colleagues. Linda Weingarten, a skilled editor and dear friend edited several chapters and provided invaluable encouragement. We regret that she died while the manuscript was still being completed. Diane Middlebrook of the Stanford Department of English encouraged our project from the beginning, and contributed careful reading of many chapters. She aided further as a co-teacher and discussant in a number of settings where the ideas were presented. The members of the Palo Alto Writers Group—Nannette Auerhahn, Susan Beletsis, Norman Dishotsky, Karen Johnson, Randall Weingarten, Emily Lyon, David Lake, Robert Harris, Deborah Rose, Alan Sklar, Harvey Weinstein, and Marequita West—read and commented extensively on several chapters in early drafts. Irvin Yalom of the Stanford Department of Psychiatry also gave us a critical reading of several chapters. Jerome Oremland contributed both close editorial reading and encouragement early in the project. Roy Schafer was particularly helpful in his reading of the *Jane Eyre* chapter as was Burton Melnick in his reading of *Pride and Prejudice*. Other members of the San Francisco Psychoanalytic Institute read and commented helpfully on one or more chapters: Owen Renik, Stanley Goodman, Alan Skolnikoff, James Dimon, Steven Goldberg, Katherine MacVicar, William Hamill, and Michael Zimmerman. The members of the Writing and Psychoanalysis Colloquium at Stanford University read several sections of the manuscript with valuable contributions from Robert Polhemus, Carolyn Grassi, Anna Holmboe, Barbara Gelpi, Thomas Moser, Jean Wildberg, Michael Horne, and Margo Horn. Our thanks to Stanley Coen for inviting us to participate in the

Colloquium on Psychoanalysis and Literary Criticism at the American Psychoanalytic Association's meeting in New York. Albert Solnit, Jerome Winer, and Morton Kaplan aided us in their capacity as editors of the publications in which some of these chapters first appeared. Finally, our heartfelt thanks for their comments and encouragement over the past several years to Stuart Hauser, Alice Rosenthal, Genevieve Dishotsky, Karin Bricker, Robert Hessen, and the late Beatrice Hessen.

THE
THERAPEUTIC
NARRATIVE

1

INTRODUCTION

The following introductory sections set the stage for discussions of specific novels. In the first section we illustrate the parallel we feel exists between life and literature. We begin with the moment in a novel that first alerted us to the idea of therapeutic narrative—the point in Jane Austen's *Pride and Prejudice* when the heroine experiences a painful moment of truth—a letter from her suitor exposes some of her self-deceptions and biases. We argue that the underlying conflict that is revealed at this moment is a universal one: the internal incestuous meaning of first serious adult attachments. Guilt and anxiety stemming from this meaning have led the heroine to deny her attraction. Recognition of her feelings, and the aspects of herself that she has used to avoid them, make this moment a turning point in the romantic plot.

We set alongside the fictional Elizabeth Bennet a real-life psychotherapy case, also of a young woman conflicted about intimacy. A similar crisis arises when she experiences an upsurge of anxiety around an increase in the intensity of treatment from once-a-week psychotherapy to four-times-a-week psychoanalysis. This panic leads her to return to a weekly format, but stimulates her self-examination of the issues that make her anxious about intimacy. As with the fictional character, the processing of the anxiety *in an activated form in relation to an important person* provides an impetus for an internal change that facilitates her capacity for closeness.

In the second section we look at the historical emergence of the novel at the beginning of the nineteenth century, and of psychoanalysis at its end. We suggest that this sequence is not accidental. Novelists (perhaps we should say artists, or narrators) are in a position to observe and even guide new cultural evolutions. We discuss why the therapeutic narrative became an important element in many modern novels, and how this same story became structured in a social/ professional relationship in psychoanalysis.

The third introductory section contains a description of therapeutic process as it is generally thought of from a psychoanalytic point of view. This framework has two purposes: it will allow us to see, specifically, similarities between psychoanalysis (or other psychotherapies) and our literary "cases," and it forms a background for the fourth section, which proposes our own schema for psychological change, the *therapeutic narrative*. There we suggest three aspects of the narrative of change—*engagement, mutual influence,* and *directionality.* We begin an examination of this narrative's substructure that will be continued throughout the entire volume. That is, what are the specific requirements and interactional patterns in each of these elements? We end the introduction with a discussion of some of the salient differences between literary and therapeutic narratives.

A PARALLEL

"Til this moment I never knew myself." This statement appears midway through Jane Austen's *Pride and Prejudice.* We came upon it when we were just beginning to think about novels and therapeutic process. Elizabeth Bennet, the heroine, has had a startling revelation, one that alters her view of several other characters, and, in turn, of herself. The sentence struck us because it refers to insight—knowing one's self—a primary goal in the psychoanalytic theory of change. We were not, at that time, reading *Pride and Prejudice* in search of therapeutic processes, but here was an illustration—in another medium —of a central feature of psychoanalysis.

Elizabeth's insight occurs at a moment of emotional intensity, and in relation to the person who is the focus of that intensity. Again, this combination is a central aspect of the psychoanalytic situation, technically referred to as "working in the transference." We were intrigued with the parallel, and began to examine this moment of the novel, and eventually all of *Pride and Prejudice,* with the psychoanalytic model of change in mind. Specifically, we became interested in the idea that there may be a pattern—a narrative—that structures how personal change occurs within a relationship.

First, we asked, what is the immediate context of Elizabeth Bennet's moment of self-revelation? The evening before, Elizabeth received an unexpected marriage proposal from Darcy, a wealthy, handsome, and proud young man who has shown an enigmatic interest in her. Despite the many advantages of a marriage to Darcy, Elizabeth turns him down. Her feelings toward Darcy—her conscious feelings— are far from friendly. At their first meeting, during a ball some months before, he had snubbed her. He had subsequently interfered in a budding relationship between her sister, Jane, and his own friend, Bingley. Elizabeth's "prejudice" against Darcy is abetted further by the complaints of another new acquaintance, George Wickham. A charming army officer, Wickham flirts with Elizabeth, and when she complains about Darcy, produces his own list of grievances against the man, grievances that sound convincing and serious.

In rejecting Darcy's proposal, Elizabeth berates him for these injuries to herself, to her family, and to Wickham. Darcy is so surprised and wounded at being refused that he departs in anger, without addressing Elizabeth's complaints. Elizabeth is left feeling angry and self-righteous, but also flattered and disturbed.

The next morning Darcy meets Elizabeth on her accustomed walk and hands her a letter explaining his side of things. Yes, he did interfere in Bingley's romance with Jane—he perceived that Jane was not deeply involved, and her motives, therefore, were questionable. This information adds to Elizabeth's resentment, for she knows how deeply the loss of Bingley has affected Jane. But the devastating revelation in Darcy's letter is that Wickham is a wastrel and gambler, who, the previous summer, had come close to seducing Darcy's fifteen-year-old sister into an elopement. Elizabeth, initially incredulous, realizes as she pores over Darcy's letter that he *must* be telling the truth—he offers as a corroborating witness a man whom Elizabeth trusts. If she has been wrong about George Wickham, she may have been wrong about Darcy too! She realizes—in a sudden moment of self-scrutiny—that it has been her own need to misunderstand the situation that has led her into these faulty judgments.

She grew absolutely ashamed of herself. Of neither Darcy nor Wickham could she think without feeling that she had been blind, partial, prejudiced, absurd.

"How despicably have I acted!" she cried; "I, who have prided myself on my discernment! I, who have valued myself on my abilities! who have often disdained the generous candor of my sister, and gratified my vanity in useless or blamable distrust. How humiliating is this discovery! yet, how just a humiliation! Had I been in love, I could not have been more wretchedly blind. But vanity, not love, has been my folly. Pleased with the preference of one, and offended by the neglect of the other, on the very beginning of our acquaintance, I have courted prepossession and ignorance, and driven reason away, where either were concerned. *Til this moment I never knew myself.*" (p. 229; emphasis added)

Once we had begun reading with an eye for the therapeutic, this passage had special significance. Elizabeth moves from a concern about her misjudgments of these two men to a concern about her judgment in general. A trait she valued highly in herself—"discernment"—turns out to be biased by "vanity." As we shall describe in detail in Chapter 2, Elizabeth is the child closest to her father, a man who uses cynicism and detachment to deal with his own limitations and his feelings about others. What Elizabeth recognizes is not simply her tendency to judge people, based on vanity, but also her identification with and attachment to her father. What is at the center of this literary moment is the combination of impulse, defense, and self-awareness, which is also at the center of a psychoanalytic moment of conflict and insight.

Four pages earlier, as Elizabeth is in the midst of her recognition about Darcy and Wickham, Jane Austen writes: "Astonishment, apprehension, and even horror, oppressed her." Why "apprehension" and "horror?" Why not simply "embarrassment" or "chagrin?" As psychoanalysts we would say that in Elizabeth's case these powerful feelings have to do with the sudden breakthrough of a disturbing understanding, a thought that is forbidden and therefore frightening. Since humans have an immense capacity for symbolization, Elizabeth does not need to think directly about sexual feelings toward her father to become anxious—her sudden discovery of a trait that *bonds* her to her father could be sufficient to represent an incestuous idea, and stimulate the intense feelings.

In human development, the child must learn ways of preventing dangerous, anxiety-provoking ideas from reaching consciousness. We call these ways defense mechanisms; each individual builds them into his or her character in a particular form. Often a dominant character defense serves both to protect and to express, in a disguised form, fended-off impulses. For example, Elizabeth's teasing, bantering, mildly cynical style is her way of being close to her father (impulse), of devaluing her mother (also impulse), and of telling herself she is really not involved seriously with the attractions and vulnerabilities of adult courtship (defense). This protects her from thoughts about love, intimacy, and sexuality, which at twenty—Elizabeth's age—are still imbued with incestuous significance. Elizabeth's relationship with Darcy threatens her defenses, but her disdain allows her to reject his proposal. When, in reading his letter, she discovers that her defense is misguided, and therefore open to question, forbidden thoughts suddenly press toward consciousness, and therefore "astonishment, and horror."

Let us illustrate how these same issues can emerge in a real-life situation.

Ms L was in her mid-twenties when she first came to see one of us (RA) for treatment. She came with concerns about her inability to follow through. In her work she would begin jobs and projects with eagerness and success, but would then lose interest, and have to force herself to complete them under the pressure of deadlines. It was notable that of all the siblings in Ms L's large family only she had entered her father's field. In her intimate life, she had formed close attachments twice, but after a year or two had decided to discontinue each relationship. When she came to see me, she voiced concern about repeating the same pattern in her important new job, and in her relationship with her current boyfriend. I recommended psychoanalysis as the most effective treatment for such recurrent patterns, but suggested that we begin with weekly therapy to explore some of her reservations.

In her first visits Ms L appeared as a pleasant young person, somewhat androgenous in appearance and manner. As our weekly sessions continued, her dress and appearance altered; she transformed herself into an attractive, feminine woman. At the same time, she began to voice greater resistance to the idea of analysis: money was suddenly a worry, even after we negotiated a fee that would fit her budget. She also began to talk about triangles in her love life. She was with one man, but another was interesting, too. Her attractiveness was not limited to therapy hours; many men seemed to become interested in her, but in each instance she played one off against the other in her mind and sometimes in reality. I was learning firsthand about Ms L's difficulty with commitment.

After several months and no decision about analysis, I raised the issue once more, pointing out that she was repeating her stated difficulty: she was not carrying through on a "project" she had begun. Ms L immediately agreed to begin psychoanalysis, but, two weeks later, when the first of the four-times-a-week sessions arrived, she was so anxious she did not want to try the couch. After a week she was comfortable enough to do so, but her ambivalence continued.

During the first weeks of psychoanalysis, Ms L's discussion of everyday concerns and her unease with treatment were mixed in with the first reports of dreams. In the third week she reported a dream in which she and I were at a remote beach. In the dream this idea did not seem unusual to her. She was feeling very warm and close to me. She awoke with the feeling she adored me, but then realized her feelings toward me were more complex; she was uncertain and mistrustful about men. She wished she were not so ambivalent.

Over the next weeks Ms L became increasingly uneasy being in analysis. She had another striking dream, one she found very embarrassing to tell. In the first part of the dream she was sitting on the toilet with diarrhea when her father walked in. In the second part of the dream her mother and a female cousin were crying about something her father had done. I interpreted to her that she was concerned about the analysis, where she probably felt she was "letting go" in an embarrassing way. While rationally she knew that analysis was all right, subjectively she felt guilty about doing something wrong, something associated with hurting other women.

Despite my attempts to help her understand her unease, a week later Ms L decided to stop the analysis. I acknowledged that she was very uneasy about something, and indicated that her need to flee would, if acted on, foreclose any understanding of her fears. She agreed to resume weekly, face-to-face psychotherapy. We continued for four months before she left the area to live near her boyfriend to whom she had now become engaged. (External progress often occurs while issues are being struggled with in the treatment situation.) During this part of the treatment my primary focus was to help her understand her uneasiness with *having*, including having a satisfying relationship with a man that would lead to marriage, having career success, or having therapy. The benefits of this understanding showed up in her decision to become engaged. She also took a leave of absence from work to do a project about which she was enthusiastic, a project that also allowed her to move to the geographic region where her fiancé lived.

During these four months of therapy, Ms L spoke more about her mother, a competent woman who was unable to finish projects that would bring attention to herself. Mother was far more effective at helping father and the children, or participating in social causes. The analytic period of the therapy became a useful reference point for both of us in acknowledging how uncomfortable Ms L was with having special things for herself, and thus having what her mother was unable to let herself have. Despite her flight from the more intense treatment, I felt some important steps had occurred.

A year later, Ms L returned, now living with her fianceé and back at her old job. She resumed weekly therapy, and continued to work on her discomfort having things. During this year she married, and launched a new, more ambitious phase of professional work with much less ambivalence than before.

Ms L's issues were very much like those of Elizabeth Bennet. She was, in her own experience of the family, the child closest to her father. While she admired and loved her mother, she saw her as blocked psychologically from personal success. So, for Ms L, doing well at work meant surpassing her mother, and being close to her father. Being feminine, and intimate with a man, created tensions about submitting to the man's importance, and effacing her own. Early in her treatment Ms L plunged into closeness with me, reenacting her wish to be close to an older man, bypassing both her guilt about this and her problematic identification with her mother. And, as with Elizabeth Bennet, this closeness led first to flight and then to insight. That is, we were able to recognize that the problem with being in analysis was that its subjective meaning had to do with being too important. "Too important" meant a special closeness with a fatherlike therapist, willing to let her come for frequent visits, use the couch, and talk as much as she wanted. The more "primitive" (unconscious) meanings of these aspects of analysis for Ms L were conveyed by the vivid imagery of her dreams, where being in analysis was equated with performing the most intimate functions in front of father. This thread—the danger of being too important—was continued in the post-analytic therapy. Ms L's gradual mastery of the conflicts this issue represented was facilitated by her relationship with her therapist, with whom she experienced a replay of her feelings toward her father. The therapist's nonshaming acceptance of her feelings and careful interpretation of their meanings allowed Ms L to modify her avoidant and self-defeating behaviors. The mastery of these conflicts, much of which took place in the second phase of psychotherapy, formed the basis for a number of life-decisions in the direction of effective action—both at work and in her intimate relationships.

The passage from *Pride and Prejudice* and this sketch of a treatment illustrate a parallel situation in life and literature.[1] For both Elizabeth Bennet and Ms L, change, in the direction of progress with the tasks of early adulthood, occurs around a sudden "horrifying" encounter with heterosexual intimacy, and defenses against its deeper significance. For both women an important relationship is the medium in which the change occurs. It is this *kind* of parallel that we shall develop in this volume. We believe that the discovery of similar experiences in our reading and in our therapy is no accident, that cure—in the sense of inner alterations that improve life for oneself and others—occurs through universal capacities for involvement and transformation. Great authors like Jane Austen capture these processes with an intuitive understanding of human psychology. They have much to tell us about how people change.

THE EMERGENCE OF THE NOVEL AND PSYCHOANALYSIS

Both the novel and psychoanalysis developed in the nineteenth century, one close to its beginning, the other at its end. We believe these two seemingly unrelated forms of human activity are connected in a significant way: both reflect the rise of an interest in individual consciousness and experience, and the translation of that interest into narrative. The *novel* describes the experience of one or more central characters. Literature, formerly the province of religion, philosophy, history, and formalized storytelling, now became, in the novel, an evocation of how people actually feel and act in the circumstances of "real" (though imagined) lives. Readers could imagine themselves as characters, and could both identify with them and think about how their own lives would look in print. *Psychoanalysis* lives out this fantasy: the patient tells his or her life story—both retrospectively and as it is currently experienced—to an audience of one. One current school of clinical theory is even based on this idea: that the patient tells and enacts a narrative with the therapist.[2] This story is commented on by the therapist, especially its gaps and illogical elements. The narrative is then added to by the patient, ultimately producing a richer set of narrative lines, resulting in a larger variety of options for action.

Psychoanalysis, of course, did not originate as an opportunity for autobiography, but as a therapy for serious hysterical disorders (the hopeless neurotic cases of Viennese neurological practice in the 1880s). Despite a variety of challenges to Freud's theories of mind, psychoanalysis has continued to be a widely practiced treatment available to those with a special interest in self-knowledge. The therapies that psychoanalysis has spawned have become increasingly acceptable. This popularity reflects not only a growing recognition of the value of treatment, but a widening of the population who feel that the subjective, the personal experience of life is important. A significant portion of society now believes that at crucial and stressful phases of one's life, it is worthwhile to talk to a therapist about oneself and one's experience. The therapeutic narrative is part of our modern, "post-Freudian" culture.

The original impetus for the introspective quest at the core of psychoanalysis and the novel came from a larger cultural shift that made the individual and subjective experience more important. This shift deprived people of convincing external definitions of who they were. The Enlightenment—a broad cultural movement associated politically with the American and French revolutions, and intellectually with new concepts of the role of the individual in society—resulted in a gain in freedom and opportunity. It also led to the gradual weakening of a great many meaning systems that previously had structured psychological life: religious belief, rigid social class lines, and well-defined occupational roles. These meaning systems had provided significant answers to questions such as: "Who am I in my immediate social world?" "What is my status in comparison to those around me?" "What do I value most highly?"

Change also was occurring in people's personal lives, the area where these central questions must be worked out on a daily basis. The family, and the concept of the individual, entered a revolutionary phase. Where once the family had been primarily an *economic* unit, it now became increasingly a focus of *sentiment*. Motherly love and nurture, paternal pride and training, family bonds—all these existed before the modern era but they had played a subsidiary role in regard to questions of personal identity. In the context of urbanization, industrialization, and the related new set of attitudes of the nineteenth century, the family—its individual members, and the quality of its relationships—became increasingly significant. For centuries parenthood had been an inevitable, often onerous, duty whose primary benefits were reaped only when offspring could participate productively in family and community life. Now mothering and fathering became active, concerned roles, and the focus of these roles, the child, became special. The "nuclear family" emerged, not only in the structural sense of a two-generation living unit, physically or psychologically separate from extended family, but also in the sense that within this group the most significant feelings, bonds, and intimate experiences of life were expected to occur. Previously, such feelings were dispersed more widely among the extended family, the community, members of the nobility, and, in Christianity, toward the major religious figures—God, Mary, and the Christ-child, and the local representatives of the church, priests and ministers.

A precedent existed for transposing such dispersed, abstract relations to a real relationship: the ideal of romantic love. In the Middle Ages, the chivalric tradition secularized worship of the Virgin Mary into an idealizing adoration of a real, but usually inaccessible, woman. Tristan and Iseult, Lancelot and Guinevere were the paradigms. Chivalric romantic love remained far removed from everyday life. Until the period that concerns us, actual relating based on romantic love was an aberrance, a symptom of social deviance, or a tragedy (as in *Romeo and Juliet*, or the Tristan story).[3] In the transformation that occurred around the beginning of the nineteenth century, these intense, idealized relationships became part of the expectations of actual relating in family life. This change began with the investment of the child and childhood with new significance. In the upper classes, initially, nurture and education became too important to "farm out" to wet nurses, tutors, schools, and other families. The ideology that accompanied this change made every child a Christ-child and every mother a Mary (or, perhaps more accurately, a Juliet). Fathers became involved, protective figures, connecting the family to the outside world and providing for it. Fathers also acquired—as inner fantasy figures—many of the attributes formerly ascribed to the nobility, the king, or God.

In other words, the nuclear family, as we have come to call it, became a highly emotionally invested social group. The importance of relations within the family led people to think more about themselves as intimates. Children grew up increasingly aware of their importance to parents and of their parents' importance to them. It was only a step from this family intimacy to an interest in feelings and personal experiences in general. This more complex version of relatedness created new difficulties. People needed to understand how to interpret this greater emphasis on the subjective in themselves and those closest to them. Just as religion had struggled with the conflict between a Judeo-Christian ideal and the harsh realities of everyday life, these new attitudes and expectations brought out conflicts between idealized images and real relationships. We are not, of course, arguing that there were no subjective feelings or awarenesses of others' feelings before the nineteenth century. Our point is that these became of *general concern* for a whole class of society—the emerging bourgeoisie—rather than the expression of a few sensitive poets and dramatists.

Here we come back to the central theme of this book. The newly defined individual inherited responsibilities along with an enhanced scope of experience. Obligation, guilt, shame, and conflict were shifted from formal relations mediated by social institutions to the arena of intrapsychic and interpersonal life. Although people always had had feelings, consciences, ideals, and values, these tended to be defined externally, and one's personal solutions were worked out privately and unselfconsciously. Often God, fate, or a deterministic personal ideal of character could be held responsible for the variations of personality and its consequences. Now the decisions, attitudes, and social behavior of daily life became the responsibility of the individual.

The Emergence of the Novel

In the midst of this historically determined, changing psychological situation, the novel began to emerge as a new literary form. In its beginnings the novel retained some of the moralizing qualities of earlier literature, of sermons or philosophical writing (Bunyan's *Pilgrim's Progress*, for example). These qualities changed as writers sought to express and answer the everyday questions people were facing (Fielding's *Joseph Andrews*, for example). Instead of a didactic tone, the novelist adopted a tone of feigned autobiography or naturalistic observation in a voice that said "here is a life story." Since the "morals" to be drawn now had to fit the particular situation of each individual, the author did not attempt to draw conclusions, but left the task of application to the reader.

In one respect, the subject matter of the novel was not new. Stories that weave the various aspects of the human condition into meaningful patterns within a particular culture are universal. The Old Testament, the Homeric epics, Shakespeare's plays—all deal with the significant themes and motives of humankind, and with a person's relation to other people, to belief, and to the Deity. To the extent that these epics and dramas deal with one figure—Odysseus or Hamlet, for example— the interest in one person's experience is centuries old. But the perspective is mythic—both formalized and external. Although the muse in Homer sings of wily Odysseus or of the wrath of Achilles (the *Odyssey* and the *Iliad* are very much stories of human envy, love, and pride), the feelings described are elevated to a static and universal status. Similarly, the *Bildungsroman* (or tale of development) in German literature describes the course of a man's life, beginning with his birth and childhood and carrying through into adulthood, again in a stylized form. Such epics mirrored life's experiences in a stereotypic way, although written in a more realistic manner.

In the novel, the subject matter of earlier literature continued, with a new twist—the universal could be explored in infinite variety by writing about individualized characters. The uniqueness of characters' personalities and interactions began to shape the plot. Rather than static representations of the solutions to life's questions, the novel presented many variations.

We have, then, in the nineteenth century, a time in which old solutions were weakened just when individuals were confronted with increasing possibilities for personal transformation and development. Concerns about adapting to change found fewer answers in traditional sources. The novel provided acceptable illustrative examples to help with this need. On the one hand, it was revolutionary: it suggested that every life and everyday life were meaningful, and thus, that whoever lived that life had an individual validity. On the other hand, the novel did not have the revolutionary potential of a political tract. Like psychoanalysis, which emerged as a formal technique at the end of the nineteenth century, the novel was more like a mirror held up to the reader, offering a reflection of oneself in the form of a story about others.

The Rise of Psychoanalysis

Although the "invention" of psychoanalysis was Freud's, it is difficult to imagine that its emergence was dependent on the genius of one individual. Like the discoveries of Darwin and Einstein, Freud's recognition of unconscious life, and of the benefits of a "talking cure" now seem an inevitable part of modern life. The challenges of the Enlightenment had been followed by the constrictions of mid-nineteenth-century Victorianism. But new questions were still in the air, and medicine was an authority that had the legitimacy to propose solutions.

Freud was broadly educated, not only in medical science, but also in classical and contemporary literature and philosophy. His writing is richly sprinkled with literary examples. Although he presented his theories as medical and scientific, drawn logically from clinical inference, Freud was, in fact, creating new models to explain human subjectivity, and experimenting in the ways a relationship could be used to ameliorate personal problems. These creations were made possible by the same social changes that led to the rise of the novel. The greater importance of individual experience made its study in the psychoanalytic situation legitimate. At a time when there was a need for guidance in the difficult questions of life, the answers of traditional medicine were as limited as those of the Church, or the old social order. Freud's psychoanalysis took the challenge in hand, saying, in effect, "The answer is in yourself; talk to me and I will help you discover it." In the next section we will describe the special relationship that is psychoanalysis, and how it evolved in the twentieth century.

HOW DOES PSYCHOTHERAPEUTIC CHANGE COME ABOUT?

It may surprise the lay reader to learn that we do not know for certain how people change in psychoanalysis or psychotherapy. The situation is this: Freud and those who followed him—both analysts and nonanalytic psychotherapists—have tended to begin with two elements, a theory of how the mind works (a "metapsychology") and a technique of interaction with the patient (a "clinical theory"). Clinical technique, in principle, would develop out of metapsychology. But, as in much of medicine, the reverse happens. Clinical technique develops empirically, for the most part. It is "what works." After observing change in the clinical situation, theorists develop or modify models of the mind to include these new observations.

Freud's first theory of treatment followed from his observation that patients improved as a result of being encouraged, first in hypnotic trance, later simply by instruction, to say what came to mind—*free association*. What emerged, in Freud's early patients, were sexual secrets—stories of actual parental abuse or reports of patients' fantasies and wishes. Awareness of these powerful experiences and fantasies allowed a discharge of the associated feelings—*abreaction*. This cathartic theory of cure has been superseded by others, but it still plays a role in treatment, and in the thinking of patients and therapists. The everyday version of this idea is expressed as "Get it out of your system!"

Freud found that the treatment situation he had developed—the technique of free association, with the patient recumbent on a couch—produced effects that were more complex than he initially thought.[4] First, he observed that despite clear instructions to free associate (report whatever comes to mind), every patient tried to hide, omit, or alter certain thoughts. This "resistance" was the effort of the psyche to keep distressing, frightening, or shameful ideas out of consciousness, and out of the analyst's awareness. This led to a new aspect of technique, the *analysis of resistance.*

Freud also found that in the analytic situation the patient began to experience powerful feelings about the analyst. While these feelings seemed, at first, to be primarily an interference or resistance to the pursuit of the patient's unconscious ideas, Freud recognized that they had a greater significance. The feelings and meanings that his patients attributed to him and the analytic relationship were not simply a reaction to the real patient-doctor relationship, but were "transferred" from other, older relationships. Furthermore, there seemed to be something about the psychoanalytic situation that promoted these "transferred" feelings.

The observation of transference led to a second phase of psychoanalytic clinical theory, in which the *analysis of transference* became the centerpiece of the process. If old relationships were inscribed in the psyche, and could become reactivated during analysis, an opportunity existed to rework the internalized childhood experiences that had led to maladaptations. Even in the healthiest environment, the child has a limited capacity to comprehend and master the powerful desires, disappointments, and frustrations of early life. Thus, even those children with the best family experience would develop neurotic conflicts. In the psychoanalytic situation, where these early experiences become reactivated, the adult could find better solutions.

In the 1920s and 1930s Freud and other analysts began to observe that problems did not always yield to approaches based on the uncovering of unconscious impulses, whether in direct form or through analysis of the transference.[5] Many symptoms were now found to be not so much the result of repressed or transformed wishes as attempts by the psyche to control impulses or massive bursts of anxiety. Attention began to focus on the extensive and complex forms of adaptation that begin to develop almost from birth in the ego—the executive portion of the psyche. Personality is formed through the choice of certain "defense mechanisms" that the individual relies upon for the management of inner life.

Clinically, this *ego psychology* phase of psychoanalytic thinking is still the dominant model of mainstream American psychoanalysis. In the treatment situation, transference is now seen as the emergence of significant conflictual issues. The patient is constantly trying to maintain a balance between, on the one hand, the opportunity the analytic situation presents for the gratification of repressed wishes, and, on the other hand, the defenses against these wishes. Any particular action by the patient is a complex compromise made by the ego between wish and defense. The analyst tries to make the patient more aware of how his or her mind is working. Clinical theory now emphasizes mastery: the more a person knows about how his or her mind works, the better he or she will be able to choose actions that are adaptive. Transference remains important in this model, because the most powerful learning occurs when the object of one's intense feelings is present in the room. One of the justifications for the frequency of psychoanalytic sessions is that this is necessary for the development of the "transference neurosis," a condition in which the patient has projected on the analytic situation not only a significant figure from the past, but also his or her most central psychological issues.

The duration of psychoanalytic treatment follows from the same premise: neurotic conflicts and their old solutions are so powerfully embedded in the psyche that it takes many repetitions and rediscoveries to enable the patient to learn about and eventually change ways of thinking and acting. Freud called this repeated processing *working through*. We have all observed the tendency in ourselves and our intimates to repeat unnecessary patterns. In analysis, each repetition can be examined and interpreted to the patient as it is played out in the transference and in external life. Psychoanalysis has also moved beyond the idea that intellectual understanding of unconscious ideas is curative in itself to an appreciation that it is understanding, coupled with a state of aroused affect and the presence of the analyst, that is the crucial aspect of insight.

In the last two decades clinical thinking has shifted its emphasis in another important direction. We no longer view the patient as the sole focus of treatment; the unit of observation has become the therapeutic dyad—patient and therapist—and their interplay.[6] "Countertransference," the therapist's emotional reactions to the patient, was once viewed as a problem to be dealt with by the therapist elsewhere—in his or her own treatment, or self-analysis. Now countertransference is seen as an important source of information about what is going on in the patient and between patient and therapist, and, in some clinical theories, is considered central to the change process. This view will fit our literary examples well, since characters in our novels are not psychotherapists, but have been given their own motivations by the authors.

In what follows we will refer at some times to psychoanalysis and at other times to psychotherapy. Although the boundaries between these techniques are not crystal clear, some definitions are in order. Psychoanalysis involves frequent sessions, four or five hours a week, and the use of the couch. The patient agrees to the "fundamental rule" of free association—to try to report every thought that comes to mind. Thus, the process of psychoanalysis is more like a monologue or reverie, with occasional commentary on the part of the analyst. He or she intervenes to clarify the patient's statements, point out resistances to free association, observe transference, behaviors and feelings, and interpret links between past and present. The analyst, though a less actively give-and-take participant, is nevertheless, in a quiet way, emotionally involved in the psychoanalytic relationship.

Psychotherapy is a broad, generic term that includes psychoanalysis as one particular subtype. The term psychotherapy usually refers to treatments that take place once or twice a week, sometimes more often. The patient and the therapist sit facing one another, or with chairs at an angle. The process has a broad range of variability. In psychoanalytic (also called "dynamic" or "expressive") psychotherapy, the approach is much like that of analysis, although the therapist may be more active in proposing ideas, in giving support, and in voicing empathy. At the other extreme are supportive psychotherapies in which the therapist is much more active, questioning, guiding, instructing, and counseling. In between these two are therapies in which the transference processes that develop are used by the patient or therapist for more specific purposes. This is frequently the case, for example, in crisis-oriented psychotherapy, where the transference basis of the relationship is not interpreted, but is used by both parties to quickly create an atmosphere of supportive trust in the interest of the patient's mastery of an immediate problem.

Because the clinical theories of psychoanalysis are the most extensively developed, we will frequently be using them for comparative purposes. When we come to talk about specific patterns in specific novels we will indicate whether we are referring to psychoanalytic or psychotherapeutic techniques.

THE THERAPEUTIC NARRATIVE

Valuable as it is in the psychotherapeutic situation, clinical vocabulary leaves us with certain problems when we try to apply it to literature. First, it is a language based in significant part on *a priori* theory. That is, it predicts in advance that certain events will occur, and that organizing them in a certain manner will make sense of the process. If it were the case that things are this predictable, we would expect to find agreement among analysts when looking at a particular case, or when discussing process in general. In fact, only when definitions are translated carefully into operationalized, behavior-level terms does reliability among clinicians become consistent. This does not mean the major tenets of psychoanalysis are wrong or even that they are too vague. It means that they are, at a descriptive level, too removed from the events of treatment.

A second limitation of psychoanalytic clinical terminology is that it was developed for the therapeutic situation. To discuss literary change alongside psychoanalytic change will require a neutral framework. We propose the following scheme of narrative structure for this purpose and will use it in our discussions as a sort of scaffolding for understanding the change process. We believe that when one says "change" one implies a process, a sequence of related, characteristic events. We believe change—if it occurs on an intrapsychic level and in relation to a real or fantasied other or others—will have these elements.

Engagement

The partners to change must link up in a special way, one that is different from an ordinary social interaction. In psychotherapy or psychoanalysis much of this aura is created by the awareness of therapy in society, and the associated attribution of special power and knowledge to the therapist. In literature the same result is created by the expectation of the role-relation of the two parties (for example, that they may become lovers), and the unique quality of their initial "match" (for example, that they meet under special circumstances, or make a strong initial impression on each other).

Strong feeling plays an important role in engagement. It must be present in the initial bond that is formed. It also helps if this feeling arises in a way, or at a moment, when the individual is off balance: suddenly alone, or in a time of external change, or crisis. A second characteristic of engagement is that there is a "fit" between the new partners. Either they have things in common or, on the other hand, they may complement each other strikingly. The well-known opening line of *Pride and Prejudice* states such a complementarity: "It is a truth universally acknowledged that a single man in possession of a good fortune, must be in want of a wife." Jane Austen tells us that the women in the story to follow are going to be looking on eligible men as potential partners. Patients entering therapy have similar anticipations and reactions to the therapist from the outset, often based on the most minimal cues.

Although initial engagement must be intense, there must also be flexibility in the bond for the process of change to proceed. Certainly there are processes of change that operate without flexibility, but these tend to be oppressive; one party ultimately bows to the greater power of the other. Such change tends to involve external behavior, as happens, for instance, to citizens in a dictatorship or members of a cult. If there is any internal change, it is traumatic and damaging. We are concerned with benign change, in which the effects are subtle, a change that reaches deep inside the psyche by appealing to latent inner capacities and potentials.

Mutual Influence

Out of the initial engagement, patterns of interaction emerge. These interactions must have the capacity to influence at least one partner in a profound, lasting way. Thus, the patterns of interaction will have enough consistency to allow each participant to orient, yet will have room for variance, so that change may occur. There must be a framework of rules, values, and conventions with which both partners are familiar. This framework establishes meaning, especially concerning issues of power, status, affection, and conflict resolution. Within these "rules" the partnership then develops an interaction pattern characterized by controlled, intermittent instability.

Instability begins when one partner does something unexpected. In treatment, for example, the therapist may ask a probing question, rather than accept the patient's initial explanation. The unexpected action of A (in this case, the therapist) challenges the capacities of B (the patient.) Will B (the patient) react in a way that attempts to restore the previous equilibrium, or will B come up with a further change in the pattern? If the latter occurs, then the situation between the two has changed, and at least one of the two (B) may have begun to change internally. B's changes may, in turn, lead to changes in how A acts. The result of the sequence also establishes a precedent for destabilization.

For example, in our literary case, Darcy's marriage proposal startles and provokes Elizabeth. Her indignant, angry rebuff, in turn, surprises *him*. (This pattern of interaction has been established between them earlier in the novel.) Here is one cycle in the process of mutual influence. The effect on Darcy begins a second cycle; now he does something new: he tells Elizabeth a family secret. We have already described the powerful effect of Darcy's revelation on Elizabeth—*her* views of Wickham, Darcy, and most of all, herself, are altered. The destabilization of Darcy's and Elizabeth's usual polite interactions in this set-to ultimately leads to significant, permanent alterations in both.

In treatment, many of the therapist's comments have disturbing impacts on the patient. Further discussion, or processing within the patient, may be necessary before a new stability is achieved. Similarly, as the therapist listens, he or she reacts emotionally to the patient (largely internally) and responds through a processing of these reactions that is both conscious and unconscious. Over time patient and therapist develop a *style* of relating, one that has predictability, yet allows for change through temporary instabilities.

Important factors in the pattern of mutual influence have to do with *intensity, sequencing, pacing, and cueing.* Just as "fit" is important in engagement, an overly strong emotional response (or one that is too mild) will disrupt, rather than move the process forward. Elizabeth upbraids Darcy after he proposes, and he is indeed shaken, but not so much that he withdraws permanently; Darcy, in turn, gives Elizabeth new information that startles her considerably, but which she can ultimately manage. *Sequencing* is a feature of most psychotherapies—certain issues cannot be approached until others have been dealt with. Ms L needed to learn—through her trial of psychoanalysis—that she was safe talking about herself at all, before she could begin to discuss specific issues in her relations with each of her parents. *Pacing* can determine whether an influence will be effective and continuing. Part of the "art" of psychotherapy technique is described in the phrase, "tact, timing, and dosage." The "right" interpretation (in the sense of accuracy) may be wrong if made too soon, or at a moment of great vulnerability. At a broader level, the imparting of new ideas may be ineffective if it is rushed; on the other hand, if it drags on, suspense turns to frustration. In Ms L's treatment, the pace of psychoanalysis proved to be too rapid; her backing away was an indication that this approach was too intense for her at this point in her life. *Cueing* refers to the way any particular dyad, or group, involved in the process of change develops special signals. These are often outside conscious awareness but nevertheless serve to inform others about readiness to proceed. Ms L's dreams cued her therapist about the power of the treatment situation, specifically about the way it stimulated disturbing exhibitionistic feelings. This made it less surprising when she wanted to withdraw from psychoanalysis, and helped her therapist to find a compromise, in resuming a once-weekly format.

Directionality

Influence is necessary but not sufficient for change. We have all had "powerful" relationships that do not alter us once the period of involvement is past. Directionality is a way to indicate that, for engagement and mutual influence to be permanently effective, somewhere there must be a pull that leads one or both parties to a new stability. In psychoanalysis we speak of the goal as "structural change" in the personality. We mean, by this, that something internal becomes permanently different, as a result of treatment, that, for example, for Ms L assertive action became less frightening because her fears of shame or punishment had been diminished by the therapeutic experience.

Further, directionality refers to a positive, salutary quality in the change process. Tragedy, too, may be the result of a process of engagement and mutual influence (see Chapter 10), but in the transformations we are describing here, change leads to the *enhancement* of the life of one or more participants.

Directionality has a great deal to do with our beliefs about good and bad. The pull toward positive change in the crucial unstable moments of interaction is fostered by a sense that the other will approve. Thus, in *Pride and Prejudice*, Darcy is deeply affected by Elizabeth's challenge that he has behaved in an "ungentlemanly" way by disparaging her family. Equally, Elizabeth is motivated—following her reading of the letter—to continue her self-scrutiny by a wish to restore Darcy's good opinion of her judgment. In other words, directionality is provided by some inspiring quality of the other partner, or by the latter's ability, as a catalyst, to bring out one's best.

In treatment, the therapist subscribes to a code of behavior, which, while it may frustrate or irritate the patient at times, represents dedication to the long-term goal of positive change. In psychoanalytic therapies, this goal is not approached by direction or coaching, but by dedication to a value internal to the therapy process—self-knowledge. Like Elizabeth, patients do not welcome this dedication, at first. Gradually, they may come to share the therapist's view, and in doing so feel they, too, are doing something "good." The therapist relies on the patient's capacity to translate self-knowledge into positive changes in other parts of life; it is the sense of movement toward a positive goal that is critical in the relationship.

THERAPEUTIC NARRATIVES AND LITERARY NARRATIVES

In the chapters that follow we will argue our hypothesis that the process of change as depicted in certain fictional works parallels psychotherapeutic and psychoanalytic processes of change, that there is a *therapeutic narrative*. It is our contention that these works serve as literary conceptions of what healing—or personal transformation—is about, and that the widespread appeal of these particular novels relates to their underlying therapeutic themes. However, while therapeutic themes may make literature interesting to the reading public, are literary conceptions of the therapeutic important or informative to the student of human psychology or the practicing therapist? Why not learn about psychological change from clinical situations alone? The powerful changes that can be engendered by therapy are surely a function of the special, technical conditions of that treatment—the therapist's training, experience, and theory of technique, the "fit" between therapist and patient, and the special aura of privacy, trust, and confidentiality that is fostered in the clinical setting. But it is the human potential for engagement with others (and its attendant wishes for closeness, gratification, and empowerment) that brings people to therapy in the first place. It is this characteristic of the human condition that writers draw upon as the source of much of their material. Our central premise is that both clinical practice and literature make use of the human capacity to resolve internal conflict and enhance development through relationships.

We are assuming the existence of a broader spectrum of transformative experiences—that occur in life, literature, and therapy—but we will focus on how these transformations are illustrated in novels. While this choice is based on personal interest, it is not completely arbitrary. The novel is available to all as a document, free of the distortions inherent in clinical reports and in personal, autobiographic recountings. (That is, we may choose to read a novel in many ways, but all readings begin with the same words.[7]) As a literary form, the novel is characterized by a focus on individual experience and relationships. The structure of the novel allows for much depiction of characters' inner states, in a kind of rambling, literary "free association." In *Aspects of the Novel*, E. M. Forster says: "That is the fundamental difference between people in daily life and people in books. In daily life we never understand each other, neither complete clairvoyance nor complete confessional exists. . . . But people in a novel can be understood completely by the reader, if the novelist wishes; their inner as well as their outer life can be exposed"[8] (pp. 46-47).

Although the novels we will examine are not "about" psychotherapy (nor are we attempting to discover "psychoanalysis-in-disguise"), we do think that treatment situations and novels may evolve in similar ways. The novels we have chosen—perhaps many novels—begin with a problem, a conflict, or an impasse. Someone feels hopeless or isolated, is unable to work, love, or grow up. Perhaps he or she loves the wrong person or chooses unsuitable partners, repeatedly. Treatments begin with such problems, too. Someone is anxious, depressed, developmentally arrested, or socially withdrawn. The middle parts of novels—in which plot and character development take place—involve action, struggle, confusion, and flight. The middle part of treatment is also characterized by struggle and confusion, which we refer to clinically as the vicissitudes of transference and resistance. These vicissitudes may also lead to action and flight. Novels have endings, happy or unhappy, in which some sort of resolution or compromise occurs. The hero and heroine marry—the hero and heroine do not marry, but remain meaningful to each other—the hero and heroine free themselves from crippling obsessions or self-defeating actions—or, alternately, the hero and heroine drag each other down to ruin, disillusionment, or death. Treatment ends, too—if not with total happiness—with resolution and compromise. Childhood wishes do not come true, but therapy can lead to better adaptations, in which satisfactions are now possible. The hackneyed plot, "boy meets girl, boy loses girl, boy gets girl," distills the idea that what is compelling in novels is this narrative of initial engagement, followed by the emergence of difficulties that must be resolved—a sequence that also characterizes psychotherapy.

In *The Literary Use of the Psychoanalytic Process*, Meredith Skura captures the phenomenon in which we are interested when she says, in talking about Shakespeare's plays: What is interesting about Shakespeare's characters is not their diseases but their movement through disease to some sort of curative reorganizations. Their proper parallel is not the neurotic but the *neurotic in analysis.*"[9] (p. 225; italics added.) Skura extends psychoanalytic literary criticism beyond the early use of psychoanalytic theory to analyze character, e.g., Hamlet as Oedipus. Skura feels the most important literary use of psychoanalytic theory is when we use the psychoanalytic process as a whole to understand the text as a whole. In so doing we can identify those moments, in both text and treatment, "of insight and self-consciousness that organize and take account of the rest." Elizabeth Bennet's realization that "til this moment I never knew myself" is an example of an insight that furthers the plot while allowing for understanding and growth. In our reading of *Pride and Prejudice*, it is a central event in the text toward which all previous events lead and from which all subsequent events follow.

We would like to expand Skura's approach by looking at depicted relationships against the background of therapy: that is, we will develop an understanding of the novel as a whole *as if it were about a therapeutic process*. At this point, however, some caveats are indicated. Our reading of these novels for therapeutic parallels is only one of many possible and fruitful organizing devices. We do not offer these readings in place of others, but rather to enrich our understanding of both literature and therapy by a study of common processes. We certainly do not assume authorial intent. How can we know what Jane Austen intended her novel to mean? How can we know if she knew? Margaret Drabble, one of the authors whose work we will be discussing, said in an interview in *Harper's* that it annoys her when people ask her the meaning of one or another of her novels because "if I knew what the meanings of my books were, I wouldn't have bothered to write them."[10] In other words, we are looking for a narrative of which the author may or may not have been conscious; its discovery, we believe, may have much to do with the appeal of the novel to readers, and with certain universals of the healing relationship.

In searching for parallels between transformative events in literature and changes that come about as the result of a psychotherapeutic process, we are not ignoring the very special conditions that facilitate the latter. This is not an attempt to simplify the essentials of arduously acquired skills and techniques: rather, we wish to document some of the ways human beings help each other change, using a medium far removed from therapy, in the hope that commonalities will help us understand elements of the process of change.

Furthermore, since we are comparing two kinds of narrative, it is important to clarify the pertinent differences in the study of transformation in literature and in clinical situations. The evidence or "clinical data" in a literary narrative is the author's creation, a product of the author's fantasy life, although often with strong autobiographical undertones. It is a narrative inevitably colored by personal history, the outcome of a complex interplay of conscious and unconscious forces. The same can be said, of course, about the psychoanalytic narrative. It, too, is its author's "creation," colored by the unconscious and by personal history, but its method of development and its purposes are different.

The psychoanalytic dialogue develops between two people: the utterances and silences of both parties influence the next utterance or silence to come. While the author, too, has a reader in mind, to whom his or her narrative is directed, and whose fantasied responses influence his or her productions, these responses are largely imaginary. They come from the author's fantasy life, not from an interaction with another person. Patients in clinical situations also respond to what they imagine their therapist thinks and feels, but here the therapist's presence and interventions correct distortions and influence the direction of the narrative. The difference, perhaps, is as much one of degree as of kind. Furthermore, the aesthetic goals of literary narratives lead to a selection and structuring of the text, while psychoanalytic therapy strives for a text that is as unselected as the patient's resistance will permit.

The purposes of the psychoanalytic narrative are primarily clinical and pragmatic, those of the literary narrative are primarily creative. However, it can be argued (and will be in Chapter 11) that the psychoanalytic narrative is a creative endeavor, albeit for a limited audience, and that the narratives of many creative writers are self-curative endeavors, and in that sense are pragmatic and clinical. Again, the difference seems to be one of degree.

We look at nine novels in depth. Eight of these are successful "cases"; one is a failed case. In each instance we try to elucidate how change takes place in a particular novel, and what elements of the psychoanalytic or psychotherapeutic process seem to be called up metaphorically by the story. For example, *Pride and Prejudice* (Chapter 2) illustrates several of the traditional psychoanalytic concepts of change, and also will serve to illustrate a general schema for change processes. On the other hand, we use *Silas Marner* (Chapter 6) to illustrate a current debate about the clinical theory of change, as well as to explore issues in the cure of a traumatic depression. In our final chapter we look at what literary conceptions of the therapeutic seem to be. That is, how does the literary imagination see healing as coming about? Will these be stories of transference cures (where one gets better out of love of or the wish to please the therapist), of corrective emotional experiences (where cure is a function of a new experience with a therapist who does not repeat the problematic behaviors of past figures), or of cures through interpretation, insight, and working through? To anticipate our conclusions, we can say that elements of all these modalities, as well as multiple sources of cure, will be discovered. Furthermore, we will be looking for the common factors all these novels share, and speculating on their relationship to healing processes in general.

2

PRIDE AND PREJUDICE:
JANE AUSTEN'S FORESHADOWING OF PSYCHOANALYTIC PROCESS

Jane Austen was an astute observer of human nature. Her best known novel has as a major theme the process of psychological change. Austen comments on this theme herself, early in *Pride and Prejudice*, through the voice of the central character, Elizabeth Bennet:

"I did not know before," continued Bingley immediately, "that you were a studier of character. It must be an amusing study."
[Elizabeth:] "Yes, but intricate characters are the most amusing. They have at least that advantage."
"The country," said Darcy, "can in general supply but few subjects for such study. In a country neighborhood you move in a very confined and unvarying society."
[Elizabeth:] *"But people themselves alter so much, that there is something new to be observed in them for ever."* (p. 45; emphasis added)

An author has an interest in the general—that which will touch every reader. Jane Austen wrote about courtship: the difficulties of two young people coming together. In *Pride and Prejudice* the obstacles to love seem, at first glance, to involve status and reputation. But Austen leaves little doubt about the important part played by underlying psychological issues. The tension of the plot in *Pride and Prejudice* is created by internal psychic conflicts, and the possibility that these will be overcome through interaction. The "something new to be observed" is that one person's behavior influences another's, in a series of actions and reactions.

As their romance develops, the novel's lovers, Elizabeth Bennet and Fitzwilliam Darcy, move from one psychological position to another. They each have difficulties: they encounter traits and attitudes in themselves and one another that block the development of their relationship. To become partners each must change. This change does not occur in isolation; one serves as a foil for the other, like parent and child or patient and therapist.

Pride and Prejudice is primarily about the evolution of Elizabeth Bennet. Every other character remains relatively static, with the exception of Darcy. Darcy's development, however, is largely offstage. In emphasizing Elizabeth, we are taking the orientation of the therapist, as well as that of the author who puts the heroine in the foreground. We will also consider how Darcy alters, and how his changes help bring about changes in Elizabeth.

In plot, *Pride and Prejudice* is romantic and comic. Elizabeth Bennet must get from her starting point—unmarried, with few prospects as the second of five daughters who have almost no dowry—to her end point as the wife of the handsome and wealthy Fitzwilliam Darcy. We will first review the events of the story, to acquaint or remind the reader of *Pride and Prejudice*, putting particular emphasis on personality, interaction, and internal change. We will also refer to those aspects of psychoanalytic process that are suggested by the events in the novel, using standard analytic terms, but also introducing our schema of the therapeutic narrative for comparative purposes. One important aspect of the reading experience that we cannot convey is the gradual unfolding of awareness. Jane Austen tells the reader only so much at a time, so that, as in therapy, crucial facts and personality traits emerge in a gradual manner. It is this unfolding, of course, that contributes to the reader's enjoyment.

THE STORY

Elizabeth begins the novel, age twenty, with a set of intrapsychic conflicts, associated beliefs, and feelings about herself and others. She is the second of five daughters; her older sister, Jane, is attractive, modest, and sees the best in everyone. Elizabeth is playful, teasing, ready to see the humor in every situation; she is a more benign version of Mr. Bennet, who takes pleasure in ridiculing the folly of others. Her younger sisters, Kitty and Lydia, are silly and flirtatious, while Mary is bookish and affected. Mrs. Bennet displays her petty, self-interested attitudes without disguise, and frequently resorts to her poor "nerves" for solace when frustrated. Where Jane is loved by all, Elizabeth is Mr. Bennet's particular favorite. She is, on the other hand, the least favorite of her mother. This position in the family creates both advantages and problems for Elizabeth. While she is valued more than her sisters and her mother by Mr. Bennet, this is an ambiguous preference. She cannot, after all, replace Mrs. Bennet.[1] Forming a positive image of a wife and mother presents problems. Elizabeth scorns her mother's embarrassing behavior; her image of an adult, married woman is a negative one. To her, the marital relationship is one that damages both parties: it makes women blithering and men cynical. Father disparages all women, especially mother, and only Elizabeth's identification/alliance with him seems to protect her from the same devalued fate. But she is still female. Identifications as a woman, and as a potential wife and mother, are conflicted. Elizabeth puzzles over her self-worth.

This situation creates another set of difficulties for Elizabeth. Late adolescence is a time of emergent sexuality and independence. Young people need to detach from the original figures in the Oedipal constellation, and turn their feelings toward peers. In Elizabeth's social milieu, this can be done successfully only through marriage. The task of courtship requires that certain developmental issues have been mastered adequately. Deficiencies in Elizabeth's experience have interfered. Her identity as a woman is shaky. Attraction to a man, and the sexuality, ambition, and wishes for intimacy this implies are—because of her particular position in the family—conflicted in their meanings. One solution to this internal dilemma is to deny these impulses—Elizabeth spends almost the entire novel oblivious to her attraction to Darcy and his attentions to her, and thus tries to protect herself from confronting these painful problems directly. Her conscious wishes for marital happiness are displaced to Jane, where they can be experienced vicariously and thus more safely.

Initial Encounters

A wealthy young man, Bingley, leases an estate near Longbourn, the Bennets' home. At a neighborhood ball, he is attracted to Jane. Elizabeth, by contrast, is slighted by Bingley's friend, Darcy:

Elizabeth Bennet had been obliged, by the scarcity of gentlemen, to sit down for two dances; and during part of that time, Mr. Darcy had been standing near enough for her to overhear a conversation between him and Mr. Bingley, who came from the dance for a few minutes, to press his friend to join it.

"Come, Darcy," said he, "I must have you dance. I hate to see you standing about by yourself in this stupid manner. You had much better dance."

"I certainly shall not. You know how I detest it, unless I am particularly acquainted with my partner. . . ."

"You are dancing with the only handsome girl in the room," said Mr. Darcy, looking at the eldest Miss Bennet.

"Oh! she is the most beautiful creature I ever beheld! But there is one of her sisters sitting down just behind you, who is very pretty, and I dare say very agreeable. Do let me ask my partner to introduce you."

"Which do you mean?" and turning round he looked for a moment at Elizabeth, till catching her eye, he withdrew his own and coldly said, "She is tolerable, but not handsome enough to tempt me; and I am in no humor at present to give consequence to young ladies who are slighted by other men.

. . . Mr. Darcy walked off; and Elizabeth remained with no very cordial feelings towards him. She told the story, however, with great spirit among her friends; for she had a lively, playful disposition, which delighted in anything ridiculous. (pp. 10–11)

Elizabeth copes with being slighted by taking a self-protectively humorous and disdainful attitude toward Darcy. Here is the "prejudice" of the novel's title.

Darcy's insult makes him important in Elizabeth's life, though negatively. The rejecting nature of Darcy's first attention helps Elizabeth hide from herself any interest in him, a handsome man with status and property. We may wonder why an insult, a rejection, would evoke involvement. Psychoanalysis tells us that transference can be triggered by any reminder of a past figure, whether positive or negative in quality. A man derogating a woman is what Elizabeth has grown up with, and the recurrence with Darcy arouses an interest more powerful than that aroused by several more admiring suitors.

On subsequent social occasions Darcy, despite himself, finds Elizabeth increasingly attractive. She, however, interprets his interest as motivated by a wish to hurt her further: "'If he does it anymore I shall certainly let him know that I see what he is about. He has a very satirical eye, and if I do not begin by being impertinent myself, I shall soon grow afraid of him'" (p. 24). Here is transference: Darcy is reserved and critical, but unlike Elizabeth's father, he is no wit! The "satirical eye" is that of Mr. Bennet looking at women, and that of Elizabeth herself.

Jane falls ill while visiting Bingley's sisters at their nearby home. Elizabeth rushes on foot across rainy fields to care for Jane, arriving with flushed cheeks and muddy skirts at Netherfield. Bingley's sisters are condescending about Elizabeth's unladylike behavior, but Darcy reacts differently. He sees her beautiful eyes, brightened by the exertion of her walk, and her loyalty to a beloved sister, a feeling he also feels toward his younger sister. Darcy also realizes, half aware, that Elizabeth is capable of a love he would like to receive!

During a week's stay at Netherfield for Jane's convalescence, Elizabeth and Darcy spend several evenings together in the company of Bingley and his sisters. Their initial pattern of relating is reversed: Darcy is polite and cautiously interested; now Elizabeth keeps a distance by teasing. Nevertheless, the visit softens the attitudes of both. Darcy realizes that he is in danger of falling in love. While Elizabeth observes Darcy's interest, and even banters and flirts with him, she is less aware of any shift in herself. One way to understand this discrepancy is in terms of the social conventions regarding love to which Austen's characters subscribe. The man is to experience the initial intensity of attraction, while the woman's interest is to be stimulated and inspired by the man's. But the conventions help Elizabeth with what she needs to do defensively—deny her interest in Darcy. After all, did Elizabeth need to rush so fervently to Jane's side? To whom was she rushing? Darcy *is* of interest to Elizabeth, but there are many reasons to protect herself from knowledge of this interest.

Wickham and Collins

Elizabeth's denial is facilitated by the arrival of George Wickham, a young officer in the militia that is camped nearby. In her first conversation with Wickham, Elizabeth discovers that he is a man with convincing grievances against Darcy. All her prejudice is reinforced. When Bingley suddenly departs for London, followed the next day by his entire party, Elizabeth suffers—not for herself of course—but for Jane. Austen tells the reader that this departure is motivated by Darcy's growing attraction to Elizabeth, and by his fear that he will wish to form an attachment that he considers beneath him. Since all that Elizabeth knows—from Wickham—is that Darcy is "intended" for his cousin, Anne de Bourgh, she has further reason to dismiss thoughts of Darcy as a lover for herself.

In a delightful comic interlude, Mr. Collins, a talkative, pretentious, and ridiculous young minister, cousin to the Bennet girls, arrives at the Bennets' home. As heir to the family's estate, he has decided to do the right thing by marrying one of the Bennet daughters. Advised by Mrs. Bennet that Jane may soon be spoken for, he attends to Elizabeth for several days, and then proposes. Backed by her father, Elizabeth rejects him bluntly. Undaunted, Collins proposes to Elizabeth's best friend and neighbor, Charlotte Lucas. Charlotte, older, plainer, and more pragmatic than Elizabeth, accepts. Elizabeth is shocked; she must have love and a relationship of mutual respect.

The Visit at Hunsford

Elizabeth and Darcy next meet while both are on visits at Hunsford. Elizabeth is a houseguest for six weeks with Charlotte and Mr. Collins; Darcy is visiting at nearby Rosings, the estate of his aunt, Lady Catherine de Bourgh, who is, coincidentally, Collins's patroness. Darcy's behavior makes it clear—to the reader, but not to the guarded Elizabeth—that he is attracted to her. When they are together, he stares at her. When she walks in the woods, he frequently appears and accompanies her. Elizabeth is faced with a dissonance—her senses tell her that Darcy is interested, but her mind insists that he still does not take her seriously. It is easiest for her to remain convinced that his attitude is condescending, that he is amusing himself at her expense. Elizabeth *is* able to observe that he shows no interest in Lady Catherine's daughter, the cousin to whom he was supposedly betrothed. When Charlotte suggests to Elizabeth that Darcy has called at the parsonage because he loves her, Elizabeth reports that he spent the visit in near silence, and must therefore merely be amusing himself.

During the visit at Hunsford Elizabeth's dislike of Darcy is heightened when she learns from Darcy's companion, Captain Fitzwilliam, that it was Darcy himself (not the scheming Caroline Bingley) who interfered in the budding relationship between Bingley and Jane. Darcy convinced Bingley to remain in London because Jane was not a suitable match. This revelation confirms Elizabeth's original sense of slight, and, by virtue of referring to an injury to Jane, elicits her righteous indignation.

Elizabeth is in this angry, injured state when Darcy comes to see her. He inquires about her health, then falls silent. Suddenly and unexpectedly, he blurts out: "'In vain have I struggled. It will not do. My feelings will not be repressed. You must allow me to tell you how ardently I admire and love you.'"

Elizabeth can still maintain her distance because in the same breath he tells her he loves her despite her family:

> He spoke well; but there were feelings besides those of the heart to be detailed, and he was not more eloquent on the subject of tenderness than of pride. His sense of her inferiority—of its being a degradation—of the family obstacles which judgment had always opposed to inclination, were dwelt on with a warmth which seemed due to the consequence he was wounding, but was very unlikely to recommend his suit. (p. 207)

Although previously she has behaved with politeness, reserve, and wit, Elizabeth is now no longer cool. Upon hearing Darcy's proposal, she gives vent to all her indignation. She accuses Darcy of interfering in the relationship between Jane and Bingley, thus doing Jane harm. She supports her indignation on this count with her "knowledge" of Darcy's misuse of Wickham. Finally, when Darcy points out his honesty in expressing his distress over her family's social inferiority:

> Elizabeth felt herself growing more angry every moment; yet she tried to the utmost to speak with composure when she said,
> "You are mistaken, Mr. Darcy, if you suppose that the mode of your declaration affected me in any other way, than as it spared me the concern which I might have felt in refusing you, had you behaved in a more gentlemanlike manner."

Elizabeth goes on to detail her criticisms:

> "From the very beginning—from the first moment, I may almost say—of my acquaintance with you, your manners, impressing me with the fullest belief of your arrogance, your conceit, and your selfish disdain of the feelings of others, were such as to form that groundwork of disapprobation on which succeeding events have built so immovable a dislike; and I had not known you a month before I felt that you were the last man in the world whom I could ever be prevailed on to marry." (p. 212)

Darcy, astonished both at being rejected and by this attack on his character, leaves. The reader, though caught up in feeling Elizabeth's indignation, may note her reference to her initial slight, and the intensity of her rejection. (Why the "last man in the world?" Surely, she knows someone less appealing!) This is not an indifferent woman, but a hurt one. Underlying her hurt feelings is rejection; deeper than that lies a wish for repair through love. For Elizabeth the wish for love is problematic, as we have noted, because she believes unconsciously that self-esteem will be lost through attachment. It is safer to be father than to love father. Thus, Elizabeth's rage, while directed at Darcy, has an older source.

Elizabeth's attack on Darcy is fortunate for the momentum of the relationship. Only at the end of *Pride and Prejudice* do we learn Darcy's side. In the moment, we see his angry, humiliated retreat. When, with Elizabeth, we read his letter the next day, we do not know that her accusation that he has been "ungentlemanly" has hit home. For Darcy loves Elizabeth, and as part of this love he has come to respect her. Her accusation makes him aware of the hurtful side of his social snobbishness. Later, he says to her, "'You taught me a lesson, hard indeed at first, but most advantageous. By you I was properly humbled'" (p. 408). From this point forward, Darcy is motivated by a desire to prove himself worthy of Elizabeth, though he clearly needs time to digest the hard lesson she has administered.

Elizabeth's crisis is foregrounded by Jane Austen; Darcy's inner state, and the alterations he undergoes are almost always out of sight. Until the proposal, Darcy's interest has been hidden behind enigmatic, often silent attention. His very silence, however, has an important function. It allows Elizabeth to project her feelings; it elicits Elizabeth's unconscious conflicts.

We have pointed out in Chapter 1 Elizabeth's emotional reaction to the letter and the information it contains: the "apprehension and horror" that reflect deeper levels of meaning implied by Darcy's "interpretation." Darcy's analyst-like behavior has created a situation in which Elizabeth has gradually developed a powerful, but unconscious, relation to him, one largely based on feelings about her father. In an analytic situation, at moments as dramatic as those of the proposal and letter, we would call Elizabeth's state a "transference neurosis."[2] That is, not just one relationship, but a whole panoply of relationships, conflicts, and parts of herself are caught up in the meanings of these interchanges with Darcy.

If she can consider loving Darcy, Elizabeth can rehabilitate her attitude toward herself as a woman. While this is represented externally by the honor of a proposal from someone of Darcy's rank, it is represented internally by the possibility that the proposal and letter come from someone whom she can respect, someone who will value her. This is the positive and more comfortable part of Elizabeth's reaction. More dangerous are the sexual and hostile feelings that account for her apprehension and horror. These feelings have their origins in the family relations we have already described: Elizabeth's sexual feelings are still intrapsychically attached to the image of her father, as attested to by her (denied) interest in a man like Darcy. (A friendly, straightforward fellow like Bingley has no romantic charge for Elizabeth, as he does for her emotionally less complex sister.) So to be loved by—and potentially to love—a Darcy evokes the horror of a sexual idea. Furthermore, the idea of closeness arouses Elizabeth's anger, both at having been slighted by her mother and at her father's derision of women. The whole experience with Darcy must be processed over and over, just as patterns in analysis are worked through in many renditions.

Mr. Darcy's letter she was in a fair way of soon knowing by heart. She studied every sentence; and her feelings towards its writer were at times widely different. When she remembered the style of his address, she was still full of indignation; but when she considered how unjustly she had condemned and upbraided him, her anger was turned against herself; and his disappointed feelings became the object of compassion. (p. 234)

Elizabeth's thoughts then continue to a new appraisal of her family, one more consonant with Darcy's point of view: she sees her father's careless indulgence of his younger daughters' giddiness and flirtations, her mother's pettiness and bad manners. She now holds these faults (rather than Caroline Bingley or Darcy) responsible for Jane's loss.

Home, Then a Visit to Pemberley

The reader now feels, "Why can't they talk it over?" A simpler romance would end at this point, with some turn of plot bringing the lovers together and enabling them to declare their feelings. Such a resolution would ignore what Jane Austen, psychologist, knew: the development of her characters is not complete. Both Darcy and Elizabeth have much to learn, internal adjustments to make. Elizabeth now knows that Darcy is not as bad a man as she thought, but not that she loves him. Time is needed. Elizabeth returns home to all the relationships and patterns of her past, questioning herself profoundly. She now feels separated from her parents—by her knowledge of Darcy's love, by her possession of scandalous information about Darcy's sister, and by her own internal reevaluation. She looks at her family with new eyes, from Darcy's critical point of view.

His attachment excited gratitude, his general character respect; but she could not approve him; nor could she for a moment repent her refusal, or feel the slightest inclination ever to see him again. In her own past behavior, there was a constant source of vexation and regret; and in the unhappy defects of her family, a subject of yet heavier chagrin. They were hopeless of remedy. (p. 234)

Here Austen introduces a long reverie on the flaws in Elizabeth's parents' marriage. The fantasy stimulated by Darcy's proposal allows Elizabeth to have such thoughts. If Darcy is, in fact, good and worthy, then she can think about marriage, but will her union be like that of her parents? In the chapters of *Pride and Prejudice* that follow, Elizabeth is concerned with understanding what constitutes virtue and moral character, clearly aligning herself with the good. She discusses Darcy's revelation about Wickham with Jane; they decide not to expose Wickham, since Elizabeth has been told of the scandal in confidence. She does urge her father to control Lydia and Katherine more, and specifically tries to thwart Lydia's plans to follow the militia to Brighton. Elizabeth confronts Wickham gently about his previous misrepresentations.

Next, Elizabeth's Aunt and Uncle Gardiner arrive to take her on a tour to the north. The Gardiners are a couple who serve as models for Elizabeth of a good marriage. Mr. Gardiner is a businessman in London, worldly, but not cynical; Mrs. Gardiner is insightful and intelligent, with some of Elizabeth's wit and wry humor. As well as being good role models, the Gardiners provide a plot vehicle for the next meeting with Darcy.

Each of these events helps Elizabeth work out better images of herself, of parental figures, and of marriage. Her activity in trying to prevent Lydia's flirtatious pursuit of officers represents an assertion of control over sexual impulses. To respond consciously to Darcy's ardor would signify a more primitive, sexually tinged attraction. Before she can love, Elizabeth must first know she is in control of her impulses.

The next meeting between Elizabeth and Darcy is the most romantic. The Gardiners are traveling in the neighborhood of Darcy's home at Pemberley, and (contrary to Elizabeth's preference) they visit his large and attractive estate, as tourists. At Pemberley, Elizabeth hears affectionate, undiluted praise for Darcy from the housekeeper. A new understanding of him breaks through her defensive denial of interest. When Darcy appears, unexpectedly—Elizabeth believes him to be in London—she is overcome. Her usual poise is gone—the power of her pull toward him overwhelms her defensive pride and its social expression, her capacity for playful teasing.

Their eyes instantly met, and the cheeks of each were overspread with the deepest blush . . . .

She had instinctively turned away; but stopping on his approach, received his compliments with an embarrassment impossible to be overcome. . . . Amazed at the alteration of his manner since they last parted, every sentence that he uttered was increasing her embarrassment. (pp. 273–74)

With the psychological work that has gone on during the intervening weeks since Hunsford, the enthusiastically positive picture of Darcy painted by the housekeeper fresh in her mind, and his sudden appearance, Elizabeth's indifference is suddenly gone. Darcy is altered, too. His hauteur is replaced by politeness toward her aunt and uncle, and he makes more active efforts to show his feelings toward Elizabeth. Invitations are made, calls exchanged, Darcy introduces his sister to Elizabeth—events move rapidly toward a second proposal.

Why does Jane Austen not resolve the plot here? It is plain that Darcy and Elizabeth love one another—plain now to them as well as to the reader. What interrupts the development of intimacy that follows the meeting at Pemberley? In the events of the story, it is the news of her sister Lydia's elopement with Wickham. Psychologically, it is the intrusion of impulsive sexuality. What Lydia's behavior represents in Elizabeth's intrapsychic experience is a breakthrough of erotic ideas and impulses, propelled by the sudden rush of love. For Elizabeth this is a devastating setback. Elizabeth's reaction to the news about Lydia is shock, anxiety, and shame. She tells Darcy of Lydia's elopement, assuming that this will confirm his earlier rejection of her for her family's crassness. It is as though in her sudden realization of love for Darcy, she is loving a forbidden object, so that the next step in love— the erotic urge—has a forbidden meaning. Telling Darcy of Lydia is a confession to the forbidden object.

Home Again

Elizabeth returns to Longbourn, preoccupied with restitution of the sexual scandal, and with the well-being of her devastated family. It would seem—at least to the conscious Elizabeth—that she is returning to her psychological state at the outset of the story, or to something worse, the proof that she, by association with Lydia, is unworthy of a man she now admires. Nevertheless, she knows that Darcy has loved her, and that she loves him: "She began now to comprehend that he was exactly the man who, in disposition and talents, would most suit her" (p. 342).

Lydia is rescued from complete disgrace by a marriage to Wickham apparently arranged through Mr. Gardiner's intervention. Following the marriage, Lydia and Wickham visit at Longbourn. Wickham tries to draw Elizabeth into criticism of Darcy but she gently chides him with her knowledge of the truth. As the first daughter to wed, Lydia is unrepentant and triumphant. In talking about her wedding, she mentions that Darcy was present, although she was supposed to keep this fact secret. Amazed, Elizabeth writes to her aunt for an explanation. Mrs. Gardiner responds that it was indeed Darcy who saved Lydia—he found the lovers out, pressured Wickham to marry, and supplied the money settlement that would make it possible. "Her heart did whisper that he had done it for her. But it was a hope checked by other considerations" (p. 359). How could the proud Darcy consider her now, when marriage would make him brother-in-law to Wickham?

Soon after the departure of the newlyweds, Bingley and Darcy return to the neighborhood. They call; Bingley is clearly still in love with Jane, but Darcy seems reserved, though polite. After a few visits, Bingley proposes, and Jane joyfully accepts. A week later Elizabeth is called on by Lady Catherine. The scene that follows is, perhaps, the most emotionally satisfying of the book. Lady Catherine boldly asks Elizabeth whether she is engaged to Darcy. Elizabeth, sensing that she is about to be bullied, refuses to answer. Lady Catherine then insists that Elizabeth relinquish her hopes for Darcy in favor of Lady Catherine's plans for her own daughter. Elizabeth holds her ground, becoming firmer as Lady Catherine becomes more insulting.

This scene represents for Elizabeth a coming to terms with guilt and anxiety about her own sexual wishes. Lady Catherine is a powerful mother, an imperious woman who, by proxy, wants the man for herself. Elizabeth's defiance obtains strength from her increased confidence in her own worth, especially in her difference from Lydia. Since she is not seeking easy, impulsive satisfaction, she can maintain her status in the face of snobbish bullying.

> "You are, then, resolved to have him?"
>
> "I have said no such thing. I am only resolved to act in that manner which will, in my own opinion, constitute my happiness, without reference to you or to any person so wholly unconnected with me."
>
> "It is well. You refuse, then, to oblige me. You refuse to obey the claims of duty, honor, and gratitude. You are determined to ruin him in the opinion of all his friends, and make him the contempt of the world."
>
> "Neither duty, nor honor, nor gratitude," replied Elizabeth, "has any possible claim on me in the present instance. No principle of either would be violated by my marriage with Mr. Darcy. And with regard to the resentment of his family or the indignation of the world, if the former were excited by his marrying me, it would not give me one moment's concern—and the world in general would have too much sense to join in the scorn." (pp. 395–96)

The resolution of adolescent issues requires the development of secure controls on impulse, and the capacity to challenge comfortably the power of the older generation. Elizabeth is proclaiming her autonomy, and asserting that the shame and guilt represented by Lydia do not apply to her. Having mastered the emergence of love and of sexual feeling, she no longer feels guilty and unworthy. She can choose Darcy as a psychological equal.

Darcy's second proposal makes for less exciting reading than the first. In fact, telling Mr. Bennet has more dramatic tension, since Elizabeth has been denying her interest in Darcy to her father all along. Of course, Mr. Bennet is surprised, but his concern (once Elizabeth assures him she does love Darcy) is that she esteem him: "'Your lively talents would place you in the greatest danger in an unequal marriage. You could scarcely escape discredit and misery. My child, let me not have the grief of seeing you unable to respect your partner in life'"

(p. 417). Mr. Bennet wants his favorite daughter spared his own experience of marriage, whose unhappiness has, in many ways, given rise to the difficulties with which Elizabeth has struggled in the novel. She describes Darcy's efforts on their behalf with Lydia, and Mr. Bennet is convinced.

THE FICTIONAL RELATIONSHIP AND THERAPEUTIC PROCESS

Our thesis in this chapter is that the evolving relationship between the protagonists of *Pride and Prejudice* is comparable, in particular, to a psychoanalytic process. In discussing this comparison we shall make use of the idea of therapeutic narrative presented in Chapter 1. Briefly, this framework involves three aspects of the process of change: the *engagement* of the two parties to change; the nature of the *mutual influence* they have upon one another; and the source of *directionality* in this influence, i.e., what makes the interaction a constructive one.

Engagement

With her opening sentence Jane Austen tells us that the story will be about courtship, about the need for men and women to join in marriage. Although Elizabeth often denies her interest, Darcy is highly eligible. He has great wealth and noble connections. In our words, Darcy's status instantly evokes a powerful, but nonspecific transference.

How does Darcy respond? Like a therapist, Darcy does not gratify this interest. In fact, he does something that hurts Elizabeth: he slights her. While the analyst at the outset of treatment does not intend to slight the patient, his or her initial role behavior has a similar effect—expected social responses are withheld, the patient is frustrated. For example, the analyst usually does not answer questions. The rationale for this is twofold: behind every question is an idea, a fantasy, an element of curiosity that is not fully conscious; answering questions may lead to a collusion between patient and analyst to avoid the patient's discomfort. In other words, frustration leads to an interaction that is better able to focus on the patient's unconscious life, since the automatic reactions and protections of the rules of conversation are not maintained by the analyst.

More specifically, Darcy's initial "intervention" evokes in Elizabeth the entire set of issues we have examined: her conflicted self-image and her ambivalence toward men and marriage. While the apparent effect of Darcy's behavior is to alienate Elizabeth, in fact she is involved by it. Her defensive derision acknowledges this: "Elizabeth remained with no very cordial feelings toward him. She told the story, however, with great spirit among her friends" (p. 11).

At their next meeting Darcy puzzles Elizabeth by his steady nonverbal attentiveness to her. Curiosity is added to her pique. The psychoanalyst can point out that Darcy has inadvertently created an ambiguity that allows Elizabeth to project meanings onto him that are associated with fundamental issues, including the form of her Oedipal romance. This powerful, attractive man disdains her, yet remains interested, perhaps to enjoy his superiority, like her father. The ambiguity of Darcy's behavior affects Elizabeth much as the analyst's does the patient: interest without clear definition of attitude and involvement. It allows her to project onto Darcy a set of meanings that are familiar, meaningful, and engaging. The result of this interest is to arouse Elizabeth's defenses also, thus bringing them into play where they may potentially be altered.

What about Darcy's engagement? Darcy seems an enigmatic figure, proud, silent, even disdainful. Austen tells us early on that he is attracted to Elizabeth. In fact, it is Darcy who brings positive attachment to the relationship. For the plot this is a necessary feature: left on her own, Elizabeth would end the novel as a spinster! But Darcy also brings a problem to the relationship, one that accounts for his silence and pride. If we read *Pride and Prejudice* back to front, Darcy makes far more sense.

> "I have been a selfish being all my life, in practice, though not in principle. As a child, I was taught what was right; but I was not taught to correct my temper. I was given good principles, but left to follow them in pride and conceit. Unfortunately, an only son (for many years an only child), I was spoiled by my parents, who though good themselves . . . allowed, encouraged, almost taught me to be selfish and overbearing—to care for none beyond my own family circle, to think meanly of all the rest of the world, to wish at least to think meanly of their sense of worth compared with my own. Such I was, from eight to eight and twenty." (p. 408)

Initial engagement is a necessary condition for the process of mutual influence. In both psychoanalysis and the novel the participants do not know just how this process will unfold. Elizabeth would deny, well into her story, that she is involved in a powerful attachment. And patients, even after they have been in treatment for some time, may resist an awareness of the feelings they have about their therapist. They may even resist knowing that they are resisting this awareness. When intimacy arouses unconscious conflicts, as it does with both Elizabeth Bennet and patients under the special conditions of psychoanalysis, it can become intense and uncomfortable. On the analyst's side, we bring a willingness to tolerate the discomfort of our side of the therapeutic relationship. By now it is surely no secret that analysts, too, struggle with their subjective feelings during treatment. As is the case with Darcy, this struggle is largely hidden from the patient's view. But, like Darcy, analysts may speak from their feelings, and the consequences, as in *Pride and Prejudice*, may be provocative, although ultimately useful.

It is, in fact, the slap in the face of Darcy's initial disdain that provokes Elizabeth's engagement. She will prove her worth—by showing him the same sort of indifference! This intrigues Darcy. At the novel's end, Elizabeth reviews his attraction to her:

> [Elizabeth to Darcy:] "Now, be sincere; did you admire me for my impertinence?"
>
> "For the liveliness of your mind, I did."
>
> "You may as well call it impertinence at once. It was very little less. The fact is, that you were sick of civility, of deference, of officious attention. You were disgusted with the women who were always speaking and looking and thinking for your approbation alone. I roused and interested you, because I was so unlike them." (p. 420)

Both parties are caught in a tension of interest, denial, and underlying intense engagement. This engagement involves the very personality elements and conflicts that are preventing their further psychological development.

Mutual Influence

Engagement is followed by a continuing pattern of interaction that both maintains involvement and steers toward change. The equilibrium of personality lies between stability and growth; internal and social signals press for development, but there are strong homeostatic tendencies. In a sense, when there is a block to development, the psyche must be misled into change. That is, available motivations are engaged to maintain and propel the process of mutual influence.

In this novel, as well as in treatment, change occurs through an extensive series of interactions. In current models of analytic and therapeutic change the cyclical nature of the process makes it possible for the patient to move from one internal issue to another, since one conflict will have implications for another, and so forth.[3] We subsume all these in the general category of mutual influence. Engagement sets the stage; mutual influence requires that a drama takes place upon it. It also refers to the attunement of the two partners in the process of change. Engagement must be followed by a continuing pattern of interaction that both maintains involvement and promotes change.

The effect of Darcy's initial snub of Elizabeth is to begin such a series of interactions. Each action by one of the two has a particular impact upon the other. This impact, in turn, evokes a further counter-reaction. Darcy insults Elizabeth; she is angry, but affected. As he becomes attracted to her, Darcy is silently attentive; Elizabeth, protecting herself, is cool and reserved, but she is curious. Darcy's reticence stimulates her doubts and allows her to fall prey to Wickham's resentment. After the prolonged contact at Hunsford, Darcy proposes;

Elizabeth is startled and indignant, but also flattered. Her angry confrontation spurs real self-examination in Darcy. Darcy writes her; Elizabeth is abashed and self-critical; she begins to examine many of the assumptions in her thinking and behavior.

As she moves from one state to another, Elizabeth has the opportunity to recognize certain habitual modes of perceiving and judging; ultimately this insight provides the impetus for change. When they meet again at Pemberley, both partners have altered, largely through self-reflection; now they can move from self-protection to attraction. But attraction triggers issues of the incestuous meaning of desire, and of sexual self-control in Elizabeth. When these are mastered, through the Lydia-Wickham episode and the confrontation with Lady Catherine, Elizabeth and Darcy can marry.

The process that brings about internal change has an external, behavioral component. That is, each partner conveys something about the impact of the last communication in the quality of the next "reply." In this way mutual influences occur. Darcy is changed as well as Elizabeth. From the point of view of Elizabeth's process, Darcy's changes bring out different and conflicting aspects of her psychology. By becoming an admirer, Darcy appeals to Elizabeth's latent desire, but evokes conflicts having to do with sexuality and competition. By being critical, Darcy impels Elizabeth to look at her defensive character style and ultimately to pass a test of self-scrutiny. In the symmetry of the novel, Darcy is changed and improved correspondingly.

Elizabeth's stay at Netherfield to care for Jane provides the occasion for several internal developments. One such development concerns her attitudes toward female rivals. Elizabeth demonstrates her love and devotion for her sister, while withstanding courageously the barbs of Bingley's sisters. In not retaliating, Elizabeth shows herself as more secure than her social superiors. All this occurs in front of Darcy, although Elizabeth would deny it is for his benefit. She is working out concerns having to do with aggression and competition in rivalrous situations. Unlike Miss Bingley, who openly fawns over Darcy, Elizabeth can keep cool in Darcy's presence and not slip into sycophancy or jealous anger.

This visit also gives Elizabeth opportunities to deal with Darcy on a daily basis. She musters her characteristic style of teasing and irony to banter with him. In her "transference" Elizabeth is standing up to the father who derides women. Darcy's interest must flatter her, but she denies any positive feelings. In many therapies, the positive side of the relationship is the most frightening for the patient. The therapeutic sessions may be dull or contentious, while the patient slowly gains confidence about the safety of positive feelings. It is safer for Elizabeth to "split" her transference and feel the positive interest in Wickham. With him there is less conflict, even while there is no love. He is flattering and satisfies the wish for easy recognition and preference. He validates Elizabeth's feelings of past injury. She does not have to modify the resentment that Darcy has stirred and the older issues it represents.

At the point of Darcy's proposal and letter, we suggested that Elizabeth had developed the equivalent of a transference neurosis. She experiences in her current relations a new version of her most critical, earlier inner experiences, conflicts, and associated defenses. Darcy, Wickham, Bingley's sisters, and other characters in lesser degree represent significant prior objects. Elizabeth has wrapped herself in a protective mantle of critical, teasing, ironic attitudes that make her safe from the feelings these figures arouse. Anxieties about her female identifications are allayed by transferring her concern from herself to Jane. Others might enlighten her and bring her projections in line with reality, but they do not: Darcy could let her know the truth about Wickham and about his feelings. Like the analyst, he lets things develop further.

The period of Elizabeth's visit at Hunsford intensifies internal tensions and then brings them to a head in the climactic proposal episode. Darcy's steady, silent show of interest, his visits to the parsonage, his explanation of his earlier behavior to her—Elizabeth absorbs the meaning of none of these actions consciously. If anything, since she must be sensing his attitude unconsciously, she heightens her defensive view. When Darcy proposes, Elizabeth explodes in indignation. Her reaction has a basis in reality: Darcy is setting his pride above his gentleman's manners; Jane was mistreated; Elizabeth is being condemned for a family that she cannot help. But the true source of her feeling is in her neurotic conflicts. What follows is similar to what often happens as an analysis progresses: Elizabeth "gets worse," that is, her misguided views and attachments intensify, as, aided by events, she protects herself from awareness of an interest in Darcy.

At this moment Elizabeth's initial psychological position is confirmed in each respect. Her latent negative self-view is confirmed by Darcy's criticism; her idea of marriage is confirmed by the idea of wedding a man who loves, but cannot respect; her anger at men for depreciating women is provoked: and her narcissistic defensive stance is strengthened (I don't need you or anyone). All of this also serves to control sexual impulses that Darcy has implicitly called forth by proposing. It is far safer to return to the family home and its substitutive satisfactions.

In terms of analytic process this phase of the fictional relationship can be seen as an intensification of the transference neurosis, which often occurs unconsciously or preconsciously. The analyst's interpretation of elements of the transference neurosis is often greeted with the same sort of surprise, denial, and indignation as Elizabeth's response to the proposal, and for similar reasons. Consciousness of the emergence of conflicted issues intensifies resistance, at least temporarily.

Then comes Darcy's letter. Austen portrays the sequence of Elizabeth's inner states vividly. Initially she reads only for confirmation of her convictions. Then, when she absorbs the significance of the revelations about Wickham, she is shaken; the whole structure of attitudes and feelings she has developed is invalid. It is here that Austen writes about Elizabeth's painful self-scrutiny.

> She grew absolutely ashamed of herself. . . . "How despicably have I acted!" she cried; "I, who have prided myself. . . ! I, who have valued myself. . . ! gratified my vanity in useless or blamable distrust. How humiliating. . . ! yet, how just a humiliation! . . . vanity, not love, has been my folly . . . I have courted prepossession and ignorance, and driven reason away. . . . *Til this moment I never knew myself.*" (p. 229; italics added)

This is the sort of self-recognition that we mean by "insight." Elizabeth has a sudden new picture of herself, one obtained in an intensely charged situation.

Elizabeth does not alter instantaneously. Her assumptions have been shaken. She needs time to assimilate the implications of the new information and what it tells her about herself and about Darcy. Darcy, too, needs time. He has been shaken himself by Elizabeth's reaction. Since he knows that he loves, it is somewhat easier for him to readjust his view of her and himself. Viewing Darcy for our purposes as the therapist, his adjustment at this point involves his altering in a way that will reach Elizabeth effectively. He must take into account her resistance to change.

Directionality

The resolution of Elizabeth's problems is not simple. Darcy's letter has a different impact on various aspects of her conflict. She feels enhanced by Darcy's regard, but at the same time her negative feelings relating to identifications with her parents are reinforced, for Darcy's judgment cannot now be lightly dismissed. Elizabeth has vented her resentment at men, but this resentment has been shown to be subjectively based. Most important, her narcissistic defenses ("I don't care") are shaken, though the hysterical ones ("I don't know I have feelings and desires") remain largely intact.[4] It is also important that Elizabeth is separated from her family by these events. Returning to Longbourn she thinks, "How much I shall have to conceal!"

In her reverie at this point on the failings in the Bennets' relationship, Elizabeth is, in effect, musing on what it is in each of her parents that contributes to her difficulties in loving. While the reverie seems to focus on her father's permissiveness and her mother's vicarious infatuation with army officers, it is also about Elizabeth's new concern—that she be upright enough in self and family to satisfy Darcy's values. The reverie indicates that she is moving away from her identification with Mr. Bennet's ironic detachment to a new attitude closer to Darcy's: a concern about principles and an acknowledgment that other people are truly important to her.

From this point in *Pride and Prejudice* there is a shift in the quality of interaction between the two lovers. Elizabeth learns more about Darcy's values, first from the maternal housekeeper at Pemberley, then through Darcy himself, in his changed behavior, and finally by learning of his efforts in rescuing Lydia. These serve to make her very much aware of him and of his positive regard for her. In psychoanalytic terms, Elizabeth must face her positive transference feelings, and their consequences. This she does in the episodes concerning Lydia and Lady Catherine. While she does not interact directly with Darcy in these scenes, it is his presence as the object of Elizabeth's desire that propels and gives these episodes significance.

Mutual influence is an important component of working through. The analyst responds out of a combination of reactivity and reserve. The analyst is *not* disinterested, but his interests are different from those of the patient. The analyst's responses provide psychologically new experiences for the patient, and are intended for his or her benefit. New perspectives on oneself require repeated iterations to become established. Because patients will quickly discount automatic, uninvolved responses, the therapist must remain personally involved in his or her communications to the patient.

The lovers of *Pride and Prejudice* have an easier time than most therapist-patient dyads. They are propelled by a normal developmental impulse to bond, rather than by a wish to relieve troubling, established symptoms. Each presents the other with challenges and encouragements, and thus they succeed. In long-term therapy, the therapist has a more difficult task because the patient is less interested in change. Because of this resistance to change, mutual influence must have a bias.

In analysis, directionality is created by the analyst's remaining true to the values of the analytic process. Gradually, the patient gives increasing weight to these values, which become merged with elements of his or her own beliefs. This is what we mean when we talk about "ego dominance" and "identification with the analyst" late in analysis. In *Pride and Prejudice* a major issue in the circular process between the two lovers is whether better values and principles will predominate. Will Elizabeth's need for superficial admiration lead her to prefer Wickham over Darcy? Will her identification with her father prevent her from loving? Will she be able to master an upsurge of sexual attraction? Will Darcy's pride ruin not only his chance for love but Bingley's and Jane's as well?

In the process of mutual influence there needs to be a tension or pull toward the ideal, toward that which will propel growth in a positive, self-enhancing direction. As Darcy eventually acknowledges,

Elizabeth's rejection is the jolt he needed to repair a distorted view of himself and his world. She has brought him up to her level.

After Darcy's letter, Elizabeth is self-critical. She sees that Darcy is well intentioned, and she strives now to be worthy of him. For Elizabeth part of this pull is represented in terms of manners and social/economic status. Various characters represent flagrant economic or social ambition. On the one hand, Elizabeth is above such ambitions, and Darcy admires this. On the other hand, Elizabeth experiences her family's crassness as a measure of herself, especially when Lydia runs off. She is convinced that Darcy will not have her now; he is too good for her. Elizabeth is struggling with the adequacy of her defenses once ironic detachment and hysterical denial have been stripped away. In effect, she is thinking, "Without these, do I have the ability to restrain the impulses to be (inappropriately) sexual, excessively aggressive? Am I capable of being the kind of person whom Darcy would respect?"

In other words, the directional pull of their influence on each other is toward that which each esteems. Each aspires to, and is pulled by, love and painful self-examination, toward the standard that the other comes to represent.

The role of Jane, and later of the housekeeper, speaks to another aspect of Elizabeth's conflict—her need to transfer her attachment from women to men. Because of her difficulties with her feminine identification and her view of marriage, Elizabeth fears and denies an interest in men and associated sexuality. Here the feminine voices of encouragement give her the push she needs to overcome her hysterical unawareness. She can move from an unambivalent, close bond with her sister to a close relationship with a man.

Having mobilized the most central tendencies of the patient through the process of mutual influence, the therapist proposes a way out. He says, "Look, you are feeling like an angry (or impulsive) child, and acting like one. You could try looking at all this from another point of view—a more objective and principled one. As you do so you may be able to see more clearly what you are involved in, and how you stay with it instead of moving ahead." The analyst, like the good mother, has in mind expectations that are just "ahead" of the patient developmentally.[5]

We believe that the mechanism of directionality involves self-esteem. Self-concept lies at the interface of the intrapsychic and the interpersonal. Internally our egos are engaged in maintaining a complex homeostasis in which stability is balanced against change. In the context of treatment we speak of these two tendencies as the repetition compulsion (which maintains the past) and the wish for mastery (which allows change to occur). Every interaction puts this balance into play. Contact with someone who is perceived as having higher status creates the possibility of our acquiring the power we attribute to that status. With such power, we hope we can improve self-esteem. Usually such changes are short-lived, because homeostatic mechanisms are not disturbed. The opera buff may feel elevated after attending a performance, but his or her life is not likely to be changed permanently. In treatment, and in *Pride and Prejudice*, the relationship facilitates mastery by way of repetitions and a steady emphasis on an attitude of respect.

Elizabeth begins with a conflicted sense of her worth. Prized by her father, and identified with him, she is superior to others; but this position makes her guilty, which makes her superiority brittle. Her mother does not like her. Her image of her mother and of herself in her mother's eyes further weakens her self-esteem. Seen in this way Darcy is, alternately, the father imago who arouses interest but bad self-feelings, and the therapeutic good parent, who encourages her to rise above her prejudices.

Darcy, by his own admission, has a similar problem. He holds to an old, but brittle, superiority that prevents attachments outside a family that consists now only of an adoring younger sister. By teasing him Elizabeth puts into play his wish for real, contemporary love and approbation. When he states his love in a superior, insulting way, she upbraids and rejects him. To win her he must aspire to a higher ideal, that of the gentleman. When he does, she can love him.

REVIEW

We have studied this early great novel, *Pride and Prejudice*, against the backdrop of the major concepts of clinical psychoanalytic theory. Without stretching either the novel or the theory excessively, we find that there are remarkable parallels. More precisely, we find that the "romantic" relationship of the novel actually derives much of its tension and interest for the reader from the fact that it is a relationship in which the "happy ending" of marriage depends on the salutary effect each lover has on the other. When we examine this effect in detail, we find that, as in a psychoanalysis, defenses emerge sequentially, and are dealt with in an active "collaboration" so that new outcomes occur. In the chapters that follow we shall pursue this parallel as a theme with variations: some novels describe both lovers' changes more fully, others describe one person's change, some deal with change mechanisms that are psychotherapeutic rather than psychoanalytic, some deal with developmental blocks, some with typical psychiatric symptoms, and some with multiple therapeutic modalities.

JANE EYRE:
MASTERING PASSION AND GUILT
THROUGH MUTUAL INFLUENCE

Jane Eyre is an immensely rich novel. Its unusually wide readership is comprised of children, adolescents, and adults. Children read it as a story of an orphan overcoming adversity in the form of wicked step-mothers and cruel schoolmasters. An aspect of the novel that appeals to adolescents, in particular, is its Gothic quality—dark, tortured Mr. Rochester; his wife, the madwoman in the attic; and Jane Eyre herself, the quiet governess whose patience is rewarded in the end. Adult readers may be drawn to the novel's implicit feminism. The heroine is a strong woman who overcomes deprivation and social disadvantage to establish herself morally and personally. But *Jane Eyre* also has wide appeal because it is a novel about psychological change—an impressive novel, in fact, because *both* its protagonists change. They do so largely through interactions with one another and these interactions are spelled out quite thoroughly by Charlotte Brontë. *Jane Eyre* is interesting to contrast with *Pride and Prejudice* where the change in Darcy is not extensively elaborated in the text. In this novel, we can compare and contrast the internal difficulties of each lover, and how the reactions of one lead to alteration in the other.

The earlier parts of the novel describe Jane's psychological development from age ten, when she rebels against the unfair treatment of her foster family, the Reeds, and is sent away to Lowood School. There, the students are ill used; Jane learns to suppress her rebelliousness, and, through her intelligence, obtains an education and becomes a teacher. This transformation has been facilitated in large part, by Jane's special relationship with Miss Temple, one of her teachers. When Miss Temple marries and leaves Lowood, Jane becomes restless and advertises for a position as a governess. She is hired to tutor a young girl at Thornfield, a large, private estate in the north of England.

JANE'S STORY

The romance of Jane Eyre and Edward Rochester is one of the best known in English literature. Jane has left Lowood School for Thornfield in search of love. She is not aware that it is heterosexual love she is now seeking. Rochester has all the romantic qualities that surround girls' pre-adolescent fantasies. He is dark, powerful, impulsive, dangerous, and sexually attractive, despite being "not handsome." But it is more than a Gothic tale that emerges in the interaction between Jane and Rochester.

The relationship that develops is one that reflects the workings of Jane's character and defenses as much as it reflects the emergence of her sexual feeling and interest. At first, Rochester deals with Jane in a circumspect, indirect manner. Like a therapist, he encourages her to voice *her* thoughts and feelings, rather than revealing his own. Their relationship, as master and governess, allows for a great deal of contact without the social constraints of the courtship situation. The protection of their roles, as well as Rochester's circumspection, allow Jane to grow into awareness of her feelings gradually, giving her time to confront a number of internal conflicts.

Their first meeting contains an element that will be emblematic—Jane assists Rochester. His horse slips and falls on an icy path. He is slightly hurt, and Jane, who happens to be walking nearby, helps him remount. Everything about Rochester—his stature, his powerful, spirited horse and large dog—emphasizes Jane's experience of his dangerous maleness. Indeed, as Jane hears the horse approach she thinks of the "Gytrash," a powerful animal in the mythology of northern England. A pubescent girl can cope with the images suggested by adult sexuality if she can maternalize the situation: the man is vulnerable, not she; she will care for him. From the start, Jane's relationship with Rochester is imbued with an aura of specialness and animal intensity, but the dangerous sexual and aggressive ideas are displaced onto the man and his animal companions.

They next meet a day later, with Rochester as the master, firmly in charge, interviewing Jane about her training and abilities. He is particularly interested in her artwork and notes three striking drawings in her portfolio. They come, he says, from "an artist's dreamland." The author's description of the drawings is hazy, as is Jane's explanation of them; she complains that she has not captured on paper the vision in her mind.

We do not have Jane's explanation of the striking images in the drawings. To guess at more specific meanings would be speculation, but some observations can be made on the incident, and, in a limited way, on the content of the pictures. Without conscious intention, Jane has exposed powerful internal imagery to Rochester, as a patient might in telling a striking dream to a therapist. Rochester comments only that "the drawings are, for a schoolgirl, peculiar. As to the thoughts, they are elfish." He notes some striking technical features of the work, and of the locations—that the landscape of one "must be Latmos," presumably one of the places Rochester has traveled. The idea that Jane has imagined a place where he has been suggests an intimacy and identity between them—her inner landscape relates to his life experience. It is a hint of the special relatedness we connect with engagement.

The images in Jane's drawings are complex and confusing, but powerful. What is significant is that the confusion and power are exposed to Rochester at an early point in their relationship. Like a patient beginning therapy, caught between eagerness and defense, Jane reveals much, but keeps meanings obscure.

A few days later Rochester initiates a conversation with Jane that establishes the quality of their future interaction. He asks her direct, penetrating, and highly personal questions. She answers with a proportionate directness, evoking half-revelations from him. The conversation begins on a note of such candor:

> "You examine me, Miss Eyre," said he: "do you find me handsome?"
> I should, if I had deliberated, have replied to this question by something conventionally vague and polite; but the answer somehow slipped from my tongue before I was aware, "No, sir." (p. 122)

Rochester notes her bluntness, contrasting it with her quiet nunlike demeanor. He prefers honesty over flattery and servility. A few minutes later, to learn more about her, he "orders" Jane to talk. She refuses; though she is a governess to his ward, she tells him, she is under no obligation to converse with him on command. They spar, and come to terms as conversational equals. With such a peer Rochester now can talk—although in a disguised manner—about *his* dilemma of wishing for love, but being prohibited from it. When Jane preaches morality, he confronts her with herself:

> [Rochester:] "You are afraid of me, because I talk like a sphinx."
> "Your language is enigmatical, sir; but though I am bewildered, I am certainly not afraid."
> "You *are* afraid—your self-love dreads a blunder."
> "In that sense I do feel apprehensive—I have no wish to talk nonsense."
> "If you did, it would be in such a grave, quiet manner, I should mistake it for sense. Do you ever laugh, Miss Eyre? . . . believe me, you are not naturally austere, any more than I am naturally vicious. The Lowood constraint still clings to you somewhat; controlling your features, muffling your voice, and restricting your limbs; and you fear in the presence of a man . . . to smile too gaily, speak too freely, or move too quickly; but in time I think you will be natural with me . . ."(p. 129)

And, indeed, further conversations with Rochester do alter Jane's response. He has addressed the defenses against expressiveness that have protected her from the danger affectionate feelings produced earlier in her life.

The ease of his manner freed me from painful restraint; the friendly frankness, as correct as cordial, with which he treated me, drew me to him. *I felt at times as if he were my relation rather than my master:* yet he was imperious sometimes still; but I did not mind that; I saw it was his way. *So happy, so gratified did I become with this new interest added to life, that I ceased to pine after kindred: my thin-crescent destiny seemed to enlarge; the blanks of existence were filled up; my bodily health improved; I gathered flesh and strength.* (p. 137; italics added)

Jane's emergence, her bodily development, is followed by a disturbing sequel: Rochester's bed is set on fire one night. Jane discovers the fire and saves the still-sleeping Rochester. After they have doused the fire, Rochester wants Jane to remain with him longer; when she insists on returning to her room, he says, "At least shake hands" (p. 141). Back in her bed, Jane is "tossed on a buoyant, but unquiet sea, where billows of trouble rolled under surges of joy" (p. 142). The sexual arousal stimulated by their growing intimacy and mutual need is dangerous; its fire must be "put out" by Jane. She can fend Rochester off, but her own desire (the buoyant, unquiet sea) has become partially conscious.

In the next plot development Rochester invites the local gentry for a stay of several weeks. When he appears to be enamored of Blanche Ingram, an attractive, but mercenary local beauty, Jane's awareness of her love and desire for him increases. During this visit competitive issues come to the fore. Rochester insists that Jane attend the social gatherings, although she is treated as a socially inferior household domestic. Jane has become accustomed to interacting with Rochester as an equal. Her humiliation and jealousy make it clear to her that she loves Rochester, and loves not as servant to master, but as woman to man. Rochester tries to get her to acknowledge her feelings to him. He points out her loneliness, her "coldness," and her refusal to "stir one step to meet it [love] where it waits for you" (p. 185). Jane stands firm; she will not be maneuvered into being the first to declare love. With admiration, Rochester then acknowledges her independence and self-sufficiency, her sound judgment and strong conscience.

Despite Jane's general clearheadedness, she remains confused about who is responsible for the fire in Rochester's room and some later mysterious events. She attributes them to a servant, Grace Poole. Many hints might alert her that something is not right at Thornfield, but Rochester's mad wife, Bertha Mason, remains unknown to her. Psychologically, Jane does not want to discover the existence of a woman who has a rightful claim on Rochester.

Jane's avoidance of the true situation at Thornfield is further dramatized when Bertha's brother, George Mason, comes to visit his sister and is attacked and stabbed by her during the night. Rochester solicits Jane's help in dealing with the incident and hiding it from a houseful of guests. She remains unaware of what has really happened and accepts Rochester's request that she ask no more questions. Jane's confusion remains in place so that she can continue to desire Rochester. He confides in her even further about his unhappy past, his dangerous present situation, and even his peace in having come to know her—but all in allusive form. In response to his distress, Jane counsels propriety; she denies her own fantasies and wishes. When she hears Rochester describe how he must live a life without love, due to a youthful indiscretion, she rejects his implicit invitation to advise him to flaunt morality in the service of love.

Now Jane is called to the deathbed of Mrs. Reed. Here she learns that, in retaliation for Jane's childhood rebelliousness, her aunt has prevented her from receiving her inheritance. This episode bolsters Jane's movement away from the [bad] mother and toward Rochester. Returning to Thornfield, Jane tells Rochester that she feels "strangely glad to get back again to you; and wherever you are is my home—my only home" (p. 233).

In the most romantic scene of the novel Jane and Rochester meet on Midsummer Eve in the Thornfield orchard. At first, he teases her about her belief that he intends to marry Blanche Ingram. Rochester then admits his attachment to Jane, and she expresses her happiness being at Thornfield and her dread of ever having to leave him. Recognizing that she will not be lured by either love or jealousy into an illicit affair, and freed momentarily from a sense of complete responsibility for his action by Jane's admission of love, Rochester asks her to marry. Jane, ignorant of the truth, happily accepts.

On their wedding day the ceremony is disrupted at the last moment by the sudden arrival of George Mason, who declares "the existence of an impediment"—a prior wife! Crushed and angry, Rochester takes the wedding party to see the deranged Bertha Mason, and explains the facts of his situation to Jane and the others. When he and Jane are alone, he pleads with her to understand his dreadful dilemma, to love him and live with him away from England as his wife. In a mid-Victorian context Rochester's plea is scandalous. Jane refuses, however, for internal reasons, not merely those of social propriety. Her *internal standards,* her superego, will not allow her to be happy or make Rochester happy under these conditions: "Conscience, turned tyrant, held Passion by the throat" (p. 282). Jane's scruples make the most sense seen in the light of how incestuous the situation must now seem to her. Certainly her next actions support such an interpretation; she flees Thornfield during the night. Taking almost nothing with her, she exhausts what money she has on coach fare to travel as far from Thornfield as she can.

Jane Eyre is read avidly by pubescent girls. It speaks, in the Rochester-Jane relationship, to their psychological situation. Psychoanalytic theory tells us that the Oedipal situation is not actually resolved until adolescence, when the emergence of adult sexual capacity makes it crucial that incestuous impulses be rejected. The recognition of sexual impulses at puberty reawakens dormant Oedipal wishes and requires drastic defensive action in the form of dramatic renunciation. Jane reacts to the emergence of sexuality with a self-destructive flight into asceticism.[1]

The next phase of Jane Eyre's life concerns her psychological reaction to this adolescent brush with incestuous temptation. All impulse, almost life itself, must be foresworn in an effort to disavow, deny, and distance the dangers just narrowly averted. "Tyrant Conscience" takes Jane close to death from cold and starvation, far from Thornfield. The imagery of the landscape into which she escapes has strong maternal overtones; it is Nature, the good mother, who keeps her alive during her flight.[2] Jane stops her ascetic flight just short of starvation; she begs at a strange home for food, work, and shelter. She is taken in by a young minister, St. John Rivers, and, as she recovers, is given a place in his household.

This new home combines the elements Jane needs at this point—kindness and love in an atmosphere of high-mindedness. St. John Rivers and his two sisters provide a peer group united by their morality, culture, and dedication to good works. This atmosphere provides external support for Jane's motives in fleeing Thornfield. There can be love without impulsive loss of control; one can love "sisters" and a "brother" rather than the dangerous Rochester. Jane is given work by St. John, teaching in the local school. This is a comfortable return to the Lowood solution—disguised in an adult role—but issues aroused earlier cannot be completely avoided.

St. John emerges as the voice of passion in this episode—inverted passion. He asks Jane to marry him and go with him as a missionary to India. St. John makes it clear that he neither needs nor loves Jane, but is drawn to her potential for submission to him—in the form of grueling religious dedication. His proposal offers a masochistic, conscience-satisfying resolution to Jane's guilt and anxiety. Now, she struggles with a new form of conflict—that between her defensive asceticism and her wish for loving attachment. Just as she cannot submit in sin to Rochester, she finds herself unable to submit in self-denial to St. John. When he makes his proposal, and presses her for a reply, she must face this conflict.

> "Once more, why this refusal?" he asked.
> "Formerly," I answered, "because you did not love me; now, I reply, because you almost hate me. If I were to marry you, you would kill me. You are killing me now."
> His lips and cheeks turned white—quite white.
> "*I should kill you—I am killing you?* Your words are such as ought not to be used: violent, unfeminine, and untrue." (p. 394)

Jane has detected the hostile component of asceticism, the invitation to join St. John in turning "Tyrant Conscience" upon love. This encounter makes Jane aware of the aggressiveness of her own superego pressures as she experiences St. John's insistence that she give up love for his life of idealistic self-sacrifice.[3] Her vigorous "no!" reflects a realization that her own actions have been motivated by guilt—in reaction to Rochester's pleas for an illicit relationship. As she questions the destructive effects of this guilty action, Jane—implicitly—begins to reinterpret her love for Rochester.

One night, soon after her confrontation with St. John, she hears the "voice" of Rochester calling to her: "'Jane! Jane! Jane!' . . . it was the voice of a human being—a known, loved, well-remembered voice—that of Edward Fairfax Rochester; and it spoke in pain and woe, wildly, eerily, urgently" (p. 401).

In turning from St. John back to Rochester Jane takes an important maturational step. The renunciation of sexuality, which seemed necessary earlier, gives way to the acceptance of intimacy. With difficulty, Jane recognizes that the appeal of St. John's proposal is masochistic.[4] Rochester's call to her is a plea from another who is truly in need, and who will offer her love in return. Unlike St. John's invitation to a fundamentally aggressive solution—sexual denial and the turning of frustrated desire against oneself—it is an appeal based on the human need for companionship and mutuality of positive feeling and desire. Jane, having experienced the dangers of excess in both impulse and conscience, is now in a position to deal with her relationship with Rochester in a more realistic way.

Jane returns to Thornfield to learn that it has been destroyed in a fire set by Bertha Mason. Rochester, who was injured trying to save Bertha, has been left blind, with a maimed hand. He is living in Ferndean, a small house a few miles away from Thornfield. Jane returns to him; in a scene that replays and reverses earlier ones between them, she teases him about his jealousy, but finally admits her love for him and agrees to marry.

The final chapter begins in an active authorial voice: "Reader, I married him." It continues with a description of the worldly and happy life Jane and Rochester lead and ends with a description of St. John's "successful" martyred death in missionary service. The tempting idealism of adolescence is part of the past for Jane; the more tangible, and less fantasy-based, satisfactions of life and love with a flesh-and-blood partner are now both desirable and acceptable. Sexual intimacy is possible now, freed from anxiety about passionate, incestuous fantasies. A combination of factors have facilitated Jane's "working through" of this issue: her experiences with St. John; the death of the dangerous mother/rival (Bertha Mason); an inheritance that allows Jane to enter marriage with a sense of equality; and the injury to Rochester that symbolizes his mortality and allows Jane to be his caretaker—he is no longer the dangerous Oedipal figure of the past.

ROCHESTER'S STORY

If the psychological story of Jane Eyre is one of traversing the developmental stages of adolescence, that of Edward Fairfax Rochester is one of arrested development and neurotic conflict. Since *Jane Eyre* is told in the first person, we encounter Rochester only through his meetings with Jane. His history and his interior consciousness are not revealed as fully as hers. Nevertheless, Rochester tells us a great deal about himself and the therapeutic narrative that heals his sense of deficit and conflict. His meetings with Jane are therapeutic encounters: Rochester talks to her about what is most on his mind. The interactions between them concern the present, and the past-as-manifested-in-the-present, far more than they do the historic past. These meetings are therapeutic for Rochester in at least two ways. When he is with Jane, he feels happy and relieved of his burden of guilt and anger. Furthermore, by having Jane in his life, he gradually ceases his restless, driven, and misdirected search for love and peace. She enables him to do this by seeing his potential for real love (even in the face of his moody withdrawals) while maintaining her own integrity in reaction to his tempting sensuality. Although his contact with Jane alone is not sufficient to cure him—the fire, Bertha Mason's death, his blinding and maiming, and Jane's return are required to achieve that—his relationship with Jane, during her stay at Thornfield, prepares the way for future changes.

Rochester is an embittered man, injured by his father's unfair behavior. To maintain the estate intact for his older son, Rochester's father marries Edward off to a wealthy heiress, whose family has kept hidden its history of congenital madness and degeneration. Rochester marries Bertha Mason because of her beauty and wealth. He finds himself trapped in a union with a woman who is, at first, merely superficial and repugnant to him, but who later turns viciously insane. Rochester becomes depressed and despondent. His "solution" is to bring his wife back to England, secretly; he puts her in the care of Grace Poole, an experienced attendant, and keeps her hidden in rooms on the third floor of Thornfield. Then he begins to travel, restlessly seeking a woman with whom he will feel loved and safe. What he finds instead are repetitions of his union with his wife—a series of affairs with women who are superficial and who ultimately betray him. He becomes increasingly cynical, angry, and impatient.

Both his inner state and the role Jane Eyre will play for him are depicted in their first meeting. Rochester is riding hard when his horse slips on the ice. He is injured in the horse's fall, and truculently demands Jane's help while blaming her for the whole situation. Jane deals with Rochester calmly; she offers help, but respects his pride and need to feel in control. The imagery of the scene is aggressive and full of animal energy. Rochester's fall suggests the self-destructive potential of this energy. It is Jane—self-possessed, interested, and helpful—who emerges as the successful figure in the encounter.

In this intial encounter, Jane has managed Rochester's feelings with sensitivity and tact. She has qualities that enable their relationship to continue in the face of Rochester's chronic mistrust. From the beginning, he associates Jane with fairies, "the men in green." This attributed magical specialness and her subordinate role render Jane benign in Rochester's eyes. Her inexperience and shyness with men reflect an innocence that Rochester values in contrast to the treacherous, worldly women he has known. But it is primarily Jane's character that establishes the salutary quality of their interactions. She is deferential when her role requires it, yet she will not yield to his attempts to dominate her. This experience is therapeutic for Rochester. As therapists, we are frequently faced with powerful pressures from our patients to respond to them in complementary ways. Our professional role and training help us hold our ground in the face of anger, demandingness, and impatience on the patient's part—hopefully, like Jane, without rancor, but with equable firmness.

Their third encounter occurs some days after Rochester has observed Jane's drawings; he seeks her out for conversation. The initial repartee involves Jane's negative reply to his question about whether he is handsome. She then asks if he is a "philanthropist"; he admits he is not, yet there is something he wants her to understand.

"But I bear a conscience . . . once I had a kind of rude tenderness . . . when I was as old as you . . . now I flatter myself I am hard and tough . . . pervious, though, through a chink or two still, and with one sentient point in the middle of the lump. . . . does that leave hope for me?" (p. 123)

Thus, Rochester expresses both his self-protective stance, and his yearning for attachment. A few minutes later he tells Jane that she has caught his interest and now he is in a mood to talk. He then orders her to speak, but she will not do so merely to "show off." Rochester notes her silence and apologizes:

"I put my request in an absurd, almost insolent form. Miss Eyre, I beg your pardon. The fact is, once for all, I don't wish to treat you like an inferior: that is (correcting himself), I claim only such superiority as must result from twenty years' difference in age and a century's advance in experience . . . I desire you to have the goodness to talk to me a little now, and divert my thoughts, which are galled with dwelling on one point—cankering as a rusty nail." (p. 124)

Jane, however, will not allow this qualification to go by: "'I don't think, sir, you have the right to command me, merely because you are older than I, or because you have seen more of the world than I have; your claim to superiority depends on the use you have made of your time and experience'" (p. 124). Jane-the-therapist has interpreted Rochester's attempt to retain a self-protective privilege in their relationship. Such privilege demands a moral core. Rochester counters with a request to Jane: "Accept my orders from time to time, without being piqued or hurt by the tone of command." Jane reminds him, with some humor, that she is his paid servant. As such, she *must* accept his orders, but she is very pleased that he is concerned for her feelings. Rochester is reassured when he sees that Jane can stand up for herself yet remain involved with him as another person, despite their differences in rank.

> "Humbug! Most things free-born will submit to anything for a salary . . . I mentally shake hands with you for your answer . . . and as much for the manner in which it was said, as for the substance of the speech; the manner was frank and sincere; one does not often see such a manner: no, on the contrary, affectation, or coldness, or stupid, coarse-minded misapprehension of one's meaning are the usual rewards of candor." (p. 125)

Their conversation shifts to the subject of goodness and badness in character, and soon Rochester is voicing to Jane concerns about himself.

> "I have plenty of faults of my own . . . I was thrust on the wrong tack at one and twenty, and have never recovered to the right course since; but I might have been very different; I might have been as good as you—wiser—almost as stainless . . . I am a trite commonplace sinner." (p. 126)

As Rochester finds himself confessing to this unworldly young girl, he explains what it is about her that enables him to do so:

> "Do you wonder that I avow this to you? Know that in the course of your future life you will often find yourself elected the involuntary confidante of your acquaintances' secrets: people will instinctively find out, as I have done, that it is not your forte to tell of yourself, *but to listen while others talk of themselves; they will feel, too, that you listen with no malevolent scorn of their indiscretion, but with a kind of inate sympathy, not the less comforting and encouraging because it is very unobtrusive in its manifestations.*"
> [Jane:] "How do you know?—how can you guess all this, sir?"
> "I know it well; therefore I proceed almost as freely as if I were writing my thoughts in a diary." (pp. 126–127; italics added)

Having asserted that Jane is an intuitive psychotherapist, Rochester continues with his central problem:

> "When fate wronged me, I had not the wisdom to remain cool; I turned desperate; then I degenerated. Now, when any vicious simpleton excites my disgust by his paltry ribaldry, I cannot flatter myself that I am better than he: I am forced to confess that he and I are on a level. I wish I had stood firm—God knows I do! *Dread remorse when you are tempted to err, Miss Eyre: remorse is the poison of life.*" (p. 127; italics added)

For the remainder of this scene Rochester tries to convince Jane (and himself) that remorse is his problem. If he can ignore remorse, he can find happiness by taking action, by following his own laws. Jane, who does not know he is alluding to his love for her, remains resolute in her views.

"... if you tried hard, you would in time find it possible to become what you yourself would approve; and that if from this day you began with resolution to correct your thoughts and actions, you would in a few years have laid up a new and stainless store of recollections, to which you might revert with pleasure. " (p. 128)

While this sounds like a moralistic scolding, it is actually an interpretation of Rochester's conflict. He has acknowledged that it is remorse that tortures him. Jane has evoked a wish for love that Rochester believes will assuage his sense of betrayal and loneliness. He is impelled to act on this wish in his characteristic, impulsive (but unconsciously guilty) way. When she counsels upright behavior and patience, Jane reminds him of how his impulsive search for love has failed him in the past. That is, his past behavior, which has led to unconscious repetitions, reflects an unresolved conflict between his wish—for gratification at any cost—and his defense—a guilt that leads to failure.

Rochester reacts to his inner conflict with the sort of creative attempt at compromise that we also see in patients struggling between an overwhelming impulse and moral scruples. He tries to get Jane to be the one who initiates a declaration of love so that he need not feel so responsible for the consequences of a bigamous liaison. Rochester does this by eliciting Jane's sympathy for his plight—which he depicts indirectly; he makes Jane jealous by courting Blanche Ingram in front of her; finally, he threatens to send her away forever by finding her a position in Ireland. At the same time, he tells her that

"... it is as if I had a string somewhere under my left ribs, tightly and inextricably knotted to a similar string situated in the corresponding quarter of your little frame ... I'm afraid that cord of communion will be snapped; and then I've a nervous notion I should take to bleeding inwardly. As for you—you'd forget me."

"That I *never* should do, sir: you know — " Impossible to proceed. (p. 239)

Now Jane gives voice to her feelings, declaring how happy she has been at Thornfield, and how miserable she is to leave. Rochester has partly succeeded in getting Jane to "go first." But in the course of clarifying that he loves *her*, not Blanche, he must be active and not only embrace Jane, but ask her to marry.

After Jane accepts, there is a further struggle between the two, a struggle that reflects Rochester's domineering and unrepentant side. He wants to possess Jane, to dress her in new clothes, to make her his emotional as well as financial dependent. He sings her a song that glorifies and idealizes love, but it is a love in which the lovers die together. Jane rebels; she refuses the new wardrobe and declares that she will "not be hurried away in a suttee" (p. 259). Rochester's mode of loving is still dominated by an aggression that threatens Jane's hard-won sense of self. If Rochester is "guilty" of a repetitive sin, it is not that of desire, but rather that his desires are expressed in an unmodified, infantile way. Regardless of consequences, he wants what he wants, and, like a child, Rochester does not give up his ways easily. Even after Mason exposes his imminent bigamy at the marriage ceremony, he wants Jane to come away with him and live abroad as a common-law wife. Jane's flight is not only from her own temptation, but because she recognizes that such a union would turn sour for Rochester, exactly because of its guilty basis.

For Jane, the exposure of the Bertha Mason mystery is a revelation of sexuality and the parental bedroom; for Rochester, it is an admission of the persistence of his inner wishes. While the plot suggests that Rochester fully intended to marry Jane, and that fate, in the form of Mason, has prevented him, Rochester has played his part. He is not able to say, "I must not have her," but he allows the discovery to take place, and, by his subsequent persistence, he drives Jane into exile.

Before Jane flees, Rochester speaks to her at length. His purpose is to possess her any way he can. In an impassioned, no longer allusive, way he tells her his history—his early rejections, the deception of his marriage, his unhappy affairs, and his final return to Thornfield "sourly disposed . . . against all womankind" (p. 297). Then he recounts his discovery of a woman he could trust and love within his own household. Now he is faced with the paradox of knowing the sort of person he wants, but finding that accepting that she is what he wants means he must be denied the love he seeks! Jane supplies the restraint. Their discussion has a meaning that is pertinent to psychological change: Jane, the one person he trusts, both listens to his story and firmly tells him its proper ending. A child cannot really accept frustration, but the next best thing is an understanding rejection from the object of desire. Sympathy, forgiveness, and hope for future satisfaction are partial solaces for disappointment.

But when Jane leaves, taking solace with her, Rochester becomes desolate. He rages, searches unsuccessfully for her, sends away everyone he cares about, and becomes a recluse. When Bertha Mason sets fire to Jane's room, Rochester shows he has not lost humanity; he stays to save the servants, and then his wife. She jumps from the roof and kills herself. Escaping the flames, Rochester is blinded and injures his hand. Here is his symbolic punishment, leaving him vulnerable but not impotent. The phallic impulse has turned in upon itself and spent its energy in the climactic, cleansing fire. While Rochester's psychological alteration must be inferred—from what happens to Jane at Morton—the story now allows him gratification, but in a compromised form. His injuries force him to accept dependence upon others, particularly upon Jane when she returns. He realizes he cannot obtain everything he wants by force. However, Rochester will not accept pity—he maintains *his* pride and his self-respect. Moreover, his relationship with Jane remains the same, in essence. They banter and test each other's honesty, frankness, and love in an atmosphere of respect and trust.

DISCUSSION

Engagement

As in *Pride and Prejudice* where the need for heterosexual intimacy provides the impetus for engagement, a similar dynamic moves Jane and Rochester beyond the impersonal roles of governess and master. Rochester needs the helping hand of a strong but loving woman. Jane needs permission for the emergence of her adult sexuality and femininity. There is a fortunate fit between what each desires and what the other has to offer. Like Darcy, Rochester is wealthy, masculine, and dangerous—the original Gothic figure. Jane, whom the reader knows to be undaunted by those in authority, is not cowed by him, but is drawn to his forcefulness and underlying vulnerability. And like Darcy, Rochester is attracted to Jane's spirit, her frankness, and refusal to flatter.

Mutual Influence

In *Jane Eyre*, the two major characters influence each other in a continuing, reciprocating manner. Characteristic and powerful internal issues are evoked strongly in one person by the other, leading to some sort of action (in the form of plot developments). The impact of each such action has an effect on the other person, who then alters his or her response, leading the two parties to a new resolution in their relationship pattern, and internal psychologies. In *Pride and Prejudice* the interventions of the "therapeutic" figure are subtle; in *Jane Eyre*, all the reactions are more forceful and direct.

Rochester demands that Jane show him her drawings, or that she sit and talk with him. Jane chides Rochester about his demands for satisfaction, and she leaves him when these demands become imperious and immoral. In therapy we might view such active behavior on the part of the therapist as manipulative and suspect. In the novel, however, the characters engage in interchanges that are the *functional equivalent* of interpretive activity on the therapist's part. That is, the comments or actions of one serve to make the other more aware of certain behaviors and tendencies, and block the automatic continuation of the behavior.

In *Pride and Prejudice* we suggested that there was a truly mutual influence going on between the two major characters, in that each of them was "cured" of intrapsychic difficulties. Elizabeth's change process was far more visible. In *Jane Eyre* the salutary influence on *each* party is made clear. The diagram summarizes some of the mutual influence patterns, for each of the two protagonists.

These influence patterns are interwoven, creating the mutuality that we feel is one characteristic of the therapeutic narrative.

Directionality

What provides the impetus, or directionality, for the positive changes that occur in fiction or therapy? Charlotte Brontë gives us an interesting answer. In her novel, it is authentic love, personal morality, and honest self-expression that characterize the responses of the two lovers as they influence each other. Differentness also contributes to the energy of their encounters. The problems of one are the stimulus for change in the other. Jane needs to experience someone as earthy, vital, and lonely as Rochester to shake loose her carefully constructed guard. Rochester needs to encounter a woman who values self-control but is capable of an altruistic love.

Jane's alternating submission and rebellion is a theme that predates her romance with Rochester and expresses an issue that is the core struggle in all her relationships. Jane learned a pattern of submissiveness, bordering on masochism, at the Lowood School, emulating the example of Helen Burns, her closest friend. This style helped her adapt to the harsh demands and cruel deprivations of the school. But submission can go only so far for Jane until she bursts out in an assertion of individuality. Her dilemma is that this individuality may mean loneliness and spiritual starvation. On the other hand, getting close is associated with the suppression of her true self. This conflict intersects with her first experience of heterosexual feeling for Rochester, as it has intersected with something or someone in each of her previous stages of development. The unique pull that Rochester exerts provides the power for her to engage with him in a way that will be mutative.

A similar argument can be made for the power of Rochester's attachment to Jane in bringing about his change. His disturbance involves his mistrust of women, although, in the plot, this difficulty traces back to his father's manipulations. (Perhaps Rochester feels, unconsciously, that his powerful father does not wish him to have a sane and healthy woman.) Jane *is* such a woman; she is truly interested in him, for himself, and she breaks through his cynicism to the "sentient point" within him that still lives. The dual elements of early, character-forming experience and the hope of transcending that experience combine to make Jane so powerful for Rochester that he engages psychologically with her.

The pattern of directionality between Jane and Rochester also involves their differentness. Jane's impulses are suppressed—"the

MUTUAL INFLUENCE PATTERNS IN *JANE EYRE*

Jane	Rochester
Problem:	Response:

Jane — Problem	Rochester — Response
1. Repression of sensuality; denial of her bodily needs.	1. Sensual expressiveness; comfort with his body and desire for hers.
2. Inhibition of impulses; defenses against all expressiveness.	2. He values expressiveness and encourages her to speak out.
3. Proud self-sufficiency dominates over taking risks in relating.	3. Confronts her defensive pride; later, expresses *his* love in a direct manner that she may emulate.
4. Mistrust in others' values and purposes, based on early experience.	4. Good-heartedness, humanness underneath his demands for gratification.
5. Masochistic, submissive style used as a solution to her frustration over limitations on her power.	5. He constantly challenges this pattern both with his own direct desire for gratification, and with his sincere belief in love.

Rochester	Jane
Problem:	Response:

Rochester — Problem	Jane — Response
1. Disillusionment with parental figures, and hence with all love objects.	1. Steady capacity to love with respect.
2. Use of indulgence as a substitute for love.	2. Capacity to manage impulses through self-control; idealization of the superego.
3. Alienation from the social contract; abandonment of social mores and ideals.	3. Acceptance of social mores; internalization of values into superego.

Lowood constraint." Rochester's are out of control—his anger, impatience, and demand for sexual satisfaction. While, for each alone, this state of things prevents psychological growth, in their encounters with each other, it is the basis for influence. The series of conversations between Jane and Rochester are confrontations between two strong-willed individuals, each convinced of the logic of his or her position. Jane is stirred up by Rochester, but her powerful conscience constrains him, first, from treating her imperiously, and, her, later, from accepting his pleas for unmarried intimacy. That Jane attributes the latter refusal to "Tyrant Conscience" is an indication that she is not simply obeying society's laws. Her internal values—which she cannot alter until she is faced with an extreme version of them in St. John—exert a relentless power over her. However, because Rochester is so passionate and unfettered, the power of her internal restrictions is first loosened in her encounters with him.

Rochester, too, is under the sway of a "Tyrant Conscience," one that takes the form of angry, self-indulgent, ultimately self-defeating behaviors. In Jane, he encounters someone who associates self-restraint with positive caring feelings. Jane's superego grew strong out of her relationships with Miss Temple and her friend, Helen Burns, both women with loving hearts. When she counsels restraint to Rochester, she conveys that one can say "no" without being rejecting or condemning. Rochester can begin to consider patience although initially this takes the form of trying to get Jane to declare herself first—a compromise between his impulsiveness and the control she represents.

Things get out of hand for both—such is the power of love and sexuality in a relationship between two lonely people. The interlude of Jane's flight and the fire at Thornfield is an externalization of a desperate defense against losing control. Both are "punished"—Jane, in the form of self-exile, Rochester in the form of Oedipus-like injuries, which stem indirectly from his loss of Jane. But the happy ending of *Jane Eyre* is indicative that the phase of punishment is only another step in the characters' growth. It is a sort of last, mighty gasp of their previous character styles, one that threatens to destroy each, but does not. They emerge free of old conflicts, and ready for intimacy, with all of its consequences. Brontë includes an afterword that shows us clearly a happy couple, with two children, Rochester's sight restored, and Jane personally fulfilled.

There is a parallel between Charlotte Brontë's vision of the directional pull in *Jane Eyre* and Jane Austen's view in *Pride and Prejudice*. One character in each novel is depicted as proper and high-minded, a clear representation of goodness—from society's point of view. In *Pride and Prejudice*, this character is Darcy; in *Jane Eyre*, it is Jane. The other character is more outspoken and unconventional. In looking at directionality in *Pride and Prejudice* we noted the importance of superior moral standards and upright behavior. *Jane Eyre* brings to our attention how impulses may also be an important part of the pull toward change. As Elizabeth Bennet points out to Darcy at the end, it was her "impertinence" that attracted him. The reader knows that Elizabeth's frankness was crucial in bringing Darcy's pride to his attention, and in helping him alter it. It is important to note that these more impulsive sources of direction are effective when they occur in a loving context. Because Darcy and Jane love their partners, they can accept confrontation and sexual intensity without being threatened.

Fictional Change in *Jane Eyre* Compared with Therapeutic Change

We shall turn now to a more specific comparison between Jane's fictional change and elements of the psychoanalytic process of change. The plot and character developments that occur early in *Jane Eyre* can be viewed as a prologue to the central action of the novel—the relationship between Jane and Rochester. Brontë describes Rochester's behavior in ways that are reminiscent of an analytic stance. Rochester listens with interest and often in silence; he draws Jane out, but is "enigmatic" about himself. These behaviors facilitate Jane's use of him as a transference figure. Jane becomes deeply involved, but resists awareness of her feelings even when Rochester encourages her to admit them. If we view the "events" of the plot that occur between Jane's talks with Rochester as the equivalent of dreams or extra-therapeutic enactments, then the parallel with analytic process is more obvious.[5] The powerful sexual feelings aroused by the episode of the fire in Rochester's room; Jane's jealousy and feeling of exclusion during Blanche Ingram's visit; her uneasiness and unconscious denial of Bertha Mason's existence—all these together may be viewed as manifestations of a transference neurosis. That is, Jane experiences the same confusion, preoccupation, intensity of feeling, and increased struggle between impulse and defense that a patient would in the midst of powerful transference feelings toward an analyst.

As this happens, Rochester serves the same dual function an analyst would; he is the object of Jane's feelings and the observer who draws her out. Jane's issues are not just *enacted,* they are also *discussed*—in highly charged moments that include the self-awareness we associate with insight. For example, Rochester reflects to Jane the defensive function of certain qualities—her pride, her self-containment, her need to be right—and ultimately he makes her *aware* of her wishes for love.

Rochester's bigamous proposal and its denouement can be reframed as if they were countertransference-induced events in a treatment. The Thornfield phase ends with an outburst of erotic feeling, abetted by Rochester's misleading presentation of himself as available for marriage. It is followed by Jane's flight into asceticism. Like many such transference-countertransference induced events in treatment, this crisis has a potentially positive outcome. In the next phase of her life, Jane uses her relationship with St. John to work through the superego problem that has been aroused. Again, Jane *articulates to* St. John the inner consequences of accepting his proposal ("You would kill me. You are killing me now.") While Rochester and St. John, the figures who stimulate Jane's insight, do not have a conscious therapeutic intent, we have shown how their interest has the *effect* of removing her resistances to self-knowledge and enabling her to change.

It can be argued, of course, that these events occur as part of the novel's plot, with meanings and purposes quite independent of the issue of intrapsychic change. We would reply that Brontë's depiction of Jane's growing insight moves the plot along, that, in essence, plot movement in *Jane Eyre* is the fictional equivalent of therapeutic movement. For example, Brontë could have resolved the problems of Jane's Thornfield phase much earlier, using the plot device of the fire and Rochester's release from Bertha Mason. The entire Rivers phase can be seen as building toward an internal resolution of tensions between desire and conscience. Immediately after her final confrontation with St. John, Jane "hears" the call from Rochester. Externally, she knows he is no different than before, but *her* internal alteration, resulting from an awareness of the devastating effects of guilt and self-deprivation, allows her to return to Rochester. In a similar manner, Jane Austen could have brought the lovers of *Pride and Prejudice* together after their meeting at Pemberley, but her heroine, too, had intrapsychic issues to resolve. We are suggesting that a novel with a narrative that involves intrapsychic change needs to provide time and opportunity (in the form of plot complexities) for the difficulties of "working through." The reader accepts and appreciates these delays because they are psychologically plausible, even necessary.

In summary, transference, resistance, transference neurosis, countertransference, interpretation, and insight can all be found in *Jane Eyre*. What is missing is the conscious therapeutic intent of the agents of change. Missing also is an initial conscious wish for intrapsychic change on the part of the protagonist. These elements—aspects of *directionality*, in our model—are provided by such "natural" motivations as desire, resentment, moral imperatives, and ambition. If analytic process is a special version of a natural process, we would expect such natural motives to function in addition to conscious wishes to get better, or to help another get better. Indeed, careful consideration of motivations on both sides in analysis reveals that behind the "therapeutic contract," lie more complex and transference-driven motives.

Observations of change in a fictional text can raise further questions: Is it possible that analytic process is, and should be, moved by more personal motivations? Does "therapeutic neutrality" mean a static, disinterested position, or a more active, flexible one, in which the analyst or therapist, deliberately or intuitively, acts differently with different patients and at different moments? This idea is subject to the challenge of the shibboleth, "corrective emotional experience."[6] But is it also possible that, in a manner more like a fictional character than like a mirror, analysts react and *transmit these reactions to patients as a necessary part of therapeutic process?* As students of countertransference would be the first to point out, this idea is hardly new, but its reappearance in this exploration of processes of change in literature affirms the value of further study of the analyst's emotional responsiveness, particularly the ways in which the analyst's ego monitors affects stimulated *by* the patient and modulates behavior *toward* the patient.

4

MARGARET DRABBLE'S
THE NEEDLE'S EYE:
A DEPRESSIVE NEUROSIS IS HEALED IN A
SPONTANEOUS RELATIONSHIP

In our study of two nineteenth-century novels (Chapters 2 and 3), we discovered parallels between elements in the psychoanalytic process and the process of change in several characters. We will now turn our attention to two recent novels. We continue our search for literary examples of conflict resolution and transformation of character, but our comparisons in these instances reveal a wider range of influences leading to change, influences more like those of psychotherapy where elements of direct support, reassurance, and confrontation exist alongside the psychoanalytic elements of interpretation of transference and resistance. Both the protagonists in these two novels—*The Needle's Eye* by Margaret Drabble and *The Accidental Tourist* by Anne Tyler—are men in their late thirties whose lives are compromised by serious long-term characterological difficulties and unresolved traumas. Both men are metaphorically "at the end of their ropes" when a new person—a woman—enters their lives. These seemingly serendipitous or "accidental" encounters become the opportunity for powerful engagements around which each man is able to resolve his psychological dilemma.

We begin with *The Needle's Eye*, a novel that illustrates the premise that transference, in its broadest sense, underlies all relationships. People constantly seek out and attempt to resume, reenact, and repair old love relationships: elements of both transference and reality coexist in all relationships, and become the focus of psychotherapeutic ones. It stands to reason that healing relationships may spontaneously arise, exist, develop, and eventually terminate, outside of any formal psychotherapeutic sphere. Falling in love is a striking example from ordinary life. Transforming, lifelong friendships; relationships with mentors and teachers; and religious beliefs connected with faith in a deity or deitylike leader all have the power to create the kind of growth and development that one also seeks in psychotherapeutic treatment.

Furthermore, we believe that works of literature, particularly "psychological" novels, often capture this process of transference repetition with startling clarity, even if this is not their primary intent. When we read the passages in *David Copperfield* that deal with David's marriage to Dora, we realize the intensity with which, to the exclusion of sound judgment and realistic assessment, he seeks to recapture and restore the mother he lost in childhood. *The Needle's Eye*, a twentieth-century novel informed by an awareness of depth psychology, depicts clearly psychological conflict and its vicissitudes in the course of a new relationship.

We will delineate the elements of therapeutic process in a fictional relationship drawn from this novel. Margaret Drabble is a contemporary English writer, the author of twelve novels, a biography of Arnold Bennett, and several works of literary criticism. *The Needle's Eye* is her sixth novel. It is written in a realistic, traditional manner, and has been compared to some of the novels of Henry James (in particular, *The Portrait of a Lady*) in its psychological complexity.[1] Drabble's earlier novels are all psychological in tone; many demonstrate intrapsychic change in major characters through the agency of new relationships. However, *The Needle's Eye* is a more developed work, one in which both major characters, Simon Camish and Rose Vassiliou, wrestle with complex moral and psychological issues. This novel is about the relationship that develops between them. It is a relationship with intense impact on both protagonists, but in Simon's case it leads to positive personal changes. Since Rose's fate is more ambiguous, we focus mainly on Simon.

ENGAGEMENT I: THE EMERGENCE OF TRANSFERENCE FEELINGS

As the novel begins, Simon Camish, a successful, married, depressed barrister meets Rose Vassiliou at a dinner party given by mutual friends. Rose is divorced and living in straitened circumstances with her three children. She lives in this way not out of necessity (being an heiress) but out of an intense moral commitment to relinquishing her wealth and living a simple, ordinary life—a commitment that most of her friends view as falling somewhere between masochism and lunacy. Rose has actually given away most of her inheritance to a struggling African nation, for the building of a school. (The title of the book is taken from the biblical quotation: "It is easier for a camel to go through the eye of a needle than for a rich man to enter the kingdom of God" Matt. 19:24 [King James version]). Rose is a woman of great individuality, and Simon, although chronically embittered and isolated, recognizes this immediately.

Prior to Rose's arrival at the dinner party we, as readers, have been inside Simon's head following an inner process that, like a patient's associations, ranges from present experience to memories of the past, from thought to feeling to fantasy. Simon is clearly depressed, and as he muses on the events going on around him—the dinner party being the manifest stimulus for his thoughts—he becomes increasingly hopeless and overwhelmed by feelings of envy and hatred. The final, painful crescendo of these thoughts occurs in the following passage:

> Suddenly, as he sat there talking about something quite different, he thought, "I am embittered."
>
> And he knew that what he was, was precisely what the word meant, and that it was what he was. When people described other people as embittered, they were describing people like himself—embittered through failure, of one kind of another, and bitterly resenting those more fortunate. He could, as yet, conceal it, but what would happen when he became like those colleagues of his who could not mention a name without a disparaging remark, who saw the whole world as a sour conspiracy to despoil them of any satisfaction or success? And even if he managed to conceal it forever, what a fate was that, to suffer and not to speak, to subdue one's resentment by reason, to exhaust oneself in concealment and the forms of charity? The continual suppression of impulse seemed an unredeeming activity, but he could not think of anything better to do, the impulses being so base. (p. 12)

Soon after this stark self-recognition, Rose arrives at the dinner party, and Simon is—uncharacteristically for him—drawn to her. He identifies with her plainness, being plain himself, and feels a bond of sympathy. He finds himself unable to resent her because to do so would be "not an act of self-defence, but an act of aggression" (p. 17). Simon perceives Rose as modest, unassuming, self-conscious, and authentic, like "ancient frescoes," radiating a "curious distinction" (p. 17). He hopes to be seated next to her at dinner. "He had not for so long experienced something like preference, something like a faintly favorable emotion, that he dispelled it from his consciousness most consciously; it would not do to fall too eagerly upon the neck of so rare and shy a visitant" (p. 18).

Their first conversation, at the dinner table, is unusually intimate. Both speak of having been born in the North, and how sad it is to hate the place where you were born. He realizes she has made an opposite journey to his. Simon has fought his way out of poverty, while she has struggled to renounce wealth and position. Rose shows real interest in his work in trade union legislation. This makes enough of an impression on Simon that he is aware of a feeling of jealousy when she is also friendly to another guest at the party. It is unusual for him to feel involved enough to be jealous.

While Simon is driving Rose home from the party, she—in a sudden, emotional outburst—enlists his aid in helping her decide what to do about a suit for the custody of her three children that has just been brought by her ex-husband, Christopher Vassiliou. She is quite distraught and is making a claim on Simon that is unfair, since she hardly knows him. He, again uncharacteristically, is not put off or offended. He trusts her immediately. He does not experience her as subversive or underhanded as he does most women. His intensely positive reaction to her has all the qualities of a transference experience.[2] It is powerful, irrational, unrealistic, and permeated with fantasy and nostalgia. He wishes to be important to her and special in her eyes; he is immediately made jealous by her approbation of others. This reaction is heightened when they reach her home. In her living room he experiences a nostalgic evocation of his childhood, of his grandparents' house, of the small, intimate, crowded surroundings of his childhood, that he has striven so hard to escape and that he now secretly misses.

> He couldn't at first work out why the room was at once so strange and so familiar: it was so entirely unlike his own home, or the homes of any of his friends or colleagues, but at the same time he recognized it, it was a known landscape, its very dimensions—for it was small, low, overcrowded with furniture—were reminiscent of somewhere intensely remembered. (p. 36)

Her home is a better version of the childhood home he hated. Rose will come to be seen (without too large a stretch of the imagination) as a new and better version of Simon's mother with whom he has had an intensely ambivalent relationship.

As is true in the therapeutic situation, the transference gives rise immediately to resistances. Simon and Rose have some mutual friends of whom Simon is contemptuous. When Rose voices admiration of them, he suddenly becomes cold and distant. The atmosphere of trust between them is broken. As he rejects her, Rose withdraws hopelessly, and Simon suddenly feels an enormous sense of loss. "She had abandoned him, she had cast him out, and it was by his own choice that he had been expelled, from this warm room and intimate, redeeming, cluttered pool of light" (p. 44). Simon's reaction to Rose's withdrawal leads him to a different kind of recognition about his mistrustful nature. He *knows* he is mistrustful, but now he sees the impact of this quality on *another person*. This insight is made more powerful by the importance of Simon's feelings toward Rose. Her subsequent willingness to forgive his narrowness has the quality of acceptance that often exists between therapist and patient; it reestablishes and reinforces the atmosphere of trust that is developing between them.

Simon agrees to advise Rose about her custody suit, read her legal papers, and see what he can do to help. Since she already has a perfectly competent lawyer, this "legal advice" becomes an excuse for them to continue to talk, meet, and spend time together. The rest of the novel deals with their developing relationship, its impact on them and their families, and the solutions they finally come to accept. While initially Simon helps Rose, it is ultimately Simon who is helped; it is he who experiences those positive changes in both character and behavior that resemble the outcome of a successful psychotherapeutic process. In these important first contacts we can see the process of engagement: inner desperation fuels powerful transference feelings that lead Simon to become involved. As the novel develops, his encounters with Rose will lead to a reworking of his major inhibitions and conflicts.

ENGAGEMENT II: SIMON MEETS ROSE

When Simon is introduced to us at the beginning of the novel, he is in a frightening inner state. Behind his diffidence and politeness lie depression and rage. He cannot enjoy life. He is caught in a crippling guilt-ridden anhedonia, and he resorts to secret criticism and loathing of those around him as partial compensation for his sense of loss and deprivation. He thinks of himself as "dry, dry as a bone" and hopeless. "There was nothing to be done about it" except to go on working responsibly. He does not really enjoy his work, but is resolved to endure it (p. 13). He is alienated from his wife and children, from his friends, and from enjoyment of his creative potential.

Simon feels profoundly guilty about what he has gotten from life. He is an only child whose father was crippled in an industrial accident when Simon was quite small. His mother, originally a spirited, hopeful woman, turned all her disappointed hopes from her husband to her son. She sacrificed to send him to grammar school, university, and law school. Her ambitions were shifted onto him, and he must not disappoint her. He is beholden to her, but also enraged with her and ashamed of her. Consciously, he blames his mother for demanding such sacrifices from them both, for being so controlling and ambitious. Unconsciously, he may feel that he is the narcissistic extension of a woman disappointed in her husband and her own personal strivings. This would certainly account for his rage. His feelings of shame about her might be viewed as a projection of the shame he feels toward himself for letting her control him, and for letting her come between him and his father. Simon attempts to "escape" her through marriage to a woman who seems generous and comfortable, but who quickly is revealed as insecure and, like his mother, burdened by a "profound, irremediable crippling social ambition" (p. 59). The escape becomes a reenactment. He becomes alienated from his wife also, suffering the same feelings of shame and rage that he feels toward his mother, toward most women. Underneath these feelings there is also guilt. Simon alludes to this directly at one point as he thinks about "his own cold, overwrought, conscience-stricken guilt-ridden childhood" (p. 55).

Simon's discomfort with his wealth, status, and success suggests intense guilt, from several sources. Simon may feel he has won the Oedipal struggle. He has had his mother's undivided attention all his life. His estrangement from her is defensive, and it will be through Rose that he will make some kind of peace with her. It is to Rose that he says, much later in the novel, something he has not said to anyone before: "'I would like to take you some day to meet my mother . . . you might like her. She's an interesting woman. It would be good to find somebody who might like her'" (p. 288).

Simon wishes he could love his mother, but he is burdened with Oedipal guilt and the rage stemming from his feeling that she has preempted his relationship with his father. He also feels guilty *toward* his mother—he feels that he has sucked her dry, that she has "fed him, pelican-like with her own blood" (p. 24), that he has taken too much from her, and owes it to her to suffer as she has suffered on his behalf. He trudges through life drearily, doing his duty, cut off from full awareness of his feelings. During his second visit to Rose's house, he puts his inner situation into words quite dramatically. Rose is telling him her philosophy of life, a philosophy he values, admires, and envies. She says:

"Being here, being myself, is something quite different. It's taken me so long to learn it and now I can't lose it. I'm happy in it. It seems to me right. People are so nervous about believing anything to be right. But what else in life should one ever seek for but a sense of being right? I explain myself badly, I put it very badly, I can't justify myself—but what I feel, now, is," and she buried her face in her hands, as though embarrassed by her own declaration, "what I feel is that the things I do now, they're part of me, they're monotonous, yes I know, but they're not boring, I like them, I do them all"—she hesitated, faintly—"I do them all with love." (pp. 99–100)

Rose asks him if he knows what she means, and he says with a sudden directness that jolts her, "'How could I know what you mean when nothing that I do is done with any love at all?'" (p. 100). She argues that his very listening to her is charitable, an act of love. Simon replies that he has done what he ought to for so long that he no longer knows what he wants to do: "'I have a strong sense of obligation. It is on this sense of obligation that I have conducted my whole life. It is very destructive of the emotions'" (p. 100).

This destructiveness has crippled his capacity to take any pleasure in his affectional or work life. We hardly know that he has three children; *he* hardly knows it, until he becomes aware of Rose's relationship with her children and the central position they play in her life. His appraisal of his wife, seemingly shrewd and insightful early in the novel, turns out to be partially wrong. Much of her difficult temper and dissatisfaction stems from his guilt-ridden rejection of her. It is possible to summarize Simon's situation in psychological language: he is crippled by neurotic guilt, anxiety about unconscious entitlement, and an outward persona characterized by a polite, conscientious, diffident reaction against his rage, despair, and envy. He is a stranger to happiness and authenticity; these words are particularly important as markers in the process of inner change that ensues from his relationship with Rose.

MUTUAL INFLUENCE: SIMON'S RELATIONSHIP WITH ROSE

What, then, is the nature of the relationship Simon develops with Rose? At first they meet privately, at intervals, in her home, a setting that is very special to him. Fantasy and memory are evoked early. Simon introspects and reviews his life. He wonders in a different way about things he has wondered about before. Why did he marry as he did? Why has it been so important to him to achieve social success and deny his roots? How does he feel about having left his father so far behind? Does his choice of trade union law have something to do with repaying a debt to his father? He comes to recognize his identification with his mother. While he may repudiate her and all she stands for, underneath they are much alike. Such insights come to him. He thinks about Rose and her appealing and idiosyncratic ideas about life, but he denies his growing feelings for her, until, on the eve of his departure for an Easter vacation, they come to him in a flash. He does not want to leave her: "I want her . . . I want what she is" (p. 176). His realization that he loves her has hidden and forbidden sexual meanings, but is experienced as a wish to be with her, to be where she is and what she is. These thoughts bring Simon peaceful pleasure as fantasies of being with Rose, compatible and fulfilled, are allowed into his consciousness. For a "mother's boy" like Simon, success may create conflict—usually because of difficulty experiencing productiveness as one's own, and because pleasing mother means defeating father. Simon believes that Rose has mastered such dilemmas; to be with Rose and to be like Rose is to be the "good" person he would like to be. His sense of peace is created by the possibility of a harmony between his ambitions, his ideals, and his conscience that until now has been lacking.

Simon's discovery of his feelings about Rose marks the beginning of the end of his private, exclusive relationship with her. Soon, Simon meets Rose's ex-husband, Christopher; Rose meets Simon's wife, Julie, and the external realities of their complex lives intrude. Nevertheless, this period of special intimacy has enabled a process of engagement to occur. Reality intrudes, but it does not stop the transformative process. Simon admires Rose deeply and feels that she has come to terms with certain problems and guilts that plague him. Her importance to him as an idealized figure survives the waning of the special, secret aspects of their relationship, and may be one key to what is therapeutic in that relationship.

In the novel all sorts of reality considerations are used to explain Simon's giving up these wishes. He and Rose are unwilling to hurt Julie or Christopher and, especially, their children. This is what both *believe,* but Simon's behavior is unconsciously determined by the incestuous meaning of his wishes. It is after he admits his feelings to himself that he first meets Christopher and "realizes" how much alike and how very involved Rose and her ex-husband still are. One might say that the early "damaged" father has reappeared and is anything but damaged—now, like a fantasy father of childhood, Chistopher is powerful and dangerous. Simon is frightened by Christopher and avoids Rose; they do not contact each other for weeks. He has already begun to give up his wishes to possess her completely.

The relinquishment of the claims engendered by Simon's transference wishes continues in a later scene in his law chambers. Rose comes to him for help. She wishes him to rescue her from her masochistic resolve to give her children up. She cannot fight with Christopher any more. She will give him the children and go away, perhaps to some poor African country. Unconsciously, she wishes to be saved. She wants Simon to declare himself to her, although she cannot let herself know this. Simon fails her; he reasons with her, and ignores her underlying emotional message. Acting on such an invitation is morally and psychologically impossible for both of them.

Simon feels guilty about his failure to rescue Rose and tries to repair it by going to see Christopher. He tells Christopher that his attempt to get the children back is doomed, and that he would do better to reunite with Rose and end the struggle over the children. Simon thinks he is doing this to help Rose. He may even be dimly aware that it relieves some of his own anxiety about his desire for her. In fact, his unconscious intentions prove quite provocative. His confrontation with Christopher leads Christopher to "abscond" with the children, on one of their weekend visits with him. This gives Simon another chance to rescue Rose and play out his fantasies of being with her.

Simon helps Rose get the children back, aiding her with complex, emergency legal maneuvers. They take a trip together to Norfolk to retrieve them. This trip, more than any of their other meetings, has the quality of a lovers' tryst. He lends Rose a scarf of Julie's for disguise when they get to Norfolk, where Rose's family lives. They are not sure they wish to be recognized until they know that it is safe to take the children back. They have to make sure Christopher will not be dangerous! As they walk through the woods toward the house, they see a dead stoat hanging from a trap. Simon suddenly declares himself to Rose. The dead stoat represents both the death of his wishes and the danger of living out incestuous impulses.

> "If I had been free," he said, "I would have asked you to marry me." They both stared at the little corpse, strung up as a warning. "Ah," she said, gently, tenderly, "ah yes. What a nice time we would have had. I too have thought of it, you know." And without looking at each other, they went back to the car. (p. 295)

Their mutual declaration is something now part of the past, something they *had* wished for. The plot devices of Simon's meeting with Christopher, of Rose's appeal in his chambers (during which she acknowledges sadly that she knows he has met Christopher), the developing friendship of Julie and Rose, and the trip to Norfolk with its outcome, the reuniting of Rose and Christopher, can all be reinterpreted in psychological language as internal events in the characters that depict the renouncing of forbidden wishes and fantasies.

Why is the relinquishing of wishes toward Rose *therapeutic* for Simon? He is, after all, someone too used to relinquishing and self-deprivation. Guilt is the coin of his psychological realm. This particular renouncement is therapeutic because it relieves Simon of his life-long guilt toward his father, of an Oedipal triumph that is unbearable to him. To take Rose away from Christopher would leave him even more burdened. As the novel ends, Christopher also becomes Simon's friend and provides him with a strong, masculine, "father figure." Simon does not lose Rose completely; he becomes reconciled to the disappointment of certain wishes toward her. What he retains is his idealization of her, and this is what is most helpful.

Before examining what makes this spontaneous process therapeutic, we may examine whether or not, from Simon's point of view, its outcome *is* beneficial. By the novel's conclusion, Simon's internal and external situations are much improved. There is a scene where Simon, Rose, and Rose's close friend, Emily, go for a walk to an old bombed-out site where there is a dusty armchair with a chicken sitting in it. This place has some sort of special meaning to Rose that Simon cannot quite grasp, but as he sits there with the two women in the sunshine, he experiences something entirely new: "So great and innocent a peace possessed him that it seemed like a new contract, like the rainbow after the flood. He could feel it, on his bare hands and face. It lay upon him. It was like happiness" (p. 216).

In another passage, later in the book, when Simon goes with Rose to her family's home in Norfolk to get her children back from Christopher, they debate whether or not Simon should come in the house with her; he decides that he will: "He seemed, for the first time in years, to be saying what he meant as he meant it. The sensation was extraordinary as though a clamp had been taken off his head" (p. 296).

Both of these passages herald new experiences, or the return of experiences lost to Simon since childhood, the feeling of happiness, the capacity for authentic action. They can be viewed as markers of more profound internal changes, as indication of shifts in character, as evidence of the beginning resolution of conflicts that have stifled his affective life and his capacity for action.

Drabble makes clear by the novel's end that Simon has gradually become less depressed and embittered, less guilty. His need for expiatory deprivation is decreased. He comes to terms with the hidden sense of specialness and entitlement that has betrayed itself in defensive devaluations and contempt for enviable others. Since Rose values and esteems his true self, he has an opportunity to assess himself more realistically.

The quality of his outer life changes for the better, evidenced by his improved relationship with his wife, his children, his friends, and his work. Simon enjoys his work now. He no longer plods through it with dreary resolution. He muses on his relationship with his wife and wonders if perhaps he has not misjudged her all along. Certainly she seems to him to have improved, to be more generous, attractive, and likable. He wonders if he has projected his own defensive mockery of her onto others, and whether perhaps she has been more likable all along. He also makes an increased attempt to relate to his children. During his Easter vacation, in Cornwall, he takes his youngest child, Katie, for a walk. This is unprecedented behavior for Simon. He has gone so far in nonintervention that he feels himself a stranger to his children. Katie talks to him confidingly, and he finds himself "enchanted, flattered by her confidences, wishing he listened to her more often" (p. 185). They feed bits of bread from their lunch to some sea anemones they find in a tidepool; in experiencing Katie's delight and fascination, Simon remembers what it is like to play.

His social life becomes less formal and limited. "He even began to enjoy his social life now that one or two of his own friends were included in it" (p. 355). In a treatment situation, if a patient's suffering and guilt decrease, if the quality of his work and affectional life improves, and if he gains an increased capacity for feeling and experience, that treatment would be viewed as successful.

DIRECTIONALITY: ROSE'S INFLUENCE

What is therapeutic in Simon's relationship with Rose? Why does knowing her, and relating to her, do him good? We have seen that Simon meets Rose at a time of personal crisis, and that her appearance—announced by a kind of invisible fanfare in the novel—catches him at his lowest ebb and marks a turning point in his life. At the dinner party, as Simon sits and muses on his own bitterness, he thinks: "There was nothing to be done about it, nothing, there was nothing in himself that could save him" (p. 13).

The analogy here might be to that of a patient who reaches a state of sufficient suffering to undertake the difficulties of treatment: that very act may mark the readiness for some new and transforming experience. We have already noted that Simon's feelings toward Rose have many of the characteristics of a transference reaction and lead to feelings of resistance that make him behave inconsistently and ambivalently toward her, while he continues to see her regularly and privately. He is aware of "a disagreeably secret and pleasantly intimate nature" to their meetings (p. 153). This awareness heralds the emergence into consciousness of Simon's love for Rose, of his wishes to marry her and have her to himself. These wishes produce discomfort and the beginning of a process of relinquishment. This process is analogous to "working through" in a clinical situation.

Simon does not simply love Rose: he loves what she is and he wants to be what she is. Rose is a person at peace with herself. She personifies a way of looking at life, of being, that Simon admires and from which he feels cut off. The passage (quoted earlier) in which Rose shares her philosophy of life with him embodies an attitude for which he hungers—to do what is right, to do things with love. It is around this issue of doing what is right that Rose is able to influence Simon in a direction that has meaning for him—to become recommitted to his ideals. Simon has traveled too far from his roots in his ambitions to leave his past and its suffering behind him. After his first meeting with Rose, he sits in his large, elegant drawing room, alone, musing about people like himself who strive so hard to leave behind the cramped quarters of poverty, only to find themselves in rooms like this with "clear empty spaces" on all sides, longing for the warmth and intimacy of the past. Rose brings the past back to him. She shows him the way not by preaching but by example, without even knowing she is showing him. Simon cannot quite understand why Rose would embrace a life of almost-poverty (although he reflects that it is easier to give up what one has *had* than what one has never had), but he admires Rose's commitment, her integrity, and, above all, her sense of meaning.

Simon possesses the capacity for commitment and integrity, but he lacks a sense of having chosen meaningfully or of being able to believe in what he is doing. In fact, his choices (of profession, for instance) have not been meaningless. He pursues a branch of law that represents some "debt repaid to his father" and he is quite interested in it, too. His sense of interest, stifled by guilt, returns to him through Rose's genuine support for what he is doing. He feels she really knows and understands him, that she values him and sees his best self.

Rose's belief in him releases Simon's pent-up and defended-against sense of specialness (the legacy of his mother's undivided attention) and gives it a more acceptable form. Since Rose is not interested in *using* Simon as he fears his mother and Julie do, her interest is not tainted by her ambitions for him. His secret grandiosity gradually gives way to more realistic self-esteem.

Through this relationship Simon's capacity to care for another person develops. "He liked her. He truly liked her. . . . He thought he understood her. He wished to understand. Such a modicum of goodwill (for so he thought it) was nothing less than a rebirth in his nature" (p. 154).

Rose is not one of Simon's black underwear "fantasy" women. She is "a whole person so entirely there and so fully existing, a person with a history survived, . . . To love her was astonishing, it was remarkable. It had amazing and *interesting* possibilities" (p. 214) [italics added]. This sense of possibilities as interesting involves a new way of looking at things; it is a sign of Simon's insight and a marker of internal change.

Simon's love survives the giving up of transference wishes for victory and possession. It becomes altruistic. When Christopher abducts the children, Simon comforts Rose. He holds her in his arms, realizing a long cherished fantasy of consoling her. But "she was too unhappy, he could not take any comfort while she was unhappy. There was no satisfaction in it. He was too unhappy on her account. He should have known that that was how it would be" (p. 275).

Through his love for Rose, Simon begins to resolve his hatred and mistrust of women. Although he overly idealizes her—this becomes very evident by the end of the novel—Rose also becomes the recipient of his "negative" transference. Simon's aggression generally takes the form of passively disappointing and withholding. His awkwardness and helplessness unconsciously express hostility. Thus, he fails Rose when she comes to his law chambers, desperate and in need of help; but, unlike Julie, Rose is able to tolerate Simon's aggression without retaliation, and this is therapeutic for him. His experience of women as exploitative and subversive is substantially modified.

Their relationship even has something like a "termination" phase.[3] Simon gradually comes to idealize Rose less and to see her more realistically without giving up his positive feelings for her. They continue to be a source of support and comfort for each other. Their friendship endures. The novel ends with a visit to a dog show, reminiscent of the visit to the armchair and the chickens, in which Simon and Rose, their crisis over, take pleasure in each other's company.

It should be emphasized that while the relationship between Simon and Rose is like that of therapy in some ways, in others it differs substantially. Rose is neither objective nor personally uninvolved, as a therapist would strive to be. Throughout the novel she actively seeks Simon's help and approval as if *he* were the therapist and she the patient: "She wanted Simon to understand. She wanted him to think well of her. . . . She desired his approbation, passionately. It was her strongest emotional need" (p. 363). Furthermore, Simon does not seek Rose out, as a patient would a therapist. He happens to meet her at a time in his life when he is ready for someone to rescue him from his despair and alienation. Simon can use Rose's help because she is the right person at the right time; he never acknowledges consciously that he is seeking help.

In this literary relationship, as in psychotherapy, both parties are impacted, but not symmetrically. Since Rose's interactions with Simon are not driven by professional role commitments, something else must fuel her continued involvement. Rose functions therapeutically for Simon, albeit unconsciously, because she, too, needs him. Unlike Simon, her intrapsychic difficulties stem more from having received too little parental attention and approbation rather than too much. She is prompted to engage with him by a strong need, rooted in childhood experience, for people with whom she can share ideals. The emotionally neglected only child of a profoundly unattuned, hypochondriacal mother and an ambitious, opinionated father, Rose's most crucial early relationship is with her religious nursemaid, Noreen. This woman is far from empathic, but she does, at least, relate to Rose; this takes the form of moral preachings on the wickedness of wealth and privilege. Throughout her life Rose reenacts elements of the relationship with Noreen through the sharing of ideals—first with a close school friend, Emily; next, and unsuccessfully, with Christopher; and, finally, with Simon. Simon understands, intuitively, how important it is to Rose to "do what is right" and his understanding, in turn, sustains Rose's interest in him.

Because Rose has found, in Simon, someone with a complementary need to share ideals, she also undergoes some change. Validated by Simon at a time of crisis in *her* life, she is enabled to resolve her painful dilemma around her children's needs. Whether this is good for her, or merely for those with whom she is intimately involved (Christopher and the children), remains highly uncertain. It is true that she becomes less dogmatic and more flexible, but she is certainly not more content. Although the relationship with Simon is very important to her, it would take a much more speculative reading of this text to demonstrate, convincingly, a positive outcome for Rose.

SOME FURTHER THOUGHTS

Like psychoanalytic narratives, works of literature may be understood and interpreted along multiple lines. Each reader brings his or her own history and transference to each text. The use of literary narratives to study processes of intrapsychic change has the potential of enriching and confirming clinical observations outside of the formal psychotherapeutic milieu. With this in mind, we may review the literary relationship between Simon Camish and Rose Vassiliou in *The Needle's Eye* along two lines—the development of Simon's self-esteem and of his capacity to relate to others.

Simon's problems in the area of self-esteem and self-evaluation are a product of his relationship with his mother. With no siblings, few friends, and a nonfunctional father, Simon becomes too important to his mother. Guilt and anxiety ensue from his sense of being special, and keep him from evaluating himself realistically and enjoying his accomplishments. Envy leads him to devalue and criticize others. Aware of his bitterness, he is disappointed in himself for failing to live up to his ideals. Rose represents elements of an ego ideal Simon admires; her tolerance and integrity are particularly important to him. His gradual identification with idealized aspects of her personality allows him to shed old self-images that were either too exciting (through unconscious overvaluation) or too depressing (through guilty self-criticism). Simon's identification with Rose resembles identifications occurring in clinical situations. Patients may identify with their therapist's values and attitudes, particularly with the therapist's observing and analyzing functions. When integrated with the patient's own personality, these identifications contribute to structural change in the form of superego modifications and the capacity for increased self-observation.

Rose *can* become the representative of a better ego ideal because she is acceptable to Simon. His defensive rejection of his mother has left him with an unfilled valence: he has rejected not only his personal relationship with her, but her ideals and her capacity to idealize as well. Since he mistrusts women as exploiters and co-opters of his success, he cannot replace the missing maternal object and her functions.[4] He unconsciously identifies Rose with his mother almost immediately; later this identification becomes conscious when he thinks about taking Rose to meet his mother because Rose "would like her" and presumably understand her. Once Simon has worked through his incestuous wishes toward Rose, he is left with a relatively uncontaminated new relationship to replace an old one. He can see Rose as a separate person, admirable and lovable, even if flawed. An important factor that allows this shift to take place is that Rose makes neither too much nor too little of Simon. She neither overstimulates nor devalues him, and reflected in her eyes, he comes to see himself more realistically. His success, as mirrored by Rose, no longer makes him guilty or anxious. His improved self-esteem allows him to experience himself as effective and valuable.

5

THE ACCIDENTAL TOURIST: TRAUMATIC LOSS AND PATHOLOGICAL GRIEF RESPOND TO "ACCIDENTAL THERAPY"

Anne Tyler is a twentieth-century American novelist who writes with humor and insight about issues of relationship and personal loss. She has a flair for describing eccentricities of character and how these impinge in situations of crisis and adjustment. *Morgan's Passing, Saint Maybe, Dinner at the Homesick Restaurant,* and particularly *The Accidental Tourist* illustrate this interplay of character and situation. *The Accidental Tourist* is notable for the sensitivity and accuracy with which it captures and depicts the process of psychological change. Macon Leary, the novel's protagonist, is mired in grief following a serious loss and hampered by entrenched characterological patterns. An unlikely "accidental therapist," Muriel Pritchett, helps him recover, while pursuing her own goal of finding a man to love.

This chapter is divided into three sections. We will first review the novel, tracing the development of Macon's psychological difficulties and their resolution. We follow with a discussion of the relationship between the two protagonists; our emphasis in this section is on the ways in which this relationship is similar to—and different from—psychotherapy. We conclude with some comments on the connections between "accidental" life encounters and psychotherapy, a connection this novel speaks about extensively.

THE STORY

Macon Leary writes tourist guidebooks for business travelers whose "concern was how to pretend they had never left home" (p. 12). His books have as their logo an armchair with wings. Macon is chronically anxious, phobic, and obsessional. His compulsive defenses form a bastion against dangers from within and without. They are an attempt to keep all the conditions of his life safe and unchanging. This attempt is not successful. His only child, twelve-year-old Ethan, is killed in a freak shooting and within a year Sarah, his wife of twenty years, leaves him. She claims he is no comfort to her in her grief. She perceives him as "muffled" in his own mourning, and she has lost patience with his finicky, controlling ways.

Deeply anguished, but frightened of experiencing the full affective impact of his grief, Macon attempts to cope by strengthening existing defensive behaviors. He shuts himself up in his house, developing elaborate techniques to increase order and efficiency in his household routines. "At moments . . . he realized that he might be carrying things too far. He couldn't explain why, either. He'd always had a fondness for method, but not what you would call a mania" (p. 11). His orderliness temporarily staves off intense and disruptive affect, but it does not protect him from loss of appetite, sleeplessness, depression, and painful loneliness. His only company is Ethan's dog, Edward, a Welsh Corgi with a mind of its own that functions in the novel as Macon's double. Edward's obvious distress at Ethan's absence foreshadows and, in fact, instigates the emotional upheaval Macon must eventually experience. Macon attempts to work but cannot concentrate. He is afraid of his own thoughts and avoids them with further compulsive maneuvers. "Maybe he couldn't get his guide-book organized, but organizing the household was another matter entirely. There was something fulfilling about that, something consoling—or more than consoling; it gave him the sense of warding off a danger" (p. 46). What is Macon warding off by shutting himself up and burying himself in a frenzy of defensive behaviors?

The author gives us some material for conjecture through a glimpse of Macon's early childhood. We learn that his father died during World War II when Macon and his three siblings were quite young. Their mother, Alicia, was youthful, impulsive, and given to sudden enthusiasms that were pursued without much thought for the consequences. Her children found her utterly unsettling. They were relieved when she remarried and sent them to live with their conservative, reliable paternal grandparents. But there are hints in the text of feelings more complex than mere relief. The children needed Alicia's mothering and she continually disappointed them. "Rose, the baby, used to wait for her return in the hall, sucking her thumb and stroking an old fur stole that Alicia never wore anymore" (p. 65). Alicia's failure to provide security and her general unreliability may have been experienced by her children as traumatic and aggressive. Alicia ascribes their personalities, already compulsive in childhood, to a resemblance to their father's side of the family, but these traits may also be viewed as attempts by the children to control their own aggressive impulses, stimulated by their mother's irresponsible and unempathic behaviors.

Macon's defenses appear to be an attempt to secure emotional closure and safety, to keep his feelings inside himself and under control. The violent events of Ethan's death—he was shot by a hold-up man in a hamburger joint—threaten Macon with awareness of his own aggressive impulses and guilt. Moreover, the losses of Ethan and Sarah "repeat" his earlier parental losses and threaten him with an awareness of his own past grief and disappointment, compounding his present bereavement.

Macon's attempt to control his feelings does not work. He experiences a minor breakdown during a telephone conversation with a grocery clerk. He is ordering dog food and suddenly finds himself saying to this woman:

"I'm all alone; it's just me; it seems everybody's just . . . fled from me, I don't know, I've lost them, I'm left standing here saying, 'Where'd they go? Where is everybody? Oh, God, what did I do that was so bad?'"

His voice was not behaving right and he hung up. . . . He was falling apart; that much was obvious. He would have to get a grip on himself. (p. 56)

Macon finds a temporary solution to his emotional crisis through a regression to his childhood world. He breaks his leg on one of his own efficiency devices and returns home to his sister, Rose, and his two brothers, Charles and Porter. All three of his siblings have lived together for years, trying to preserve their safe and idiosyncratic way of life. Rose alphabetizes her groceries as she stores them. They eat baked potatoes every night for dinner, preparing them exactly as they have since childhood. All three get lost whenever they leave the house for errands, confirming the confusing, dangerous nature of the outside world. Often they do not answer the telephone: they do not like surprises. Their eccentricities are familiar and endearing to Macon: "He almost wondered whether, by some devious, subconscious means, he had engineered this injury—every elaborate step leading up to it—just so he could settle down safe among the people he'd started out with" (p. 63).

At first Macon's return home brings him relief, but a gnawing discomfort follows. While he seeks safety, a part of him wishes to be different—the part that has been awakened by the loss of the two most important people in his life. The loss of what was most meaningful to him highlights the emptiness of what is left and creates a readiness for something to replace what was lost. Macon looks at a portrait of himself and his siblings as children and sees them now as adults: "Was there any real change? He felt a jolt of something very close to panic. Here he still was! The same as ever! *What have I gone and done?* he wondered, and he swallowed thickly and looked at his own empty hands" (p. 81).

At this juncture, Edward, the Welsh Corgi, begins acting up. He becomes increasingly unruly, threatening strangers, on one occasion biting

Macon. Macon is curiously unable to discipline Edward. He thinks it is because the dog was Ethan's: "He was sympathetic and cared about Macon and plodded after him wherever he went" (p. 93). Macon is baffled at his own helplessness. Perhaps he does not want to control Edward because he is secretly gratified by Edward's aggression, enjoying vicariously in Edward what frightens him in himself. Edward does not take Ethan's death lying down. He is fighting back!

Under pressure from his family, Macon finally hires a dog trainer. Muriel Pritchett is a young woman who works at the kennel where Macon boards Edward during his travels. She is interested in Macon and already has attempted to get to know him by suggesting that she train Edward. Macon thinks she is "bizarre"—she is young, impulsive, outspoken, flamboyant—but he hopes she can handle Edward.

Muriel, for all her flighty, unsettling mannerisms, is a firm, consistent trainer. She insists that Macon, still on crutches, help with the training and practice with Edward between lessons. She lets him know that training takes time, that she cannot perform magic, and that he will have to do most of the work if he really wants Edward's training to succeed. She is talking about Macon, also. After their second lesson, Macon has a dream about Muriel. In the dream he is sitting in his grandfather's car with some girl.

> The bitter smell of her perfume seemed familiar. . . . It was Muriel. He drew a breath to ask what she was doing here, but she put a finger to his lips and stopped him. She moved closer still. She took the keys from him and set them on the dashboard. Gazing steadily into his face, she unbuckled his belt and slipped a cool, knowing hand down inside his trousers.
> He woke astonished and embarrassed, and sat bolt upright in his bed. (pp. 110–11)

This dream disturbs Macon's equilibrium more than he realizes. He does not want to have feelings, erotic or otherwise, toward Muriel. Shortly after the dream occurs, he precipitates a rift in their relationship. During a training session Edward becomes angry and lunges at Muriel, his teeth bared. She disciplines him immediately, holding him in the air by his choke-chain for longer than Macon can bear. Edward accepts this treatment meekly, but Macon becomes furious and fires Muriel. He wonders how she can be so heartless.

What has happened in this passage? Macon is struggling with his own affects and impulses, expressed at this point through Edward. He fears that expressions of impulse may become destructive, but underneath his fear lies a wish for omnipotent control; it is this wish that he cannot stand to have thwarted. He sees Muriel, correctly, as someone who can tame the hidden unruly part of himself but he does not yet see how taming will make the expression of sexual and aggressive impulses safer. At this point Macon is like a patient who consciously wants to change but is loathe to give up unconscious gratifications. In Macon's case, aggressive impulses are gratified through controlling behaviors. These behaviors—which range from the withholding of love and its expression to correcting other people's English—are partially responsible for his wife's alienation and departure. Muriel, unlike Sarah, seems impervious to this veiled hostility. She does not try to correct herself in Macon's presence, and she does not let him drive her away. What is most disturbing inside of him does not upset her. Macon senses this and is both reassured and threatened by it. This is apparent even in their very first encounter:

> "My speciality is dogs that bite," the woman said.
> "Specialty."
> "Pardon?"
> "Webster prefers 'specialty.'"
> She gave him a blank look. (p. 42)

By firing Muriel, Macon hopes to escape dealing with his own sexual and aggressive wishes, but his unconscious betrays him again. Soon after his cast is removed, he goes to New York on a business trip. He does not feel ready to travel. He is upset about his sister Rose's burgeoning romance with Julian Edge, the young man who is Macon's boss. He does not like changes in his family constellation, and he does not want to be reminded of his growing feelings for Muriel. He finds himself behaving differently around Muriel, and this makes him feel excited and anxious. In an unusual act of adventuresomeness, he goes to a restaurant on the top floor of a very tall building while in New York; there he experiences a panic attack.[1] "All of a sudden he thought he had died. . . . It wasn't the height; it was the distance. It was his vast, lonely distance from everyone who mattered" (p. 159).

Macon is aware, during his attack, of a wish to be comforted and carried out of the building like a baby. He calls home to Baltimore frantically, for help, only to discover that once again Edward is out of control and has cornered his brother Charles in the pantry. He cannot reach Sarah either and, in desperation, calls Muriel. She *is* home, and she gives him exactly the responses he needs. She offers to go get Edward and keep him until Macon returns. He then tells her, somewhat shamefacedly, about his panic attack: "'See, I'm up on top of this building,' he said, 'and I don't know what it is but something has scared the hell out of me'" (p. 164). The "something" is compounded of his own loosening controls (enacted by Edward) and his longing for human warmth and contact. It is a longing that early losses have rendered threatening and shameful. Muriel's reaction reframes the whole experience for him.

> "Oh, Lord, I'd be scared too after I went and saw *Towering Inferno*. . . . Boy, after that you couldn't get me past jumping level in any building. I think people who go up in skyscrapers are just plain brave. I mean if you think about it, Macon,

you *have* to be brave to be standing where you are right now."

"Oh, well, not so brave as all that," Macon said.

"No, I'm serious."

"You're making too much out of it. It's nothing, really."

"You just say that because you don't realize what you went through before you stepped into the elevator. . . . Why, you ought to be walking around that building so amazed and proud of yourself!"

Macon gave a small, dry laugh and gripped the receiver more tightly. (p. 165)

Muriel's description of Macon's experience relieves his shame, and this allows him to hear an "intervention" that gets to the heart of his trouble:

"Then when you get back from your trip, we need to talk about his training. I mean, *things just can't go on this way*, Macon."

"No, they can't. You're right. They can't," Macon said. (p. 165; emphasis added)

Macon knows Muriel is talking about him. It is *his* difficulty with impulses that needs training. After she hangs up, he feels "soothed, tired, and terribly hungry."

In this episode, Muriel has proven to Macon that she is not frightened by his feelings and that she does not view his vulnerability and neediness as weak or shameful. Macon feels understood and, reluctantly, allows a relationship to develop between himself and Muriel. As they train Edward, Muriel talks about herself, her son Alexander, her life as a single parent. Macon admires her courage and her capacity to take action. She has the resilience he lacks. Like a therapist, she is interested in him and available; she does not take offense when her interventions are ignored or rebuked. In Muriel's case these interventions are suggestions that Macon try some new things, that he take her to a movie, for instance (he hates movies—"They make everything seem so close up"), or that they have supper together one evening. Although attracted, Macon fights involvement. He is ambivalent about substitutes for his wife and his own son. He does not want time to move on in the form of new people, and new experiences.

In a second key passage, Muriel, by dint of persistence, gets Macon to agree to a date. He fears the sexual and emotional involvement; Muriel's assurance that it is "just for supper" does not convince him. He goes to her house the night before their date to tell her he must cancel. Muriel listens silently. Suddenly, Macon finds himself telling her the whole story of his son's death, something about which he has never spoken openly to anyone. He talks about his grief, about the failure of his marriage and how lonely and far away from everyone he feels. She draws him into the house gently, but insistently. She puts her arms around him and continues to listen silently. Then she leads him upstairs to the bedroom, and, in a motherly way, she suggests that he go to sleep. This is what he needs. She creates an atmosphere in which he can confide in her, and, later, when he is ready for sexual involvement, she is available. Like a good parent, Muriel expects just a little more from Macon than he does from himself; she pulls him gently to the next step. Unlike Sarah and his family, she does not see him as unable to change. This passage is reminiscent of a situation frequently encountered in the psychotherapeutic situation. A patient disturbed by an onrush of transference feelings may threaten to terminate abruptly. If the therapist listens carefully without becoming controlling or defensive, the patient may reveal what is really troubling him or her and not be impelled to act.

Macon gradually moves in with Muriel and her son, Alexander, bringing Edward with him. Although he is reluctant to admit it, he is aware of being different when he is with her. The following passage has the sense of fresh discovery that we may associate with insight:

> Then he knew that what mattered was the pattern of her life; that although he did not love her he loved the surprise of her, and also the surprise of himself when he was with her. In the foreign country that was Singleton Street he was an entirely different person. This person had never been suspected of narrowness, never been accused of chilliness; in fact, was mocked for his soft heart. And was anything but orderly. (p. 212)

Macon's developing relationship with Alexander is a signpost in his psychological progress. Alexander cannot really replace Ethan, nor does Macon wish this; but through encouraging the fatherless, physically vulnerable Alexander, Macon expiates some of his guilt over Ethan's death. His own fatherlessness has made him uneasy about parenting. Could he have done more? Could he *somehow* have prevented Ethan's death? Such thoughts plague him. Elements of hidden Oedipal rivalry and hostility toward Ethan may operate in Macon's psyche, making the resolution of his grief more difficult. Sarah *does* leave him once Ethan dies. Macon may feel that Sarah preferred Ethan and has no use for him, or the marriage, now that Ethan is dead. Macon's relationship with Alexander allows a new relationship to attenuate his guilt over the previous one.

Macon is developing insight and undergoing internal shifts. He is changing, but slowly and with considerable resistance. Just as Edward had to progress and regress in his obedience training, Macon takes steps forward and then retreats. He tries to convince himself his life is really "on hold," that this is a sort of interim period which does not count. His ambivalence about Muriel is expressed through his family's disapproval. Charles says to him:

> "She's some kind of symptom, Macon! You're not yourself these days and this Muriel person's a symptom. Everybody says so."
> "I'm more myself than I've been my whole life long," Macon told him. (p. 249)

While he defends Muriel and what she means to him, he soon starts thinking about Sarah. He and Muriel meet Sarah at his sister Rose's wedding. Muriel guesses immediately that Macon will leave her to go back to Sarah. She feels he has used her up and will now discard her. As it turns out she is right, but only temporarily.

To Macon, Sarah represents the past and the familiar. In that sense she is a respite from change and its difficulties. But he also wants to impress Sarah, as one would want to show a parent a new accomplishment. As his mother did, Sarah sees Macon as fixed and unchangeable; this troubles him. He is not convinced himself of his change.

> Macon . . . had a sudden view of his life as rich and full and astonishing. He would have liked to show it off to someone. He wanted to sweep out an arm and say, "See?"
> But the person he would have liked to show it to was Sarah. (p. 285)

Perhaps Macon wonders if he can be a different person away from Muriel. Patients in therapy often use the therapist's absence as an opportunity to see whether insight and new behaviors will hold. What we sometimes view as "acting out" can also be trial action in a sphere outside of the therapeutic setting. If Macon and Sarah can interact differently, he will feel more secure in his new sense of himself. He loves Sarah; she is part of his past, and he does not want to give up the past. Nor does Sarah, it turns out. She feels she is too old to change, and she wants the familiarity of her relationship with Macon. She *does not* acknowledge his change. Nevertheless, he continues to have novel experiences. He now talks to people in airplanes, where he used to hide behind a book. On one occasion, he thinks of himself as "a merry, tolerant person." He notices tact and delicacy in a bank clerk. His self-protective shell is dissolving. As he thinks about his relationship to Sarah, he comes to a difficult but insightful conclusion:

> He began to believe that people could, in fact, be used up—could use each other up, could be of no further help to each other and maybe even do harm to each other. He began to think that who you are when you're with somebody may matter more than whether you love her. (p. 317)

Since Macon does nothing impulsively, these thoughts do not lead to immediate action. The final episodes of the novel take him on a business trip to Paris with both Muriel and Sarah in pursuit. Macon is forced to make a choice. His thoughts at this time reveal his dilemma about making decisions.

> He reflected that he had not taken steps very often in his life, come to think of it. Really never. His marriage, his two jobs, his time with Muriel, his return to Sarah—all seemed to have simply befallen him. He couldn't think of a single major act he had managed of his own accord.
> Was it too late now to begin?

Was there any way he could learn to do things differently? (p. 351)

He makes the more difficult choice: to return to Muriel, a choice that means moving forward in time and taking risks. Not insignificantly, his final thoughts have to do with Ethan. As he is leaving Paris, he sees a French boy who reminds him of his son.

> If Ethan hadn't died, Macon thought, wouldn't he have grown into such a person?...
>
> And if dead people aged, wouldn't it be a comfort? To think of Ethan growing up in heaven—fourteen years now instead of twelve—eased the grief a little. . . . Macon gazed out the cab window, considering the notion in his mind. He felt a kind of inner rush, a racing forward. The real adventure, he thought, is the flow of time; it's as much adventure as anyone could wish. And if he pictured Ethan still part of that flow—in some other place, however unreachable—he believed he might be able to bear it after all. (p. 354)

The resolution of Macon's grief and of his limiting defensive behaviors are captured in his thoughts about time and its flow. He has partially overcome a major roadblock for obsessional personalities, paralysis of action in the face of uncertain outcome. He can now allow an unpredictable future to be part of his life.

DISCUSSION

We have used Anne Tyler's novel, *The Accidental Tourist*, to examine the influence of a new relationship on the parallel processes of grief resolution and the modification of defensive obsessionality in the novel's main character. In the discussion that follows we will describe the nature of Macon Leary's personality change, and examine the ways in which Muriel does and does not function like a therapist for him—that is, how the process between them is similar to, and different from, psychotherapy. We will highlight the roles of transference, resistance, and working through in this process, but we also will connect these phenomena to our overall therapeutic narrative.

If we view the central characters in this novel as parts of Macon's psyche, the following picture emerges: Macon represents the besieged ego, under stress internally and externally: "I'm frightened of anything new and different, especially of losing control. I'm frightened of experiencing my feelings. I cannot make decisions."[2] His family embodies portions of his superego and ego ideal—the comfortable, older parts of the ego ideal, the nonpunitive aspects of his superego: "This is how one should be, how one should live. Here is righteousness and safety." Sarah, on the other hand, stands for punitive and shaming superego elements: "You are narrow and constricted. You can't change. You are a failure as a person." With a little imagination, Edward represents Macon's id: "I am out of control. I bark and bite at will. Try and stop me." Macon longs to indulge his Edward part, but he is frightened. "Look at what happens when aggression is unleashed. Look at my mother's destructive impulsiveness. Look at how people 'murder' the English language. Look at what happened to my son!"

While Macon cannot fully give in to Edward, he mediates these longings through his reality ego and superego and comes up with a new self-concept, embodied in Muriel: "I can take action. I can be imaginative, occasionally even outrageous. I am not frightened that my impulses will lead to chaos. I can be around other people's intense affect without becoming frightened myself." Macon wishes to integrate this new self-concept, but this involves compromises. He cannot continue the fantasied omnipotent control of his universe that is so secretly pleasurable to him. He must relinquish old aims and objects. The completion of his grieving process is necessary if his ultimate outcome is to be successful. He develops ego controls over both id and superego with an attendant increase in both his range and capacity for action. His object world broadens to include new people and the possibility of a future, and his self-esteem is enhanced.

These kinds of changes do not occur in a vacuum. Muriel is central to Macon's progress. She is not a therapist in any conventional sense of the word; yet she *functions* in this capacity for him. At first, certain qualities we might not think of as therapeutic—her intrusive curiosity and brashness—mask subtle capacities that will influence Macon in a positive direction. Muriel has neither the objectivity nor the absence of personal agenda that is associated with the therapist's role. She wants something from Macon—marriage and commitment—and she is quite outspoken about these wishes. However, her "nontherapeutic" qualities are deceptive. Therapists are driven by curiosity also, and by a kind of personal agenda: they wish their patients to form a therapeutic alliance with them to allow participation in a process that will eventually enhance the patient's capacities to work and to love. A point of difference is that Muriel wishes to cure Macon so that he can love *her*.

Where Macon is concerned, Muriel is intuitive and empathic, but also confrontational. She cuts through Macon's avoidance when she tells him what he does not want to hear, but she waits until there is some readiness on his part to absorb what she has to say. While no clinical theory guides her, she is usually correct in both content and timing. In two different situations (the panic attack episode, and the first date) she shows remarkable tact in her interactions with Macon. In the first instance, she reframes a shameful experience, allowing for relief and mastery on his part. In the second, she does not allow him to retreat from his own needs. Her sensitivity and availability allow Macon to talk about his son's death directly, and in so doing to resume a stalled grieving process. (Muriel, an intuitive "therapist," knows how to use the psychotherapeutic techniques of reassurance, reframing, and confrontation. At the same time, she seems to have a sense of the three difficult essentials of psychoanalytic interpretation—tact, timing, and dosage!)

In no interaction does Muriel ever resort to shaming Macon. She does not hesitate to try to evoke guilt, when he is leaving her, or when he will not make a commitment to Alexander, but this is not damaging because she is so clear about her own needs. Macon has reason to feel guilty and gains nothing by avoiding it. He has made use of Muriel's interest and generosity, and in normal social (nontherapy) interactions, obligations are incurred. Shame, on the other hand, will only lead him to further self-protection and retreat. Sarah shames him, and this shame increases his resistance to change and his unwillingness to take risks.

Muriel has another important therapeutic quality, her delicate ability to balance limit-setting and permissiveness. She is exquisitely attuned to Edward's capacity to obey and she never pushes him further than he is really able to tolerate. She is patient, but very persistent. The same qualities are present in her interactions with Macon: she knows when to move forward and when to back away. Since Muriel is comfortable with her own impulses and remarkably free of shame, she is not made uncomfortable by Macon's forays into new territory. She does not have a preexisting set of expectations for him as do Sarah and his family. In this instance, like a therapist, she accepts *his* view of himself and reality, and sees possibilities that he has not yet considered.

Her own behavior is unselfconscious and adventurous. Macon admires this, even when it makes him uneasy. His admiration of her is an aspect of her ability to influence him. She is feisty and courageous. No dog frightens her; she stands up to a teenager who tries to snatch her purse in a store. "He had to admire her. Had he ever known such a fighter?" (p. 279). She can take action, and she is not troubled by her own failures or mistakes. She has had to fight for everything in life; for her, the future is always exciting and full of possibility.

Muriel has many therapeutic qualities for Macon, but this does not explain why he can and does make use of them. He could have avoided her entirely, and found someone else to train Edward. He almost did; his first impression of her was that she was bizarre. Here, we may consider the issue of "readiness," and the idea of transference as a motivation for making new connections. Macon is desperate when he meets Muriel. He knows his desperation has to do with losing Ethan and Sarah, but he is not aware that these new losses have opened old intrapsychic wounds—those of early parental loss and failure. He is aware of feeling limited and unhappy, and of the need for both relief and change. The awareness, referred to earlier, that he "might be carrying things too far" in his household routines is a sign of readiness. Perhaps it would be more accurate to say Macon would like to *be* different without having to *do* anything differently. Muriel frightens him in that she knows that training involves a lot of risky work. But whatever his ambivalence about action and his resistance to change, it is outweighed by a longing to have richer, more varied relationships and experiences. Using the language of our therapeutic narrative, we can say that Macon *engages* with Muriel because he senses she has what it takes to help him move on with his life. Furthermore, she fills an important valence in Macon's object world.

Macon's readiness for new relationships is intensified by his recent losses. His basic transference needs for someone nurturing and trust-worthy are consciously mobilized in his decision to move back to his family home. Unconscious transference needs motivate his choice of Muriel. At first, he is not aware of Muriel's resemblance to his mother, Alicia. Later in the novel, he makes the connection between the two women, with some dismay, but by then Muriel has other important meanings to him. Is Macon's devaluation of his mother and her flighty ways really an attempt to deal with his disappointment at her erratic unavailability? If so, those same impulsive, flamboyant qualities in someone essentially *available* would be very compelling. Macon never knows why Muriel is so attractive to him. He is truly puzzled and tries over and over to talk himself out of his feelings. He is uncomfortable with what his unconscious understands very well. Muriel represents the lost, loved, Oedipally attractive mother whom Macon cannot acknowl-edge; to do so might mobilize his fears of loss and disappointment.

These "negative transference" feelings intensify Macon's ambiv-alence toward Muriel. (This ambivalence is the equivalent of resistance in a therapeutic situation.) The "heartless trainer" he fires and later leaves is really the heartless mother who fired him. Muriel's con-tinued availability, then, is especially important. It means he can have revenge, without punishment, paving the way to forgiveness on his part. Macon's feelings toward his mother were complex and included admiration. Muriel represents a blend of Alicia and Macon's grandparents. She is exciting and adventurous, but also disciplined and reliable. On the other hand, Sarah, who is also a transference figure for Macon, repeats, through shaming and criticism, the empathic failures of his mother. Macon can become involved with Muriel because she does not reenact the seduction and abandonment of his past. In the transference reenactments of therapy, and of real life, the script must end differently for change to occur.

As we examine the process between Macon and Muriel, we see that Macon has engaged with Muriel based on unconscious need, readiness, and a sense that *she*, because of the kind of person she is, can help him. We have seen that she *does* help him, and in what ways, but what happens in between their attachment and his change? In the middle part of their relationship, Macon goes through a period that resembles the therapeutic process of "working through." This is the period of *mutual influence* in which insight and longing for more gratification impel him to behave differently, to do something "out of character." Repeatedly, as resistance (based on fears of loss) enters the picture, Macon backs away, becomes anxious, or denies the significance of what is happening. His feeling that his life is really "on hold" is a form of resistance. He does not want to admit that something is changing inside of him. He devalues his own experience. He uses the obsessional's constellation of defenses—denial, negation, isolation of affect, undoing, and devaluation—as the building blocks of an overall resistance in which he has to experience time as standing still, and inner experience as not really mattering. It is therefore significant that his final thoughts have to do with the adventure of time moving on, and his ability to move on with it.

Macon's need to see himself as someone who cannot take action is also a major resistance. He sees himself as impotent to act while enacting his hostility everywhere. His hostility does not alienate Muriel. She is not unaware of it; rather, she is able to absorb it without losing her equilibrium. Here is another analogy with therapy worth noting. Muriel, like a good therapist, has enough countertransference awareness to know what Macon is doing to her and to be able to confront his withholding behaviors: "You're so self-centered! You've got all these fancy reasons for never doing a single thing I want" (p. 284). However, she is not so caught up in her reactions that she loses perspective. This may be why she is able, despite the personal involvement that marks this relationship as different from therapy, to function therapeutically.

This relates to the overall question of why in certain life situations (depicted occasionally in literature) people are able to function therapeutically for each other. Transference needs alone cannot account for therapeutic effects. Transference may be the hook that brings people together, but it does not necessarily drive them in a therapeutic direction. It may lead to destructive repetitions. Macon is drawn in a positive direction by several factors in addition to transference need. Muriel has a sense of where he needs to go. She has the ability to withstand and, in effect, to interpret his resistance and to pass certain crucial tests of the transference.[3] Muriel continually refutes Macon's central fear that the expression of impulse or affect will lead to loss and destructive outcomes. She does not merely react to *his* impulses without fear; she is not afraid of her own. His wish to identify with that courageous part of her, and to incorporate her admirable qualities, is a primary force moving him toward intrapsychic change.

It is Muriel's ability to withstand Macon's ambivalence that allows the process of mutual influence to succeed. Her admirable qualities—emotional honesty, flexibility, and acceptance of others provide the direction for Macon's change for these are qualities he would like to have himself. Although Muriel, like Darcy, remains more in the background of the novel, she is also influenced. Macon represents maturity, stability, and a higher social status to her. He teaches her to parent Alexander more appropriately, modifying her overprotective and infantilizing bond with her son. He does this by providing her with the care and stability she needs. Muriel can then allow Alexander to become, with Macon's help, a separate male person rather than the weak and feminized receptacle of all the fears she disavows in herself.

COMMENTS ON "ACCIDENTAL THERAPY"

We may summarize the process of change that takes place in Macon Leary as follows: Transference needs are mobilized in him by contemporary losses that evoke old parental failures. A new person enters his life at this point. She has the ability to withstand the negative forces, or resistances, that ensue. In a process that resembles working through, she does not allow him to repeat the past. His admiration of her allows a partial identification with her that contains its own rewards: He likes himself better as the person she wants him to be.

The searching out, or accidental encountering, of growth-enhancing figures is a feature of normal development, recognized as especially important in childhood and adolescence, but going on beyond those developmental phases. As we noted in Chapter 4, the combined transference and reality elements of relationships with friends, teachers, mentors, lovers, spouses, and children all provide opportunities for growth and repair throughout life. Perhaps people who are successful at finding accidental therapists never need to consult real ones.

It *is* striking how frequently people come for treatment when they have exhausted outside sources and outside searches. Often a hoped-for, but failed, self-rescue attempt in the form of a divorce, a new love affair, or a career change is the precipitant for seeking treatment. Shame expressed by patients early in treatment that they are "unable to do this on their own" also may reflect their sense of failure in not finding an outside therapeutic figure. Another way of putting this is that those people most likely to turn their outside relationships into transference repetitions quickly exhaust their interpersonal worlds. They need the special conditions of psychotherapy where transference wishes and enactments can be interpreted and worked through.

The work of psychoanalytically oriented therapy involves, in large part, this recognition of transference repetitions motivated by unconscious wishes for inappropriate gratification or punishment. But despite the emphasis on transference interpretation and resolution, many therapists recognize the importance of new or modified outside relationships, modeled on patterns established with the therapist, as a sign of solid intrapsychic change. Perhaps one of therapy's salutary outcomes is the more adaptive utilization of accidental or spontaneous therapeutic situations encountered during and after therapy. Macon's ability to father Alexander in a less anxious and driven way than he was able to father his own son, Ethan, is one example of this.

What is happening in these "accidental therapy" situations? Some are supportive experiences, where confidence is enhanced but defenses remain unchallenged. Others are corrective emotional experiences where the therapist's understanding and control allow a new interaction to take place. We would not characterize these situations as primarily interpretive, yet certain events and encounters have interpretive results: people take a new look at themselves. Sometimes the accidental therapist achieves an effect by being an idealizable other, a model. The operant factor in this modality may be that the therapist is perceived as someone who has worked out the very conflicts and problems with which the patient struggles. Patients in therapy often have just this fantasy about their therapists. The therapeutic model in this story seems to contain all of the above elements to some degree. Muriel supports Macon; she interprets his resistance; she does not participate in destructive reenactments; and she provides an idealizable model.

Another important factor in the relationship between Muriel and Macon is Muriel's control over what we call, in a clinical situation, her countertransference. Lucia Tower, a psychoanalyst, makes the point that if the therapist does not develop some countertransference reactions to the patient's material, the process does not engage both parties enough to be successful.[4] If countertransference is too powerful, reenactments are likely to occur; but if, like Muriel, the therapist knows, in a visceral way, what is going on and is able to resist participating in the reenactment, the results are likely to be more optimal. The ability of accidental therapists to avoid repetitions is as central to their success as it is to the efforts of professional therapists.

Interestingly, in Muriel's case, her capacity to control countertransference manifestations is almost entirely lacking in her relationship with her son, where, as we have noted, she is overprotective, inconsistent, and neurotic. Here is where her nontherapeutic qualities are most evident. It is Macon who functions as an accidental therapist for Alexander, providing the kind of parenting opportunities the boy needs. Professional therapists depend on clinical theory, training, and personal treatment in the management of countertransference. This allows them to treat a wider range of patients and problems than the accidental therapist, where a meshing of personal needs is *necessary* to the process.

When we compare clinical situations with relationships in literature, we find many areas of overlap. While we know they are not the same, understanding each modality enriches our appreciation of the other. Psychoanalytic insights enhance our reading of literary texts, and these texts, in turn, illuminate human situations of conflict, resolution, and growth in ways that may broaden and confirm our clinical observations. There is one particular way that literature captures an important aspect of the therapeutic encounter. For many reasons, both therapists and patients may experience the clinical relationship as artificial and unnatural, outside the bounds of normal social intercourse. The more healing and "human" aspects of this relationship often remain unarticulated but are deeply felt. This is, in part, a consequence of the necessity for maintaining role relationships in the therapeutic situation. Clinicians focus on the transference and let the real relationship quietly cement the process. Literary works often capture the rich emotion and fantasy that lie behind all kinds of role-structured relationships; they illuminate both transference and reality, the fantastic and the genuine, in a way that allows us to experience the healing nature of certain interactions. What therapy often maintains as a subtext, literature makes explicit.

SILAS MARNER (GEORGE ELIOT): CHRONIC DEPRESSION RESOLVES IN A COMPLEXLY LAYERED THERAPEUTIC PROCESS

The hand may be a little child's

Those among our readers who are products of the American public school system may remember *Silas Marner*—perhaps with mixed feelings—as required reading in high school. We feel that this unusual novel deserves a second chance; from the vantage point of its underlying therapeutic themes, it is sensitive, astute, and surprisingly complex. *Silas Marner* is the story of a man in midlife who recovers from chronic depression and social withdrawal. Embedded in the plot, characterizations, and descriptions of this novel is a "subplot" that concerns psychological change. George Eliot, of course, does not consider change in terms of psychotherapy or psychoanalysis, but—taken in the fictional context—we can recognize many of the elements of process we know from the clinical situation.

We shall pursue our discussion of *Silas Marner* at two levels. First, we shall examine the story of Silas, his traumatic departure from the community of his youth, subsequent retreat to the rural village of Raveloe, and his eventual healing after he adopts the little girl, Eppie. Second, we shall examine the novel as a whole, emphasizing in particular the role of two other major characters, the brothers Godfrey and Dunstan Cass, whose lives are interwoven with that of Silas. This analysis enables a deeper interpretation of George Eliot's depiction of personality and change. We shall argue that the latent meaning of *Silas Marner* involves a richer, more complex understanding of intrapsychic change than the more apparent version we experience in reading about Silas alone. Eliot has elaborated different aspects of the change process in a way that can be used to understand and integrate different *theories* of psychoanalytic change. Specifically, we shall suggest that *Silas Marner* integrates elements of psychoanalytic libido theory, ego psychology, and self psychology, using the persons of the three central male characters of the story.[1]

While *Silas Marner* reads as a morality tale, a story of faith lost and regained, a strong case can be made that its central narrative is therapeutic, that the reader is interested in the story because it concerns psychological recovery. In the nineteenth century the therapeutic was conceived as moral. What, today, we would call a psychotherapeutic approach to mental illness was known then as "moral treatment." Silas's initial, disillusioned retreat is discussed in the novel as a loss of faith. In psychoanalytic language it is the loss of confidence in object relations: loss of confidence that one can be effective and trusting toward others, and that others will behave predictably and sympathetically.[2] *Silas Marner* is the story of such a loss, of the substitutive activities Silas undertakes to ensure his psychological survival, and of the slow restoration of his trust through caring for a child. Taking a wider view, this novel can be interpreted as a commentary on the multiple strands of the process of psychological recovery.

THE STORY

At the beginning of the novel, Silas is already an isolated man, living on the outskirts of the village of Raveloe. We learn quickly how he came to be there. As a young man, Silas was a devout member of a religious community in an unnamed city. Soon after Silas became engaged to marry, his closest friend, William, betrayed him by stealing the community's funds, planting the incriminating evidence in Silas's room, and then denouncing Silas as the thief. In biblical fashion, lots were drawn to determine whether Silas was indeed responsible; they declared Silas's guilt. He was suspended from membership in the community, unless he confessed. Silas responded angrily by accusing William, and by denouncing "a God of lies, that bears witness against the innocent" (p. 15).

For the reader, it is unclear why Silas has been singled out in this way. The elements of a jealous triangle are present—Silas has just become engaged—but Silas also appears to be a victim of his friend's ambition, and of his own overtrusting nature. Later in the novel we learn of an earlier trauma—the loss of his mother and sister during his childhood—that may have sensitized Silas to the impact of this adult betrayal. Eliot makes none of this clear. The true problem—its origin and nature—remains obscure, hidden like the crucial wounds of childhood behind a protective amnesia.

After this betrayal, Silas turns to his loom for solace. His fiancée, one of the community that has condemned him, sends a message rejecting him, and within a month she marries William. Silas leaves the town. He wanders through the country, disoriented, adrift both personally and spiritually. What is unmistakable in the following passage is the presence of unresolved mourning and depression: "Minds that have been unhinged from their old faith and love have perhaps sought this Lethean influence of exile in which the past becomes dreamy because its symbols have all vanished, and the present too is dreamy because it is linked with no memories" (p. 16).

Silas settles in the village of Raveloe, where his skill at weaving is useful to the local women, who need their spun flax woven into linen. He works for long hours, losing himself in repetitive activity. "Every man's work, pursued steadily, tends in this way to become an end in itself, and so to bridge over the loveless chasms of his life" (p. 18).

For his first work he is paid five guineas. Eliot makes it clear that the monetary value of the gold is of no great significance to Silas:

> But what were the guineas to him who saw no vista beyond countless days of weaving? It was needless for him to ask that, for it was pleasant to him to feel them in his palm, and look at their bright faces, which were all his own: it was another element of life, like the weaving and the satisfaction of hunger, subsisting quite aloof from the life of belief and love from which he had been cut off. (p. 18)

At this point in the narrative, there is an interesting disruption of Silas's isolation; he heals a woman with congestive heart failure. Using herbal knowledge obtained from his mother, Silas administers a concoction of foxglove, and the woman recovers. When the locals come to him with further requests for herbal healing, Silas refuses. He knows the real limits of his healing powers and fears further rejection should he fail. The villagers are already suspicious of the weaver; he has "fits" in which he falls into trance states (probably petit-mal seizures), and he is reclusive and miserly. His refusal of their requests for healing alienates them further. Now, Silas turns to his gold with increased need. He becomes obsessed, not so much with the gold itself, but with its characteristic feel, shine, and capacity to grow in amount. At night, when he is done weaving, he takes out the gold and plays with it, as though it were animate: "He would on no account have exchanged those coins, which had become his familiars, for other coins with unknown faces" (p. 21).

Eliot inserts here a psychologically telling incident. Silas trips and breaks a brown earthenware pot he has used to carry water for twelve years. Like the gold, the pot has obtained semi-animate status. It has "been his companion . . . its form had an expression of willing helpfulness" (p. 22). When the pot breaks, Silas props the three pieces together "for a memorial." Despite his withdrawal, the ability to appreciate, to care, and to feel loss remains. He has not lost the capacity for attachment, but only turned away from human objects, and from God, the ultimate symbol of trust.[3] At the same time, Silas does not want to risk the complete sense of isolation that he fears would follow new trust and new disappointment.

Paradoxically, it is a second traumatic loss that begins Silas's process of psychological recovery. Silas's precious hoard is stolen. He turns to the villagers—not for solace—but for recovery of his gold. But this desire to regain his loss forces him to leave his isolation.

> This strangely novel situation of opening his trouble to his Raveloe neighbors, of sitting in the warmth of a hearth not his own, and feeling the presence of faces and voices which were his nearest promise of help, had doubtless its influence on Marner, in spite of his passionate preoccupation with his loss. *Our consciousness rarely registers the beginning of a growth within us any more than without us: there have been many circulations of the sap before we detect the smallest sign of the bud.* (p. 59; italics added)

The theft alters Silas's situation in two respects. In the eyes of the villagers he becomes more human. Now they can feel sorry for him; he is vulnerable and needy, not an object of fear and suspicion. His misfortune also gives Silas an opportunity to heal the deep depression that has kept him isolated. He has scorned human society, in effect damning his Raveloe neighbors along with his friend, William, and his congregation family. Eliot tells us, though, that this disillusionment is not unyielding, that hope has not been given up:

> To anyone who had observed him before he lost his gold, it might have seemed that so withered and shrunken a life as his could hardly be susceptible of a bruise, could hardly endure any subtraction but such as would put an end to it altogether. But in reality *it had been an eager life,* filled with immediate purpose, which fenced him in from the wide cheerless unknown. *It had been a clinging life;* and though the object round which its fibres had clung was a dead, disrupted thing, it satisfied the need for clinging. (p. 78; italics added)

Silas is thrown into acute grief once again, by the loss of his gold. He returns to his loom. "As he sat weaving, he every now and then moaned low, like one in pain" (p. 79). His prior mode of dealing with loss, through withdrawal and substitutive investment in his weaving and its golden yield, is no longer effective. Now Silas truly grieves. Sympathetic visitors come. The pastor urges him to attend church. Silas listens, though with little clear effect. Dolly Winthrop, a good-hearted neighbor, visits with her youngest son, Aaron, bringing Silas cookies. Silas accepts them, and in turn offers one to the shy boy, who has sung him a carol. Their exchange foreshadows the means of Silas's recovery: caring and being cared about. The coin-shaped cookie is exchanged rather than hoarded.

Interwoven with the story of Silas and his gold is another story; this involves the two sons of Squire Cass, the richest landowner in the village. Godfrey Cass, the oldest son, is being manipulated and blackmailed by his profligate younger brother, Dunstan. Out of lust, Godfrey has married an attractive, but penniless, woman in another village; he has kept this marriage a secret from his family and his neighbors. His wife has borne him a daughter, now two years old. Dunstan uses his knowledge of the marriage to extort money and favors from Godfrey, who fears being disinherited if his father discovers his secret.

It is, in fact, Dunstan who has stolen Silas's gold. A series of misadventures leads him to the weaver's cottage where he finds the door open and Silas away. Dunstan, who has heard of Silas's hoard, locates the gold and takes it. Wandering drunkenly into the foggy night, he falls into the quarry pit with the treasure and is drowned.

On New Year's Eve, a few weeks after the theft of Silas's gold, Godfrey's wife, who is now an opium addict, sets out with her two-year-old daughter to expose her husband by appearing at Squire Cass's annual celebration. On the way she collapses from the effect of the drug, just outside Silas's cottage. There, as the night turns colder, she freezes to death. The child, who has been asleep in her mother's arms, awakens and toddles toward the light of Silas's hearth. Silas, hearing the New Year's revels, has stepped outside to listen. He falls into one of his fits, leaving the door open. The child enters and goes to sleep near the fire. When Silas recovers consciousness and sees her, he initially—being nearsighted—mistakes her golden hair for his lost coins. As he realizes it is a child, Silas makes an immediate connection to a younger sister he helped care for, a sister who died in childhood. He feeds the little girl.

When Silas discovers the body of the child's mother outside his hut, he goes for help to Squire Cass's house. Godfrey returns with the rescue party but does not acknowledge that the body is his wife's nor does he claim his child. Silas *does* want the little girl, though his thinking, at first, has a quality of ownership, like his relation to the inanimate gold: "'No—no—I can't part with it, I can't let it go,' said Silas, abruptly. 'It's come to me—I've a right to keep it'" (p. 119). Silas has transferred his wish for possession from the gold to the child ("it"). Dolly Winthrop observes the child's attachment to Silas, and supports his plan to care for her over the succeeding days with practical advice and hand-me-down clothes. Silas insists on managing the child himself, possessively fending off any suggestions of outside aid.

"Eppie"—Silas names the child for his mother and sister—becomes the link to renewed psychological development, and to social participation. The gap is bridged through the renewal of relatedness—with Eppie, and with the community that parenthood opens to Silas. "As the child's mind was growing into knowledge, his mind was growing into memory: as her life unfolded, his soul, long stupefied in a cold, narrow prison, was unfolding too, and trembling gradually into full consciousness" (p. 131).

As Eppie grows older, Eliot makes this causal sequence even clearer. By "seeking what was needful for Eppie," Silas embraces the customs of local life; this involvement, in turn, reawakens his faith and trust. He now wants to understand what has happened to him, to connect his past and his present. He talks to Dolly about his history. After much mulling she tells him that his error was the abandonment of faith in God—the abandonment of trust. This conclusion, the only explicit "moral" Eliot gives us, feels incomplete. It is a harsh moral, requiring faith and trust when events and people go terribly awry; it is faith in the God of Job. When Silas takes Eppie to see the places and people of his youth, he finds them gone without a trace; his past now exists only in memory, and in the characterological developments time has engendered.

The idea that relatedness now matters more than possession, for Silas, is reinforced by events that occur many years later. The nearby quarry pit is drained, exposing the skeleton of Dunstan Cass with Silas's gold. Despite his vindication and financial recovery, Silas says of the gold: "It takes no hold of me now" (p. 169). What is satisfying is realization of his love for Eppie, and the value the gold will have to help her.

A third iteration of the idea that in the curative process altruistic love replaces possessive attachment is expressed through Godfrey Cass. Godfrey has remarried, this time to a woman of his own class, Nancy Lammeter; the marriage has been happy, but childless. Moved by the uncovering of Dunstan's crime and punishment, he confesses his prior marriage to Eppie's mother. His wife forgives him, and in their reconciliation Godfrey acknowledges the teenage Eppie as his daughter. He offers her the benefits of his status and wealth by suggesting she come live with him and Nancy. Silas is horrified at the prospect of losing Eppie, but he puts the choice in her hands. Without hesitation, Eppie decides to remain with Silas. The Casses are hurt and disappointed, but they recognize the fairness of her decision. Godfrey Cass continues his support of Silas and Eppie. Godfrey thus pays the price of fearing to lose his position as first son, and of wishing to marry well. Like Silas's, Godfrey Cass's life is resolved but only partially fulfilled. Marner has had no wife; Cass has had no child.

DISCUSSION

In our analysis of *Silas Marner* we shall proceed in two steps. First, we will examine the most obvious process of change: Silas's recovery, through his relationship with Eppie. Second, we will suggest that a full appreciation of how this novel renders the question of change involves looking at the three major male characters—Silas, Godfrey, and Dunstan and their interplay in the plot. We take each character as a psychological principle, an aspect of the personality that comes into play during the psychological development necessary for change.

The novelist, especially a pre-Freudian one like George Eliot, is free of preconceptions—or, at least, free of *our* current clinical preconceptions. In devising the plot and characters of *Silas Marner*, Eliot gives us not only an accessible, "manifest" story about change in Silas, but a "latent" story woven among several characters.[4] This story contains what we might term a speculation about how change occurs, a latent level of interpretation. Interestingly, we will find in each of the major characters of *Silas Marner* a recognizable psychoanalytic point of view. That is, the character exemplifies some aspect of mind that has become important in psychoanalytic discourse. Since Eliot brought these themes together in a plot, we can look for the respective roles of each, and thus identify how she makes them work toward change.

It can be argued that the requirements of plot are different from those of personality function and change in real life situations, let alone in psychoanalysis. We agree; we only suggest that this interpretation of a novel presents a *possible* integration of the elements of the process of change. In favor of this approach, though, we are suggesting that the enduring popularity of certain novels is an indication that they speak successfully to core psychological themes. This was, of course, why Freud appealed to literature so often for support of his ideas.

Eppie: The Therapeutic Effect of an Idealized Child

Our first level of interpretation concerns Silas's recovery from a depressive state after he adopts the child. Eppie, the child of Godfrey's lust, becomes Silas's healer. Whether we take her literally—as a child whom Silas must feed, protect, and nurture—or symbolically—as the child in himself with whom he reconnects, Eppie is the central figure in Silas's process of internal alteration.

Like Silas, Eppie experiences directly; she also acts, like any child, with spontaneity. Eppie has little complexity, but embodies an idealized developmental process. In this process, Silas relives development from the parental position, and is able to provide Eppie the loving, empathic conditions needed to undo the traumatic experiences of his own past.

First Silas must learn to feed and clothe the child. His initial wish to possess her leads, through the gratification of relatedness, to a wish for what is best for her, which in turn means involvement in the social life of Raveloe. He agrees to her christening. The same protective-possessive stance leads Silas to take Eppie with him on his rounds, and the child, of course, provides him and his neighbors with a focus for socializing.

Later, Silas must deal with Eppie's innocent mischievousness, as she wanders away from the cottage and almost falls in the quarry pit. Dolly Winthrop says he must correct her behavior with physical punishment or rejection, but these are too disturbing to Silas. Instead, punishment is replaced with solicitous close observation. His parenting contrasts with that of Squire Cass, who is permissive but inattentive with his sons and tenants, then overly harsh when they misbehave.

The bond of attunement, loyalty, and gentle concern between Eppie and Silas is also idealized. As she emerges into consciousness, Eppie is as much a mother as a daughter, caring for Silas; later, she approaches marriage in a way that reassures Silas that she will never abandon him. While this bond seems too good to be true, it is intuitively convincing in describing the degree of conflict-free relatedness Silas needs to recover from the wounds of his youth.

Eppie also represents the hope a child often signifies for a parent: the chance to "start over."[5] We find this idea in various forms in clinical theory. Each of these formulations of process involves the idea that the treatment situation offers the opportunity to resume the developmental process in the treatment relationship. In *Silas Marner* the child represents the birth of new possibilities in a depressed man. Starting over taps into his vulnerability by discovering hidden hope.

Unlikely as it seems on first consideration, Eppie has important qualities in common with the therapist. Eppie is functionally similar to a central aspect of the analytic attitude. In recommending that we listen neutrally, nonjudgmentally, and with "evenly-hovering attention," Freud was describing desirable role qualities much like Eppie's traits; she, too, is attentive, loyally available, and uncritical. She makes few demands for herself beyond the expected needs and foibles of childhood. The idealized, harmonious quality of the relationship between Silas and Eppie allows him to rebuild a feeling of trust. It is this aspect of the psychoanalytic relationship—the establishment of trust—that enables the patient to tolerate the intense affects and distortions that appear in the throes of the transference neurosis. However, *Silas Marner* is a more complex novel; the lives of the Cass brothers are inextricably woven into the plot. Silas, Dunstan, and Godfrey can be seen as representative of three major psychological themes that play significant roles in change.

Three Characters as Three Aspects of Change

Silas: Silas *experiences,* and reacts to his experience in a reflexive, automatic fashion. Rather than give up all hope, he turns away from social attachment, in a reaction to trauma. His unconscious goal is equilibrium—the maintenance of psychological balance or wholeness in the face of massive disappointment. Social ties have been the source of his disillusionment; Silas withdraws from them. He does not give up hope for connection and love, but his caring is now directed toward his gold and the round of his daily activity.

Like many defensive compromises, Silas's is severely limiting. Whatever the psychological nature and meaning of his original injury (e.g., whether we ascribe it to early maternal loss or traumatic betrayal by his friend), Silas must feel enraged, powerless, and rejected by his religious community. In turning to his work, Silas "pulls in" his world. Dangerous archaic, aggressive impulses are controlled by a withdrawal of involvement. The world is killed off and protected at the same time by withdrawing oneself behind a safe barrier of isolation.[6] Within his limited domain, Silas can retain the purity of his "eager" and "clinging" life, by limiting his emotional involvement to the gold, over which he can experience complete control. The trauma has been too great for Silas to mourn; he has transferred the object ties his loss has left behind to the simple activities and objects of his solitary existence.

This depiction is a psychologically accurate account of an adaptation after a traumatic experience. (Recall how Macon Leary, too, "pulled in" his world, avoiding social contact and focusing on compulsive household routines to manage his grief.) But, somehow, *Silas Marner* does not make sense as a novel if we view it as solely about recovery from trauma and withdrawal. Why the other characters and plot elements? It is through Godfrey and Dunstan that we learn about sin, anxiety, and guilt—and about impulsive action. We believe *Silas Marner* is phenomenologically accurate in this sense: we do not *feel* impulses, sin, or the resulting guilt directly; what we feel is disapproval and rejection by internalized parents and their values. Silas's "unjust" condemnation by his congregation (and God) is felt subjectively as overwhelming repudiation by his human environment, as abandonment, and as loss. Although Eliot assigns Silas no responsibility for his initial betrayal by his friend, other characters in the novel deal with issues of sin and morality. We shall see, through analysis of these other characters, that a person can bring such punishment on himself or herself, and that impulse may be a factor in cure as well as a component of conflict.

Godfrey: Like Silas, Godfrey Cass also wishes for love and connection. Unlike Silas, he has the *capacity for self-observation*, for feeling accountable for his actions. Godfrey has also lost a mother during childhood, and like Silas he may be struggling with the effects of unresolved mourning: yearning, rage, and guilt. By marrying the attractive, alcoholic, and lower-class Molly Farren, Godfrey expresses all of these: yearning is gratified by sex; rage, by binding himself to a woman unacceptable to his father; and guilt, by depriving himself of marriage to his social equal, Nancy Lammeter. This is speculation; it is more important to observe that Eliot has portrayed Godfrey—unlike Silas—as a man *aware* of his actions and of his responsibility for them. Hamlet-like, when opportunities arise for facing consequences, Godfrey is unable to act. His dilemma is that he wants to serve both desire and conscience; he balances guilt and wish in a way that prevents action and resolution. Godfrey's problem is self-doubt, and the desire to have his patrimony while at the same time misbehaving behind his father's back. He wants status without the risk of coming to terms with guilt and responsibility. When, years later, the truth emerges, he is a sadder, wiser man, more aware of the consequences of sin and his hesitation to confess. He recognizes the consequent limitations on happiness. But until the end of *Silas Marner*, Godfrey's self-awareness does not bring about action in a new direction.

We can compare Godfrey and his situation in *Silas Marner* to that part of personality we term "ego"—a significant character in the psychic drama, but one required to serve several masters. In particular, the ego mediates between wish and conscience. We know how, in analysis, the multiple tasks of the ego may sometimes result in endless loops of resistance: how entrenched patterns may be repeated without significant structural alteration, reflecting the stability of compromises arrived at early in life. Godfrey represents such a tendency: the different calls on him lead to inaction.

Dunstan: Dunstan Cass is a significant linking figure in understanding the change process in *Silas Marner*. He is all impulse and ruthlessness, a depiction of drivenness, of Freud's "pleasure principle"—a man in a constant search for satisfaction or relief of discomfort. Duncan knows about right and wrong, but does not care. He is a character with energy. In contrast, neither Silas nor Godfrey have available motivational energy for change. Dunstan does not have purpose, in the sense of long-range goals—his direction is formed out of wishes or exigencies of the moment—but he acts continuously, and almost always destructively. Yet his destructiveness also *propels* the novel, creating the turn in Silas's affairs that brings him back to society. He is connected with Godfrey's sin and repentance, and is the instigator of events that bring Eppie to Silas.

How is it that what seems like a purely evil, impulsive, destructive figure is the catalyst of positive change? We would suggest that this can be understood if put psychologically. Dunstan, representing impulse unrestrained, is dangerous—a source of guilt and anxiety for Godfrey, and the cause of Silas's second traumatization. But he also represents, like the id in Freud's structural theory of mind, the source of motivation and action. Without his presence there would be no movement in the plot of *Silas Marner*. In psychoanalysis, a crucial aspect of movement in the process comes from the impulses that the analytic situation stimulates. (This is a significant part of what we mean when we speak of "regression" in treatment. Wishes that are hidden or defended against are released.) Impulses are disturbing to patients, and lead to extensive resistance to change. But impulses are also what moves the process along, creating the intensity that is part of transference and the transference neurosis.

In *Silas Marner*, Dunstan's role in the story is brief: he blackmails Godfrey with his knowledge of Godfrey's secret marriage into covering a debt he himself has incurred. Then, to pay the debt, Dunstan suggests that he sell Godfrey's valuable horse at the hunt. Godfrey agrees. During the hunt, Dunstan impales the horse and kills it while taking a fence. Walking home, passing Silas's cottage, he thinks of the weaver's gold as a solution to the loss of the horse; when he finds that Silas is not at home, he steals the hoard. Then, mysteriously, he disappears.

For Silas, the loss of the gold jolts him out of his deeply embedded, depressive, narcissistic retreat. Only a significant disruption will imbalance this internal equilibrium. Dunstan's impulsive, selfish act has the explosive energy to do this. Dunstan's theft triggers Silas into a grief that reopens his need, and makes him receptive to the sympathy of others, and then to Eppie. Dunstan's disappearance with the gold is then necessary in the plot to provide Silas with opportunity, motivation, and time to change.

Again, there is an analogy to psychoanalytic process. Regression releases old desires into the therapeutic relationship. Like the near-sighted Silas groping about his cottage, confusing Eppie's golden hair for his coins, patients seize on the analyst as the object from whom they hope to obtain what they feel was denied them in the past. And also like Silas, their motivations are initially selfishly determined. They wish to possess and control the analyst completely; they want to "start over" with life on their terms. Yet, as with Silas and Eppie, there is, in the new relationship of analysis, a potential for concern for the analyst, for guilt about wishes to harm and exploit. This capacity for concern stems from a relationship with a new figure who, like Eppie, is empathic, noncritical, and appropriately caring. Identificatory processes are inevitable in analysis, and these traits in the analyst begin to become internalized by the patient. Hopefully, the patient can then recognize previous maladaptive compromises and substitutions. This, in turn, frees up capacities for taking action toward better adaptation.

Dunstan's drowning can be read psychologically in relation to both other characters and what they represent. For Godfrey, Dunstan's disappearance is a metaphor for the repression of an impulse-guilt constellation. Freed from the threat that Dunstan might reveal his prior marriage, Godfrey can marry the woman he wishes. The barrenness of their union seems a representation of punishment for his past sins; Dunstan has disappeared, but he could always return. When Dunstan's body is revealed fifteen years later, Godfrey is finally motivated to confess his previous marriage to Nancy. Though he fails to reclaim Eppie as his child, his conscience is now clear; there is no longer a guilty secret separating him from his wife. For Silas, the disappearance of Dunstan with his gold is a metaphor for the disappearance of the gold from his own psychic life as a substitutive satisfaction.

The sequence of internal events that the characters in *Silas Marner* experience resembles a sequence that might occur, in reality, in the course of psychological arrest and subsequent therapeutic change. Traumatic early experience and conflict are followed by withdrawal. Infantile wishes are not given up, but rather are redirected from relationships, and the hope of good experiences with others, to controllable physical objects and soothing, rhythmic bodily activity in work ("an eager life . . . a clinging life").

It is the forced breakdown of Silas's defensive position that allows change. When Dunstan steals the hoard, Silas is acutely grief-stricken. He reaches out to the villagers in a desperate attempt to retrieve his gold. In their own way the villagers now reach out to him. Silas is engaged once again in the social matrix. This sets the stage for the correction of his pervasive, protective mistrust.

Silas Marner and the Therapeutic Narrative

We believe George Eliot's depiction of the process of change—illustrated through the three major figures of *Silas Marner*—illuminates the therapeutic narrative. It does so by teasing out different strands of the experience of change that are ordinarily so densely interwoven that they are difficult to recognize:

(1) Every patient experiences events, whether intrapsychic or external, as happening to himself or herself; at any given moment life is experienced, not observed. Eliot represents Silas this way—as a man to whom events happen. Awareness of experience tends to focus on feeling states, especially signal affects, cues that operate to stimulate equilibrium seeking. Each of Silas's actions is taken in this protective manner, even his attempts to take control or to understand. While he is still alone, Silas's actions are only marginally successful in creating a satisfactory equilibrium. Like a depressed patient before treatment, his world is severely limited by the adaptations that have followed the loss of faith in a caring, concerned world.

When Eppie first appears, Silas—in a desperate state himself—reaches out for the child almost in the same way he cared about his gold. She is an "it" that will relieve his painful inner state. Thus Silas's *engagement* in change begins with a self-deception similar to that many patients create—that the change agent will be a reassuring, magical replacement that will not stress them further.

Once Eppie is part of his life, Silas is inevitably drawn into a process of *mutual influence* as the activities of childrearing awaken old capacities and new social patterns. Silas's sense of safety in being an adult caring for a child, and in relating through the child to others, is akin to an important part of the therapeutic relationship. This is its reassuring, empathic, caring quality, a quality that has different names in different clinical theories—the "basic transference," "self-object transference," "maternal transference."

Finally, the *directionality* of Silas's change is maintained by the reassuring quality of the relationship with a child. Eppie is depicted as benign and kind, a model for Silas's renewed involvement with humanity and trust in God.

(2) Like Godfrey, patients become more aware of their motives and

conflicts over the course of treatment, as they become less paralyzed by ambivalence and avoidance. Godfrey begins, frozen by his conflict. Time and events guide him toward confession, atonement, and awareness. These relieve his guilt and allow him to enjoy the satisfactions that are really available to him. From the point of view of our model, the awareness that Godfrey represents serves primarily an after-the-fact function. It is not insight that leads any of the characters to change or improve. But once they have begun to change, their awareness increases, and serves to stabilize the alteration they have made. This picture is not our accustomed view of psychoanalytic change, but it does correspond to recent proposals that action occurs first, followed by insight.

(3) Finally, for therapy to progress and carry over into outside life, there must be the Dunstan Cass element of *driven action*. During a successful treatment, action comes under greater ego control. Taking Dunstan, the theft, and the quarry pit as metaphor, action begins as ruthless and destructive, but is repressed until it can reemerge in sublimated form, its old quality now just a skeleton. Action becomes less impulsive and, at the same time, freer.

The action aspect of the change process serves all three components of the therapeutic narrative. It promotes *engagement* by jarring Silas traumatically back into the social world. Action motivates *mutual influence* in the form of the demanding presence of the child's needs and attachments. And, at the end, action—brought under control—is the fuel of the richer, positive social life Silas leads with Eppie and her husband as a new family.

As a thorough psychologist, Eliot moves us back and forth between these three views, just as we believe skillful analysts and psychotherapists move between empathic acceptance and confrontive interpretation of impulse derivatives, affects, or defenses. In the plot of *Silas Marner*, Dunstan and Godfrey go offstage during the period of Eppie's childhood, i.e., during Silas's recovery. Only near the end, with Silas again a part of the community, fully re-engaged with people, do Dunstan and Godfrey reappear. Dunstan is now known to be dead; the threat he represents to psychic equilibrium is now past. Godfrey reappears to confess his past sin, resolving the unstable neurotic compromise of concealment. In the end, Godfrey also represents the capacity for understanding. He recognizes the justice of his punishment of childlessness—one cannot have it all.

In long-term psychoanalytic treatments the course is often the same as in this story: for most of the treatment we are caught up with the patients' sensitivities, their struggles for control, their need for us to listen, or contrariwise, to care about them more actively. "Starting over" in treatment means forming a new object relation, and then struggling through a whole series of developmental issues in that relation, just as Silas and Eppie do in the novel. Only after much reworking, frequently near or even after the completion of treatment, does the patient become capable of self-awareness, of being able to think and act comfortably, more contented with his or her lot in reality.

Silas, Godfrey, and Dunstan do not come from different species of humankind; their qualities have to do with different, but not irreconcilable, aspects of human experience. It is interesting that sophisticated descriptions of analytic process by representatives of self psychology and of ego psychology include both aspects—experience and reflection. The common elements in their conceptions of clinical process are quite similar to those we have delineated in our study of *Silas Marner*. To change, we need to be comforted and confronted, cared about and encouraged out of withdrawal—in a process that is both new and a reworking of the past. To complete change, and to retain it, we need to understand ourselves, and gain a greater capacity for self-awareness. *Silas Marner* enables us to see that there may be a core psychoanalytic process that transcends theoretical differences in conceptualizing the mind.

In summary, a picture of psychoanalytic therapeutic process is suggested by this study of *Silas Marner*. A sufferer such as the depressed weaver enters a state of narcissistic withdrawal, reflected in symptomatic behavior and social isolation. Crucial human needs are met in safe, controllable ways. Subjectively, the patient experiences a limited, unhappy life, but one that exists in some equilibrium. Even when treatment is voluntarily sought, the sufferer is not truly ready to relinquish this safety. Instead, he or she must be helped, as Silas is by Eppie's golden locks, into forming a new attachment. Once the new relationship takes hold, it is the arena for a developmental process, not identical to original development, but taking a course necessary for the sequential mastery of prior problem points. Motivating all this is drive, in the sense of the wish for erotic and aggressive satisfaction as well as a more neutralized urge for mastery. The process is kept on course by the equilibrium-maintaining tendency that is associated with self-states. Ultimately, if a new equilibrium is reached, it can be stabilized by the self-awareness we signify as insight.

7

FRANCES HODGSON BURNETT'S *THE SECRET GARDEN:* MULTIPLE CURES, MULTIPLE PROCESSES OF CURE

It was the sweetest, most mysterious-looking place anyone could imagine.

In this chapter we analyze a well-known children's classic to illustrate a more complex therapeutic process, one that combines elements of the therapeutic milieu with those of the psychoanalytic relationship. A whole genre of children's literature exists in which the child hero or heroine is responsible for the healing of other children or adults. *Heidi, Anne of Green Gables*, and *Little Lord Fauntleroy* are classics in which these themes appear, but Frances Hodgson Burnett's *The Secret Garden* is a particularly rich example of transformation of character and attainment of developmental goals within this genre. In clear, old-fashioned language Burnett spells out certain universal themes and problems for latency age children in an appealing and relatively undisguised way. *The Secret Garden* has been a perennial favorite, particularly (but not exclusively) with girls, since its first publication in 1911.

Bruno Bettelheim maintains that, in listening to fairy tales, children are drawn to those stories that have themes with meaning to them at that moment in their lives. These special tales allow the child to experience mastery through fantasied solutions of current conflicts. Children "choose" the tale they need and request repetitive tellings or readings until they are ready to move on to another tale with new meaning. By latency, children can read to themselves and pick their own literature, but those choices are also determined by current unconscious conflict and the need for solutions. Latency age children reread novels whose central metaphors are of particular importance to them and process their contents in the service of their own continued development.[1]

The Secret Garden is a text well suited for our purposes—studying therapeutic process in literature. In this instance we highlight developmental elements in latency and pre-puberty and connect them to intrapsychic growth in two major characters, Mary Lennox and Colin Craven.

Authors writing about latency and pre-puberty differ in the ages they assign to these stages. We will use the classification of Sarnoff, who divides the years six through twelve into true latency (six to eight and a half years) and late latency, or pre-puberty (eight and a half to twelve years).[2] The former stage is characterized by the extensive use of fantasy to control impulses, making the child amenable to learning. Pre-puberty is characterized by a diminution in fantasy and a turning to reality for gratification, with a strong emphasis on peer group relationships. Harley (1962) considers pre-puberty to begin at about nine or ten years of age, coincident with the appearance of secondary sex characteristics. The children in this book are ten years old chronologically, and thus potentially in the stage where fantasy turns to activity and peer relations.

The centrality of peer group experience, with its accompanying search for new attachments and models, and the need for separation from the regressive pull of attachments to parents, both real and fantasied, are features of *The Secret Garden* that relate to a therapeutic outcome. This novel was not written as a case study, but it lends itself to this use because of an astute psychological subtext. There are elements in this story that would not make sense in a real clinical situation, but some leeway may be allowed for poetic idealization.

This chapter is divided into four sections. First, we synopsize *The Secret Garden*. Next, we present a brief description of the protagonists' psychological problems. Then a description of the process of change within the text of the novel is followed by a discussion of that process.

THE STORY

The Secret Garden begins as follows: "When Mary Lennox was sent to Misselthwaite Manor to live with her uncle, everybody said she was the most disagreeable-looking child ever seen" (p. 1). Mary is the "spoiled" only child of an upper-class English couple living in India. Her mother, "a great beauty who cared only to go to parties and amuse herself . . . had not wanted a little girl at all" (p. 1), and her father is always busy or ill. During early childhood Mary is left entirely in the care of servants who are frightened of her, but instructed to obey her every wish. She emerges orphaned from a severe cholera epidemic during which everyone forgets about her. Once found, she is sent to live with her only remaining relative, an uncle, Archibald Craven, in a gloomy old manor house in Yorkshire. He is a widower, who has been severely depressed since the death of his wife ten years earlier. He pays no attention to Mary, leaving her in the hands of servants once again. But these servants—sturdy, independent Yorkshire natives—are not afraid of Mary and, although kindly, not at all inclined to indulge her. She is forced to rely on her own resources; she discovers the outdoors, and, in particular, the secret garden.

The secret garden, shrouded in mystery, has been locked up for ten years. Mary, initially bored and sullen at her new home, gradually develops a consuming interest in finding the garden and making it her own secret place. She is aided in this by Dickon Sowerby, a local Yorkshire boy, who understands about all sorts of growing things—plants and animals.

The garden, however, is not the only mystery at Misselthwaite Manor. Mary, driven by curiosity about strange sounds of crying during the night, discovers that she has a cousin, Colin Craven, a boy her own age who has been an invalid since birth. His existence is kept secret (much as Mary's was when she lived in India) and he, like Mary, also is attended by frightened servants who indulge him. He suffers from paralyzing hypochondriacal fears, loneliness, and a self-centered, tyrannical nature that keeps him isolated from human warmth and contact.[3] He and Mary are very much alike, except that she has already begun to develop and change by the time she encounters him. Colin is immediately interested in Mary, who, unlike the servants, is not frightened of him. When she shares the secret of the garden with him, he is motivated to leave his sickroom and become involved in the world. Mary, Colin, and Dickon restore the garden to full bloom, and the garden, in turn, is both the scene and the means of their return to health.

One of the secrets of the garden is that it belonged to Colin's mother. It was a special romantic retreat for his parents until the day a rotten tree branch broke, injuring her. The accident precipitated Colin's birth and led to his mother's death in childbirth. His father, a hunchback already prone to black moods, became severely depressed and could not bear to see the baby. He fears Colin will be a hunchback too. He provides for the boy physically but shuns him emotionally. He locks up the garden and travels the Continent compulsively, seeking respite from his grief. When, at the end of *The Secret Garden*, he discovers Colin returned to health, his depression lifts and he and his son are psychologically reunited.

THE CHILDREN'S PSYCHOLOGICAL PROBLEMS

The problems Mary and Colin face are complex. They suffer from partial developmental arrests, pathological character defenses, and hypochondriacal concerns. Mary is described as thin, yellow, tired, and listless. Colin's hypochondria has reached more dangerous proportions. He is convinced that he cannot walk, and that he will become a hunchback and die young.

The developmental arrest is similar in both children. They have been unable to progress to latency and pre-puberty in any solid or sustained manner. Since both are motherless and—essentially—fatherless, no one has monitored their development, particularly the development of relational and peer group capacities. No one has invested the outside world with interest for them, or helped them tame and sublimate their desires. As a result they are given to uncontrolled outbursts of aggression, and suffer from boredom and loneliness that can be understood as the punishment a child receives for being bad, selfish, and out of control. Colin is described as a "young rajah" in his manner. He and Mary (when she was still in India) order the servants about, call them names, and experience no affection for anyone. When thwarted or fearful, Colin throws frightening tantrums.

This book was written in 1911, for children; no direct mention of sexual drives ever appears. We have to surmise that both children suffer from failure to sublimate their sexuality as well as their aggression. Frequent references to secret, shut-up rooms in the house, to strange sounds in the night, and to the garden as the site of romantic trysts in the past and as the present mating place of robins and other creatures provide allusions to Mary and Colin's sexual curiosity and concerns. Since no one has told them what they need and want to know, their curiosity is consuming.

Mary and Colin do not use their bodies actively as do other children of their age. Neither of them is involved in the kind of industrious pursuit of learning and purposeful play that characterizes normal latency, although both can read and are interested in books. Mary liked to play at making gardens in India. They are hungry for the company of other children and the activities of latency, but the intrusions of unbridled aggression and self-indulgent wishes interfere. They cannot get past their distorted defensive postures to the kind of cooperation, industry, and solid gender identity that would prepare them for puberty and adolescence.

The healing process for both children involves the sublimation of disruptive drives and drive derivatives, the gradual replacement of restrictive narcissistic defenses with more adaptive ones, and the cure of hypochondriacal feelings and fantasies.[4] At the end of the book they have moved from distorted caricatures of the "spoiled" child—weak, ineffectual, hated and self-hating—to physical strength, emotional empowerment, healthier relating, and secure gender identity.

DESCRIPTION OF THE THERAPEUTIC PROCESS

A therapeutic process may be traced through the story. We have seen Mary Lennox as a disagreeable and unwanted child, left in the care of servants who indulge her. The cholera epidemic that leaves her orphaned occurs when she is nine years old. She is abandoned by her caretakers. "Everyone was too panic-stricken to think of a little girl no one was fond of" (p. 5). She survives, frightened, angry, and alone, for several days, caring for herself, until discovered. These traumatic events highlight Mary's internal isolation and narcissistic defenses. She does not miss either her ayah or her parents. "She was not an affectionate child and had never cared much for anyone" (p. 5). When she is orphaned, she thinks only of what will happen to her and whether she will continue to be indulged.

She is informed abruptly that she will be sent to England to live with an uncle she has never met. She denies that this news has any impact on her, but these dramatic incidents begin to breach her narcissistic defenses.

> Since she had been living in other people's houses and had had no ayah, she had begun to feel lonely and to *think queer thoughts which were new to her*. She had begun to wonder why she had never seemed to belong to anyone even when her father and mother had been alive. Other children seemed to belong to their fathers and mothers, but she had never seemed to really be anyone's little girl. She had servants, and food and clothes, but no one had taken any notice of her. She did not know that this was because she was a disagreeable child; but then, of course, she did not know she was disagreeable. She often thought that other people were, but she did not know that she was so herself. (p. 12; emphasis added)

In the moralistic language of old-fashioned children's stories, Mary is neglected because she is disagreeable, not the other way around! Her tendency to project and externalize are clearly noted in this passage; at the same time introspection and insight are beginning.

The series of crises in Mary's life that began with the epidemic give her an opportunity to wonder about herself. She is gradually shaken out of her complacency and habitual defenses. Mrs. Medlock, the housekeeper who comes to take her to England, tries to tell her about her new home. Mary feigns indifference while listening closely, remembering unhappily that no one has ever explained things to her. Children reading this book may understand intuitively that Mary's self-centered, disagreeable ways are a result of such neglect, and that her indulgence at the hands of servants is a poor substitute for real parental affection and investment.

When she reaches Misselthwaite Manor, it seems as if this neglect will continue. Mary hears from Mrs. Medlock that her uncle is a hunchback whose wife has died. This elicits an unusual moment of pity. His story reminds her of a favorite fairy tale. Mrs. Medlock tells her, "You mustn't expect that there will be people to talk to you. You'll have to play about and look after yourself" (p. 10). The realization that her uncle is not interested in her leads to the disappointment of hope. Things will not be different in England. She suppresses her compassionate feelings toward him, becoming more "contrary" than ever.

Her first day in her new home involves a series of encounters and experiences that continue to shake up her equilibrium and offer her new opportunities. She meets Martha Sowerby, the young housemaid who is to look after her. Martha does not behave like an Indian servant. She is independent and does not understand why Mary cannot be likewise. She will not dress her, wait on her, or coddle her. Mary finds this so upsetting that her controls break:

> She was in such a rage and felt so helpless before the girl's simple stare, and somehow she suddenly felt so horribly lonely and far away from everything she understood and which understood her, that she threw herself face downward on the pillows and burst into passionate sobbing. (p. 28)

Martha comforts her, but does not give in to her demands. Rather, she engages Mary's interest with stories about her own large Yorkshire family, particularly her brother Dickon, who tames animals and has many pets. Mary "began to feel a slight interest in Dickon, and as she had never before been interested in any one but herself, it was the dawning of a healthy sentiment" (p. 31). Martha inadvertently arouses Mary's interest even more deeply by her mention of the secret garden. Mary overcomes her chronic lethargy enough to go outdoors. She does not know how to amuse herself generally, but she wants to find the garden.

What has happened in this encounter, and why is Mary's interest so aroused? She has had a tantrum that has not brought the usual results, gratification of substitutive, infantile wishes. Perhaps she is unconsciously relieved. She has a choice now. She can continue to seek old solutions with increasing frustration, or she can begin to learn a new idea her environment offers: you cannot have everything you want right now, but you can have something very interesting later, if you work for it. At this moment Martha is like a therapist who does not join in the reenactment that the patient attempts to establish. Patients who can tolerate this frustration can move to new levels of experience and integration.

The garden quickly becomes a consuming interest. Mary wonders if she can find it, if it will bloom in the spring, if it can be saved. She unconsciously identifies the secret garden with her own lonely, wintry, unknown, and defended self. The garden has been locked up for ten years. "Ten years was a long time, Mary thought. She had been born ten years ago" (p. 64). She wants to see the garden because it has been shut up for ten years, as she herself has been. The story suggests that her passion for finding out secrets may represent attempts to solve the mystery of why she is unloved. Is there hope for something or someone who has been shut up for ten years? The process of discovery and exploration of the garden will become a metaphor for Mary's resumed growth and development.

As she wanders about outdoors she meets another plain-speaking servant, the gardener Ben Weatherstaff. They spar irritably with each other, and she suddenly realizes she is lonely and perhaps this has something to do with how "sour and cross" she always feels. Ben tells her that they are two of a kind, both nasty tempered and unattractive.

This was plain speaking, and Mary Lennox had never heard the truth about herself in her life . . . . She had never thought much about her looks, but she wondered if she was as unattractive as Ben Weatherstaff. . . . She actually began to wonder also if she was "nasty tempered." She felt uncomfortable. (p. 40)

In this new setting Mary repeatedly encounters people who do not respond to her in accustomed ways, forcing her to recognize her shortcomings. If she wants different responses, she must behave differently. Eventually she will feel differently. This will not happen quickly or easily, but Mary is helped along by developmental needs that are searching for an outlet. She needs to be interested in something, and the secret garden fills that need. She shows determination in her search for it. When she finds it, the garden becomes the object of fantasy and sustained play. Mary's increased capacity for satisfaction through fantasy and the repetitive, systematic activities involved in restoring the garden (her first "hobby") are behaviors of normal latency.

At this point in the story Dickon makes his appearance. He is a natural, unspoiled moorland boy. He befriends Mary at a time when she is ready for a friend, although she would not be able to articulate this to herself. He is a model to her: he has the skills and knowledge she now strongly desires. He knows how to make living things grow. Mary thinks he is a kind of magician. She, who likes no one, especially not boys, trusts him immediately. In a dramatic and revealing passage she tells him the secret of the garden's existence:

"I've stolen a garden," she said very fast. "It isn't mine. It isn't anybody's. Nobody wants it, nobody cares for it, nobody ever goes into it. Perhaps everything is dead in it already; I don't know."

She began to feel hot and as contrary as she had ever felt in her life. "I don't care, I don't care! Nobody has any right to take it from me when I care about it and they don't. They're letting it die, all shut in by itself," she ended passionately, and she threw her arms over her face and burst out crying—poor little Mistress Mary. (pp. 99–100)

At this moment Dickon is like a therapist, someone who can be trusted with secrets and painful affects. Mary is telling him about herself, reliving the shame of having wished unsuccessfully for her parents' love and admiration. Perhaps she becomes "hot and contrary" because she anticipates a repetition of their indifference. Dickon listens with interest and sympathy. The negative reenactment does not occur, and her trust can continue.

Needs for human relatedness have been gradually mobilized in

Mary. She has suffered many losses for which she hopes her new environment will compensate. Martha, Dickon, and perhaps most important of all, their mother, Susan Sowerby, become objects of fantasy, idealization, and potential attachment. The garden, too, has meanings that connect it with a lost object. It is beautiful, as Mary's mother was. Although Mary barely knew her mother, she admired her and liked to look at her in her pretty clothes "full of lace." She longs for a maternal figure after whom she can model herself.

In the presence of an environment that provides her with new experiences and people who meet her needs, Mary begins to develop. In numerous ways the author makes it clear that this process involves repeated regressions to entitled, self-centered behavior followed by steps forward into relatedness. Dickon, Martha, and Ben do not reward sulking or imperious demands, but they respond to Mary's age-appropriate activities with interest. The vicissitudes of Mary's growth resemble the working-through process in a therapy situation.

Mary is already well engaged in her own healing process when she discovers Colin. He is her cousin, and male counterpart, and his problems seem even more crippling. In addition to his fear that he will become a hunchback and die, he is deeply concerned about his mother's death. He hates her for leaving him and says so. He may wonder, as children often do, whether he is somehow responsible for his loss, whether her death is his fault. He lives as an invalid, hidden in his room. He is "spoiled"—as Mary was—but longing for companionship and activity. He is as ready to meet Mary as she was to meet Martha and Dickon. When she casually mentions her interest in finding the garden, he embraces the idea with great excitement. Mary does not yet trust him enough to tell him she has discovered the garden. "But it was too late to be careful. He was too much like herself. He had had nothing to think about and the idea of a hidden garden attracted him as it had attracted her" (p. 129).

Colin latches onto Mary and tries to control her with the same imperiousness he has used with others. In Mary, however, he has met his match. She understands his use of his illness for secondary gain, to manipulate others powerfully. She will not be controlled by him. In an important sequence of scenes, she thwarts his wishes to have her with him all the time. She neglects him in favor of Dickon and the garden. He is furious and frightened of further loss. That night he has a tantrum so severe that Mary is summoned to help contain him. The servants know that she will be able to confront and help him. "It was funny that all the grown-up people were so frightened that they came to a little girl just because they guessed she was almost as bad as Colin himself" (p. 175).

She will not be intimidated by him; she shouts him down. His fear of becoming a hunchback, which he has kept a secret, emerges during their fight. Mary assures him gruffly that he has no hump and will not die. This fight is not simply a contest of wills. Mary is angry at Colin for reflecting her worst self, but she also pities and understands him. She struggles with her old self and her new self, trying to find her position in relation to him. Compassion and self-protection war inside her, with compassion winning. She tells him she has found the secret garden and will take him to it. In her role as limit-setter for Colin, Mary finds a healthy channel for her own needs for power and control.

Colin now becomes involved in a process of healing similar to Mary's. She "teaches" him what she has already learned. He is gradually able to master unruly impulses and sublimate them in healthy activities. He learns to walk and do calisthenics, determined to become strong, as strong as Dickon, and perhaps behind this, as strong as his father. He feels there is magic in the garden, and he wants to become a great scientist and find out all about that magic. His new goals are still somewhat grandiose, but represent a compromise with his previous psychological position of holding onto the sense of infantile omnipotence. Mary and Dickon befriend him, a friendship of equals engaged in group activities. This kind of peer group activity, the secret club which excludes parents and other adults, so very important to children in latency and pre-puberty, plays a central role in helping Colin modify his narcissistic claims. He must depend on others, learn from them, and cooperate with them if he wishes to be part of their select society.

Colin's psychological position is difficult. His hunchback fear is multidetermined. It is a wish when it represents an identification with the father he longs to please. It is an unconscious punishment for both hating his mother, and keeping her with him secretly. (He has a portrait of her near his bed, covered with a curtain. He tells Mary, "She is mine and I don't want everyone to see her" [p. 133]). His fear is also a bid for the special claims and privileges of illness. Colin does not know if his father wants him well or ill. If his invalidism also represents passive submission, will health make him a dangerous rival, a man without a handicap? He must take that risk.

As it turns out, his father is greatly relieved by Colin's recovery. His own depression lifts. Presumably this depression was more than pathological grief over his wife's death.[5] He feared his hunchback "taint" would pass to his son, and he struggles with feelings of hatred for the child that give rise to powerful guilt feelings. Seeing Colin strong and well relieves enough guilt to allow father and son a chance at managing normal levels of ambivalence as they attempt to repair their relationship.

DISCUSSION OF THE THERAPEUTIC PROCESS

The nature of therapeutic process in this novel may be viewed from two complementary perspectives: that of the therapeutic milieu and that of the psychoanalytic encounter.[6] Neither model alone quite explains the whole process. Together, they provide a more accurate template with which to understand what happens to Mary and Colin as they proceed from "patienthood" to healthy functioning.

We have seen that both are disturbed children, in that sense, patients. Neglect and continual low-level trauma in the form of indulgence and absence of appropriate parental concern and limits have left them at the mercy of a defensive adaptation that fosters anxiety and isolation. Personal crisis provides a chance to resume development. The excitement and absorption with which these children respond to each other, and to their shared project, the garden, suggest an underlying longing to be well, which makes them ready for the therapeutic experiences they encounter.

These experiences involve a new environmental setting, and a set of environmental expectations (the "milieu") in which previous behaviors no longer lead to expected gratifications. Intense social pressures motivate new behaviors. Mary cannot remain infantile and self-involved. If she wishes to find the garden, she must learn to dress herself, and she must risk going outdoors. If she wishes the garden to survive, she must work at tending it. If she wants friends, she must develop the capacity for concern and cooperation.

Mary approaches these challenges with some ambivalence, at times eager for progress, at other times regressing. She cooperates with Dickon, but becomes furious with Colin for his claims on her. She loses sight of her previous compassion for him and becomes cruel and imperious herself. She struggles inwardly and softens towards him. In the dramatic tantrum sequence, Mary is threatened by Colin's outburst of aggression. It is too close to her own previous reaction to frustration. Her controls are still shaky. In an intrapsychic sense, Colin represents her own insight into whom she was and whom she still can be. In the terms of a milieu setting, she is like the patient further along in treatment who confronts the new patient and sets different standards.

Mary's initial changes are attempts to get some gratification in the form of attention and approval. Her behavior is still imitative. She has not yet internalized the values of her new environment. She gives up some of her omnipotence, but keeps part of it intact by pursuing secrets that are forbidden to her. She is quite ruthless in her pursuit of these secrets (the garden, the closed rooms in the house, and the crying sound in the corridor that turns out to be Colin). She does not really respect the adult authority that forbids her to investigate. Her previous situation was one in which adults were helpless themselves, unable to help her control herself and unable to teach her.

The first person she is able to trust and admire is another child, Dickon. Mary intuitively understands that Dickon has the power she lacks. She is awed by his capacity to tame animals and to entertain himself alone on the moors. Equally important, she senses he is capable of a loving and considerate interest in others. If she can tolerate the compromises she must make, she can be like him. In the way that patients in a milieu setting model themselves after staff members or other more advanced patients, Mary emulates Dickon. She even learns to speak with a Yorkshire accent! As she and Colin experience success and empowerment from their new behaviors, they begin to internalize the values and attitudes of those they admire. They now behave differently not only to obtain attention and acceptance, but because they believe what they are doing is right.

The milieu is important but would have little effect on these children were it not for their intense needs for relatedness. Their curiosity and the capacity for intellectual development remain largely intact, despite emotional impoverishment and isolation. This may say more about poetic idealization in literary texts than it does about clinical verisimilitude; in any case, the children's impairment is depicted largely in the area of relationships. They cannot love or admire their caretakers, much as they need them, because they do not experience them as competent parental substitutes who will facilitate development. As characters appear who *are* capable of helping these children through their emotional impasses, the children form powerful attachments to them. Modified behaviors are now dually rewarded. Ego capacities are enhanced, with attendant mastery and knowledge, *and* the admiration and respect of idealized others is gained.

Transference, the impulse to renew and replay the past, is the engine that drives all elements of the therapeutic process in our story. Central to the psychoanalytic process, it is also a powerful force within the milieu. It is the point at which these two therapeutic modalities cross paths. In the psychoanalytic setting the development and exploration of transference feelings and behaviors toward the analyst are central to the attainment of insight and change. Within the therapeutic milieu this single intense dyad does not exist. Instead, the transferences are multiple and partial, focused at times on individuals and at times on the institution itself.

In this novel the whole environment is full of therapistlike figures and influences, both animate and inanimate. Martha is like an occupational therapist for Mary. She buys her a skipping rope and arranges for Dickon to bring her seeds and garden tools. Ben Weatherstaff is like a physical therapist for Colin, encouraging him to walk and become strong. The garden itself takes on the character of a therapeutic influence, as if it were animate. The children become transference figures to each other. Mary "mothers" Colin. She sings him to sleep when he is upset, as her ayah did with her. Dickon "fathers" both Mary and Colin, teaching them to deal with external reality and to solve problems. Perhaps the term "transference," as usually understood, does not quite capture the power of the treatment milieu to influence its members. This influence depends on the "charismatic appeal" (the capacity to evoke idealization and awe) of its members and of the organization as a whole. Of course, idealization and awe may be important factors in transference, also, and in that respect the two concepts overlap.

The garden itself is the institution to which the children "transfer" wishes and fantasies. It is a private place, in which special activities and rituals take place daily: work, exercise, meals, and prayerlike chantings in which the magic of the garden is invoked. Colin says, "There is Magic in there—good Magic, you know, Mary. I am sure there is" (p. 234). Like a milieu treatment setting, it is a place where people become immersed in group activities that propel them in the direction of new adaptations. In an earlier study by one of us (R. Almond, *The Healing Community: Dynamics of the Therapeutic Milieu*), the term "communitas" was used to conceptualize an important quality of this kind of organization. Communitas describes the absorbing and self-esteem enhancing experience of being a member of a group that is imbued with special qualities. In this case the specialness also extends to a place, the garden itself.

The understanding of the therapeutic process in *The Secret Garden* would be incomplete without a discussion of the role of Susan Sowerby, Dickon's mother. She does not appear in person until the final two chapters, but she, more than any other character, represents a single therapistlike figure. She is like a therapist in her relative anonymity, receptivity, and essentially supportive attitude, and in her knowledge of what children need to be healthy. She does not interpret or confront, in a conventional sense, but everything she says, either directly or by report from Martha or Dickon, is of great importance to the children. Mary and Colin develop intense transference-like fantasies and wishes toward her. Colin wishes she were his mother: "'Even when I was ill I wanted to see you,'" he said, "'you and Dickon and the secret garden. I'd never wanted to see any one or anything before'" (p. 275). Susan acknowledges his progress and recognizes those inner conflicts that are most disturbing to him: his fear that his aggression has somehow destroyed his mother and that his father hates him and wishes his destruction. In a moving passage she reassures him that his mother would have loved him had she lived, and that his father will love him, that he may grow up to be a man.

He stood quite close to Susan and fixed his eyes on her with a kind of bewildered adoration and he suddenly caught hold of the fold of her blue cloak and held it fast.

"You are just what I—what I wanted," he said. "I wish you were my mother—as well as Dickon's!"

All at once Susan Sowerby bent down and drew him with her warm arms close against the bosom under the blue cloak—as if he had been Dickon's brother. The quick mist swept over her eyes.

"Eh! dear lad!" she said. "Thy own mother's in this 'ere very garden, I do believe. She couldna' keep out of it. Thy father mun come back to thee—he mun!" (pp. 279–80)

Mary also needs maternal support. She has been trying to establish her feminine identity through the garden. She will soon face puberty. Her curiosity about secrets goes beyond a concern about why she is unloved. She has specific sexual and gender concerns. What does it mean to be a girl? What will happen to her, to her body? What are the secrets of sex? What do the grown-ups do, in gardens or rooms? Can instinctual drives be controlled and made safe? She hopes the garden, described over and over in imagery that suggests the female body—hidden locks and keys, tangles of roses, tendrils of ivy, budding plants, and blooming flowers—holds the answers to these secrets. The burgeoning of her femininity (and presumably the development of secondary sex characteristics) is represented in the book by descriptions of changes in her health and appearance. From sour, thin, and ill she becomes stronger, plumper, with color in her cheeks, and thickening hair. Susan notes all of this with approval in a passage that links Mary with her own mother.

> She put both hands on Mistress Mary's shoulders and looked her little face over in a motherly fashion.
> "An' thee, too!" she said. "Tha'rt grown near as hearty as our 'Lisabeth Ellen. I'll warrant tha'rt like thy mother too. Our Martha told me as Mrs. Medlock heard she was a pretty woman. Tha'lt be like a blush rose when tha' grows up, my little lass, bless thee." (p. 276)

Susan Sowerby encourages growth and reassures both children that their aggression has not killed or alienated their real mothers and that their interest in sexuality is normal, even helpful, in preparing them for puberty and adulthood.

Susan exerts her powerful influence on the children through the medium of transference feelings and fantasies. She is an idealized figure who represents the pull toward healthy development, and as such, she is the recipient of their positive transference wishes, for love and admiration. Negative transference feelings are more diffuse, devolving on others in the environment: for example, Colin's tantrum, when he fears Mary is deserting him, as his mother did; or Mary's withdrawal of sympathy from Mr. Craven, when she understands that he will neglect her emotionally. Mrs. Sowerby inspires both children to relinquish infantile patterns in favor of growing up, but her influence is powerful precisely because it is embedded in a milieu that conveys the same messages she does.

The elements of a psychotherapeutic dyad intertwine with those of a therapeutic milieu. In both modalities we see engagement by "patients" in a state of readiness to relieve psychological suffering. Transference fantasies and behaviors occur in characteristic ways in each setting. These wishes lead to attachments, and the development of ambivalence and resistance. These attachments are tested repeatedly, with advances and regressions—the working-through process. Along the way insight is gained, and more adaptive solutions become internalized. The two processes reinforce each other to create a powerful depiction of healing, self-realization, and fulfillment.

We may also describe the therapeutic process in *The Secret Garden* using the concepts of our therapeutic narrative—engagement, mutual influence, and directionality. The urge to resume arrested or distorted development is a powerful one—particularly in childhood. Under the pressure of developmental needs, children explore and use their environment—including their human environment—in more naive but also more creative ways than do adults. To a child anything may become an object of curiosity, a toy, a pastime, or a friend. In the sense that children do not have a fully formed sense of how things "should" be, they are at one and the same time less discriminating than adults and open to more possibilities.

Mary and Colin need to resume development. They need relationships and activities that will enable this process. Therefore, they are ready to engage with any aspect of their milieu—the garden, the servants, and particularly Dickon and Mrs. Sowerby—that will serve these developmental needs. In all of our previous literary examples, engagement occurred in a more *particular* way, between two people who had some degree of mutuality in their need for each other. Here, it is more diffused.

The process of mutual influence is also somewhat different in this chapter. The milieu demands new adaptations that both children want and fear. Their movement back and forth between old behaviors and new adaptations—which we have characterized as a metaphoric working through—represents the operational level of the phase of mutual influence. As is appropriate to children's development, where involvement with peers and nonparental adults is so vital, the children here, once mobilized, seek out that part of the environment that will aid them in their next steps.

There is *some* of the process of dyadic mutual influence we have seen among the lovers and parent-child surrogates of our other "cases," but it is of a simpler sort. Mary knows what reactions are right for Colin because he is a male mirror of herself and what she has recently been through. They interact as do patients in the therapeutic milieu; the more experienced patient confronts the more symptomatic one in a way that helps both. Mary is a powerful influence in preventing Colin from retreating to sicker behaviors because she is also a child. At the same time, by confronting him, Mary confirms changes she herself has recently made.

What *is* clear is that Martha, Dickon, and Mrs. Sowerby provide the directionality of the process. All are highly admired figures who represent competence, maturity, and the capacity for love and cooperation. While these Yorkshire farming folk may seem idealized, it is the significance of this portrayal that gives them their therapeutic directionality in the narrative of *The Secret Garden*. The children not only wish for their approval but wish to emulate them. In so doing, they make significant gains in self-esteem, and resolve a multitude of particular conflicts and worries.

THE APPEAL OF *THE SECRET GARDEN*

The garden itself is the central healing metaphor of this novel. It represents growth, development, and the restitution of loss. It is the locus of a private children's world where passivity and handicap are overcome through the support and empowerment of a peer group. Within its walls ego functions develop and relationships mature. The ability to learn and to persevere in the attainment of goals, the cultivation of friendship with its sense of shared purpose and ideals, and the capacity for loyalty and altruism are the fruits of the children's labor in the garden. These skills and relationships bring great satisfaction, and compensate Mary and Colin for earlier losses: their disruptive aggression, engendered in part by these losses, is substantially modified. The hidden garden may also represent, to its child readers, an idealized and not yet attained part of the self that will emerge through "cultivation" as part of the ego ideal.

The "secretness" of the garden has metaphoric meanings as well. So much is mysterious to children. They long to know the secrets of life; of their parents' world, of their own pasts; of their sexual and gender roles; and of their future identities. They wonder what they will be allowed to know, and how they will find it out. Sometimes they transgress boundaries, as Mary does when she explores the forbidden house and garden. The children in this book have their *own* secret, guarded jealously from adults. This fascinates the young reader who may enjoy the revenge this exacts for children's exclusion from the adult world. The child may also experience vicariously the sense of specialness inherent in being able to exclude others, and the sense of power that results from finding out what is forbidden. Another aspect of secretness has to do with the meaning of private peer groups, formed apart from the family. These allow children to learn about a different kind of relationship, one that is autonomous from relations with parents. New ways of relating prepare the child for the relationships of adolescence and adulthood.

These aspects of *The Secret Garden* may appeal to children of both sexes, but we are convinced that this story has a special fascination for pre-pubertal girls. We might add, parenthetically, that many adult women of our acquaintance, friends as well as patients, spontaneously (or when asked) remember this book with a particular fondness and nostalgia, and refer specifically to its mysterious, romantic, healing, inspiring, and "therapeutic" qualities. We propose the following explanation for this gender difference.

The appeal of a book at any age has to do, in part, with the day-dreams and fantasies that lie at its core and with the solutions to inner problems that the author proposes, through the devices of plot and character development. In *The Secret Garden* arrested development is resumed and normal latency, with its emphasis on fantasy, industry, and peer group activities is attained. But this is not a book that appeals to children in early latency. The devoted reader of this novel is likely to be a girl between nine and eleven years old, the age of the pre-pubertal heroine, Mary.

The pre-pubertal girl loves this book because it deals with the issue that is uppermost on her mind: the development of her own sexuality and femininity as she approaches puberty. The garden is a sexual metaphor in several ways. It may represent the female genital, a hidden place that must be opened up and, ultimately, planted. The nine- or ten-year-old girl must make a transition from vague, magical ideas about how she is to produce babies, to a more specific anticipation that this event will occur somehow *within* her own body. Recent psychoanalytic theories of female gender development are arguing convincingly that there is a positive "primary femininity" in which the body interior, especially the infolded genital region, represents the rich world of feelings, and empathic, nurturant, and procreative capacities.

The garden is also a place where feminine *roles* can be learned and rehearsed. The themes of reproductive and nurturing activities permeate the scenes that take place within its walls. The children watch the robins mate and hatch their young. Dickon brings an abandoned newborn lamb to the garden, "and when Mary had sat under a tree with its limp warmness huddled on her lap she had felt as if she were too full of strange joy to speak. A lamb—a lamb! A living lamb who lay on your lap *like a baby!*" (p. 197; emphasis added).

For the girl reader, this passage taps into the enormous interest in and longing for a baby that is a hallmark of pre-puberty. Despite successful sublimation, latency age children are highly invested in their sexual feelings and theories, and need to share them and play them out with other children. The phase-specific interest in babies, human and animal, of pre-puberty involves caretaking rather than creating. An interest in playing at parenthood takes precedence over those fantasies of becoming parents, with the attendant sexual involvement and acts, which will predominate in puberty. An important aspect of the pre-pubertal girls' baby worship is that the defenses of latency help separate the wish for a baby from the earlier wish for father's baby, thus protecting the impulse from excessive anxiety. In the garden Mary can take care of baby animals, and enthusiastically support Colin's recovery, as preparation for her own future maternal role.

The Secret Garden has been a great favorite for over eighty years.

We think the "secret" of its appeal lies in the way it addresses young girls' specific concerns about their sexuality and feminine development in a disguised, nonthreatening, but very accurate way. Although most children reading the book do not suffer the debilitating history and conflicts of Mary Lennox, they identify with her. In her motherlessness lies their hidden wish to be free of the pull of a regressive maternal attachment. They wish to be free to explore and play, to develop their identities and learn about their sexuality. Mary's mastery of her conflicts (depicted as illness and cure), and her ensuing sense of power and satisfaction, is the happy ending they wish for themselves.

8

HEIDI (JOHANNA SPYRI): THE INNOCENCE OF THE CHILD AS A THERAPEUTIC FORCE

Heidi is a novel about cures. It has been translated into many languages and has survived as a children's favorite for over a century. Because of its widespread popularity and its emphasis on healing, it is interesting to compare it to some of our previous studies to see what similarities and confirmations it provides. The *psychological* story of Heidi is complex; it concerns developments and changes in many characters. Most readers recall best the cure of the little paralyzed girl, Klara Sesemann. Klara's recovery is like Colin's in *The Secret Garden*, where multiple influences, including that of nature, contribute to the overcoming of developmental blocks. Klara, the only child of a widowed father, presumably fears growing up, and has lapsed into a symptom that makes her passive and helpless as she anticipates puberty.[1] Her cure is facilitated by the interweaving of healing relationships and dramatic events—the positive support and encouragement provided by Heidi and Heidi's grandfather, the healthy mountain air, and the jealousy of Peter, the goatherd, who destroys Klara's wheelchair. (Recall how another destructive act—the theft of Silas Marner's gold by Dunstan Cass—also propelled a recovery.) The fabric of mutual aid in *Heidi* is so like that of *The Secret Garden* that we will not elaborate it any further. Rather, we note that the story of *Heidi* lends support to a number of the ideas about therapeutic narrative in *The Secret Garden* cited in Chapter 7: (1) the relationship of man (or child) to nature and the "natural" (i.e., the core of human experience in the body) is crucial to emotional health; (2) helping others helps oneself; and (3) a dyad, triad, or group may develop a healing ethos. Embedded in Johanna Spyri's main story is a significant subplot, the healing of Uncle Alp, Heidi's reclusive grandfather. We shall depict his cure in this chapter because it is very close to that of Silas Marner and it enhances some of the conclusions of the previous two chapters.

Uncle Alp, the elder of two brothers, had charge of his parents' property, "the finest farm in Domschlag," which he lost through gambling. His parents died of grief, and Alp went to Naples where he was not heard from for fifteen years. When he returned, it was with a half-grown son and the rumor of having killed a man in a brawl. The farmers of Domschlag refused to take father and son in, and Uncle Alp moved to the mountain village of Doerfli where he settled. His son grew up, learned carpentry, and married. Two years later the son was killed by a falling beam; his widow died of grief leaving the infant Heidi orphaned. The Doerfli villagers took this as sign of Uncle Alp's evil nature, and the pastor urged him to repent. Instead, embittered and isolated, Alp took to the Alm (the foothills under the Alps), where he lived alone for some years before the story of *Heidi* begins.

Like Silas Marner, Uncle Alp is a recluse, occupied only by the routine of everyday life and soothed by the presence of the mountain environment. Alp has sins to account for his self-exile—he is directly or indirectly held responsible for the deaths of his parents, a man he has killed in a fight, his son, and his daughter-in-law. He has not "repented" because, like Silas Marner, he feels he is being held accountable for too much. His behavior was wild, but his intent was not to destroy. To confess to guilt for all these crimes would be to accept himself as worse than he feels he is. Withdrawal to the hut on the Alm, with its beautiful, natural surroundings is his compromise position, akin to Silas Marner's isolation with his loom and his gold.

When Heidi, his five-year-old orphaned grandchild, is thrust upon him by the impatient, uncaring aunt/foster mother, Dete, he reacts resentfully: "'Suppose the child begins to fret and whine for you, as is usually the case with the unreasonable little things, what shall I do with her?'" (p. 15). Dete responds by citing her other responsibilities, and addressing his guilt, "You don't want anything more laid to your charge" (p. 16).

Initially, the grandfather is reserved and gruff, but Heidi's charm, curiosity, and excitement about life begin to soften him. When he seems indifferent to her needs, she provides for herself. He then begins to help her adapt to her new setting. Like Eppie, Heidi is an idealized child, positive and spontaneous. The psychological importance of the loss of her parents is suggested only indirectly, through her sympathy for one of the goats, Schneehöpli, who has just been separated from its mother and is unhappy. In contrast to her grandfather, Heidi has the optimism of a child *for whom loss can be repaired*. (In reality, a child who had just been dumped unceremoniously with a total stranger would be frightened, depressed, and suspicious. The appeal of Heidi to her young readers must, in part, have to do with her heroic response to such adversity.)

Uncle Alp's depressed state is suggested in their inital encounter: "After Dete had disappeared, the uncle sat down again on the bench and blew great clouds of smoke from his pipe, while he kept his eyes fixed on the ground without saying a word. Meanwhile Heidi was content to look about her" (p. 17).

The beginning of change in Uncle Alp is stimulated by the contrast between his inner state and Heidi's. Heidi looks into the goats' shed and listens to the wind in the fir trees. Then she returns to her grandfather.

> When she found him in the same place she had left him, she placed herself in front of him, put her hands behind her, and gazed at him. Her grandfather looked up.
> "What do you want to do?" he asked, as the child continued standing in front of him without moving.
> "I want to see what you have in the hut," said Heidi.
> "Come along, then!" and the grandfather rose and started to go into the hut. (p. 18)

When Heidi asks where she is to sleep, the grandfather says, "Wherever you like." She looks about and climbs a ladder to the hayloft, where she finds a window with a view down into the valley. Announcing that she will sleep here, Heidi demands a sheet, and proceeds to make herself a bed out of hay. When her grandfather comes to look at it, he admires her creation, and adds more hay so that she will not feel the hard floor.

In a series of similar interactions, Heidi arranges the necessities of her new life—a place to eat, a chair to sit on at the table, and a place setting for herself. Heidi's initiative and interest engage her grandfather's help. The grandfather, stimulated by a growing admiration for the child, thinks to himself, "She knows what she sees; her eyes are in the right place." During the night, after Heidi has eaten and gone to sleep, the wind howls, and branches crack off the trees. The grandfather awakens and thinks, "She may be afraid." He climbs the ladder, and sees that Heidi is sleeping peacefully, with a look of happiness on her face. "The grandfather gazed long at the sweetly sleeping child until the moon went behind a cloud again and it was dark. Then he went back to his own bed" (p. 25). From this point we see the same pattern repeated: grandfather's reserve and withdrawal encounter Heidi's unfailing interest, curiosity, and compassion. He responds in kind, becoming a caretaker, first for Heidi, then at Heidi's prompting for Peter the goatherd's family.

Heidi's cheerful appreciativeness provides a yardstick against which Uncle Alp measures his bitterness, cynicism, and depressed withdrawal. The child's lack of expectations, beyond those necessary for her bodily needs, assures him that humans are not what he has come to expect—the representatives of punishment and rejection, the reminders of past disappointments and sins. Heidi simply lives her life—a child, optimistic about the world despite multiple losses of her own. She provides her grandfather with requests that are simple, and free of selfish baggage. She makes no judgments about who her grandfather is, or what he has been in the past.

Uncle Alp does not give up his position of self-exile quickly. He trusts only Heidi, not others. When the parson comes to urge him to move to the village over the winter, for the child's sake, he refuses. He provides for Heidi's need for activity during the shut-in cold months by helping her visit down the mountain with Peter's family, where she becomes attached to Peter's grandmother. This relationship has special meaning to Heidi. She was cared for between one and five by her own grandmother.

In this novel, as in *Silas Marner* (and many of our examples), it is the helper who is helped. Through aiding Heidi, Uncle Alp begins to care for and trust human company again. When Dete returns after two years to take Heidi to the Sesemanns in Frankfurt, Uncle Alp is resistant, but unable to protect his newfound relationship. In effect, he has enlisted Heidi in his uncivilized, reclusive retreat; hence, he is vulnerable to Dete's worldly plans and threats. When he relinquishes Heidi, he tells Dete never to bring her back. Nevertheless, when, after her long, unhappy sojourn in Frankfurt, Heidi returns, rushing up to him and hugging him, he responds with feeling. "Neither did the grandfather say anything. *For the first time in many years* his eyes grew moist, and he had to pass his hand over them" (p. 166; italics added). As was the case with Silas Marner, Uncle Alp has had to engage in a new attachment, and experience a new loss, to begin mourning his earlier losses.

Soon after their reunion, Heidi addresses Uncle Alp's outcast position more specifically. While at Frankfurt she has been taught by Klara's grandmother about God, and about trusting in his plan. She conveys this to her grandfather in the following interchange.

"Now I will always pray as the grandmamma told me, and always thank the dear Lord, and if He does not do what I ask, then I will surely think all the same, it will just be as it was in Frankfurt; the dear Lord is planning something much better. But we will pray every day, won't we grandfather? And we will never forget Him, so that the dear Lord may never forget us."

"And if one should do so?" murmured the grandfather.

"Oh, it would not be well for him, for then the dear Lord would forget him, too, and let him go away, and if he should get into trouble and complain, nobody would pity him, but everybody would say: 'He first ran away from the dear Lord; now the dear Lord, who might have helped him, lets him go.'"

"That is true, Heidi; how did you know it?"

"From the grandmamma; she told me all about it."

The grandfather was silent for a while. Then he said to himself, following his own thoughts,

"And if it is so, then it is so; no one can go back, and whomever God has forgotten, He has forgotten."

"Oh, no, grandfather; one can go back; that I know, too from the grandmamma; and then it says so in the beautiful story in my book; but you don't know about that; we are almost home, and you shall see how beautiful the story is." (p. 177)

Heidi then reads her grandfather the parable of the prodigal son. Uncle Alp is deeply moved. When Heidi is asleep, he prays to God for forgiveness and the next morning he takes the child to church. Afterward, he tells the pastor that he will come to the village for the winters, so that Heidi may attend school. With the grandfather restored to human society, the focus of the story moves on to the healing of other characters. Uncle Alp becomes an agent of cure for others. He intuitively recognizes their needs and refashions his retreat on the Alm into a place where health is restored.

DISCUSSION

We want to flag certain commonalities between *Silas Marner* and *Heidi,* because their recurrence suggests that authors are, again, tapping into some universal process or narrative. In both stories, the "patient" is a man in or beyond midlife. The problem is not one of a delay in development, but of a major divergence from a satisfying life course. Each man has fashioned a substitutive existence, in which human relatedness is replaced by some other source of satisfaction, more controllable and predictable. A child enters the scene. The child's simple needs, straightforward communications, and potential lovingness engages the man's otherwise inaccessible capacity for involvement with people, and seems to tap into a hope about starting over that has survived.

In the course of both stories there is a repetition of trauma: in *Silas Marner,* the loss of the gold; in Heidi, the loss of Heidi herself. In *Silas Marner,* the second loss is necessary to stir the weaver out of his retreat; in *Heidi,* the loss seems to release the affect of sadness, and the process of mourning for the past. These two reactions are related. In adults, the deficiencies and conflicts engendered by childhood experience do not sit quietly in the psyche waiting for better, corrective experiences to become resolved. If people worked this way, treatment would be a simple matter of supplying what the past has omitted, or providing reassurance that the conflicts of childhood are no longer pertinent. Adults, like our two fictional old men, have formed protective shells of character to immunize themselves from the repetition of injury or the danger of intense feelings. These shells must be opened in the therapeutic process, but in a context that is safe. Furthermore, the inner coating of pain must be acknowledged emotionally as the mourning of past losses, deprivations, and disappointments.

The final step in the process seems to be to help someone else. This can be a part of healing itself, but it is also an external sign and ratification that there has been internal change. Both men in these stories have been selfish—or accused of being so—in youth. Now, through caretaking they show that they have a capacity for altruism, that the positive directionality of their cure has been internalized.

9

THE MAGUS (JOHN FOWLES):
A LITERARY PSYCHODRAMA

The Magus, unlike the other novels discussed in this volume, portrays a deliberate transformative process, though a highly unusual one. It is a form of psychodrama, drawing on the past of the "therapist," as well as that of the patient, and ranging in style from formal drama to guerrilla theater, drawing the "patient" into personal relations with the actors. *The Magus* is ambiguous about outcome—at its conclusion we are left feeling that its protagonist is a better person, but he does not clearly reap the benefits of internal change in the form of a "happy ending." This places *The Magus* closer to *The House of Mirth*, our "failed case" where the hero and heroine attempt internal change but reach a tragic outcome.

Nicholas Urfe is a young Englishman just out of Oxford, and at loose ends in his life. He meets an Australian woman, and despite her being "below" him socially, they become romantically involved. Nicholas's fear of intimacy leads him impulsively to take a job teaching English at a private boys' school on a Greek island. While there he searches out a mysterious, wealthy eccentric—Conchis—who owns a large estate on the other end of the island. Nicholas has a series of meetings with Conchis, punctuated by sudden tableaux and dramatic scenes that appear while they are talking. Gradually, the actors in these scenes become real people, and Nicholas becomes entangled in their supposed, offstage lives. This "treatment" can be seen as a metaphor for therapeutic influence. In our discussion of how therapeutic influence works in *this* novel, we will view the psychodrama from three different perspectives—as the protagonist's reality, as transference fantasy, and as dream. Furthermore, since *The Magus* deals with a relationship that almost fails to produce change, analysis of this novel highlights those factors that may prove to be useful in understanding unsuccessful or "failed" encounters.

In his preface to the revised version of *The Magus*, John Fowles describes his work as "a novel of adolescence written by a retarded adolescent."[1] He gives us permission to read this text as we would a Rorschach: "Its meaning is whatever reaction it provokes in the reader, and so far as I am concerned there is no given 'right' reaction" (p. 10). Fowles tells us further that his intention, insofar as he can specify one, is the humanist aim of destroying human illusions of "absolute knowledge and absolute power." He accomplishes this aim by leading his hero, Nicholas Urfe, through a series of adventures and encounters in a complex "masque" or psychodrama (the Godgame) that force Nicholas to face his illusions and self-deceptions.

The Magus is a work of considerable, perhaps excessive, complexity, but a therapeutic theme can be effectively extracted from its Byzantine plot. The author not only gives us permission to do so ("read it as you will") but, in effect, *invites* this treatment of his text since he has written a novel about the deliberate influence of one character on another. Fowles reifies what we have attempted to demonstrate about fictional plot and interaction in previous chapters. However, the actual transformative process is more complex and richly layered than the central location of the Godgame theme within the narrative implies. That is, Fowles presents what looks like treatment in the form of a complicated "play" enacted around the central character. The true healing process is actually more subtle than this heavy-handed manipulation.

This novel relates to two novels we have previously discussed, *Jane Eyre* and *The Secret Garden*. Like *Jane Eyre*, *The Magus* is a novel about late adolescence and the overcoming of adolescent and young adulthood barriers to heterosexual love, but the two protagonists are very different. Jane Eyre is honest with herself as far as her intrapsychic and reality situations permit. She struggles with a conflict that creates unconscious barriers to further development. Jane loves Rochester, but guilt over sexual impulses leads her to flee. A harsh superego must be modified for Jane's transition to adult sexuality to succeed. In this sense, her problems are developmental as well as neurotic. Unlike Jane Eyre, Nicholas Urfe resists self-knowledge. He deliberately deludes himself; he is largely unaware of his characterological behaviors and defenses. Nicholas's problem is not the avoidance of sexuality—quite the contrary—but the fear of non-sexualized intimacy. He thinks he is one kind of person, and he convinces the reader of this very effectively. Only in his final personal crisis does a truer understanding of his character emerge. His is a story of healing through love, of healing the capacity to love, and of healing through disillusionment.

The Secret Garden also offers suggestive points of comparison to *The Magus*. In *The Secret Garden*, developmentally arrested and emotionally inaccessible children evolve through a combination of therapeutic influences—environmental and transferential. In *The Magus* the "environmental" influences are more calculated and deliberate, less benign and natural; in *this* novel the motives of the participants remain obscure. However, as in *The Secret Garden,* the combination of a meaningful personal relationship and outside influences condenses to produce an effect that neither one could accomplish alone.

THE STORY

Mystery and ambiguity characterize the plot of *The Magus.* In first person voice we are introduced to Nicholas Urfe, the only son of an English brigadier and his conventional wife. *The Magus* takes place in 1954 when Nicholas is about twenty-seven years old. His parents had been killed in an airplane crash six years earlier. After the initial shock of their deaths, Nicholas experiences relief to be free of parents who did not understand or appreciate him. He views himself as a "wartime aesthete and cynic," a would-be poet, perhaps with hidden talents waiting to be discovered. He graduates from Oxford to find that his ideas of what he is entitled to in life make all the ordinary work of teaching (for which he is trained) unattractive—boring and ordinary. Seeking novelty and excitement, he accepts a more exotic teaching job at the Lord Byron School on Phraxos, a Greek island. But "that same evening by a curious neatness of fate, I met Alison" (p. 23). In his relationships with women Nicholas is a successful seducer. He sees himself as a "cad," able to blend his attractive cynicism with what he calls the "solitary heart," his lonely, sensitive, orphaned state. To certain women, he tells us, this combination is irresistible.

Alison is an Australian woman Nicholas's age. Sexually experienced and superficially worldly in her relationships with men, she is, like Nicholas, alienated from her origins. This similarity draws them together. Alison is bored and disappointed with her stolid, insensitive Australian friends, but insecure in the more sophisticated atmosphere of English middle-class society. Because she is insecure, she can be devious and unstable in her behavior, but she is always direct, candid, and honest about what she feels. She also sees through Nicholas's affectations. She loves him, but "she didn't fall for the solitary heart; she had a nose for emotional blackmail" (p. 36). Nicholas knows this is no ordinary affair; Alison is unlike anyone he has ever met before. Conflict leads him to deny his involvement and his feelings for her. Causing her considerable pain, he takes the job on Phraxos.

Greece is his new mistress, but despite his enchantment with Phraxos' beauties and novelty, he becomes depressed. Three factors contribute to his depression. He has had to face his lack of true poetic talent. He feels abandoned by Alison, who writes that she has returned to an old boyfriend. Furthermore, he believes he has contracted syphilis from a prostitute in Athens. Narcissistic wounds and the loss of a relationship he unconsciously needs but consciously devalues, precipitate fantasies of a suicide he cannot bring himself to carry out. In the state of readiness that often accompanies a psychological crisis, Nicholas seeks out Bourani, the summer estate of an elusive and wealthy Greek islander, Maurice Conchis.

It seems that Conchis has been anticipating Nicholas's arrival. A carefully orchestrated series of weekend visits to Bourani ensues, with Conchis determining when Nicholas shall arrive and when he shall leave. During these visits they talk. Conchis asks Nicholas many questions, but reveals information about himself only on certain occasions. Nicholas has the impression that Conchis is interested in him as a kind of "syndrome." He is fascinated and flattered by this interest, but confused. Conchis tells Nicholas a series of stories about his own life—most of which turn out to be untrue—which are veiled references to the relationship between himself and Nicholas or "morality" tales for Nicholas's benefit. Pieces of these stories are enacted at unexpected times and places in a sort of spontaneous guerrilla theater. For instance, Conchis tells Nicholas of a powerful benefactor of his own, Alphonse De Deukans, who "adopts" him in his youth and makes him his heir. This story suggests that Conchis intuits Nicholas's fantasy of himself as Conchis's protégé. A story about Conchis's desertion from the army in World War I follows a mock Russian roulette challenge between Conchis and Nicholas. In both the game and the story Conchis demonstrates to Nicholas that the wish to live is greater than the pleasure derived from self-dramatizing and pseudo-heroic gestures, symbolized by Nicholas's failed suicide attempt.

Nicholas's fascination with the masque staged for his benefit becomes an obsession with the appearance of "Lily," a beautiful young woman who was, supposedly, once Conchis's fiancée and who died of typhoid in 1915. Nicholas knows, of course, that the woman playing Lily is an actress, but who is she and why is she doing this? Lily immediately becomes the romanticized and unattainable woman whom Nicholas must possess. He tries to enlist her allegiance against Conchis, to get her to reveal the secrets of Bourani, its inhabitants, and the masque to him. Meanwhile, Conchis tells Nicholas that Lily is a schizophrenic (whose real name, in fact, is Julie), a patient of his whose delusion is that she *is* Lily. Throughout most of the novel Conchis presents himself, quite plausibly, as a psychiatrist, which, in fact, he is not.

As the Godgame progresses, the reader shares Nicholas's continuing confusion as to what is real and what is fantastic. Nicholas cannot suspend disbelief as Conchis requests and let himself be immersed in the experiences he is having. In seeking the answers to the secrets of the masque and its actors, he wants to know, not in order to understand, but in order to regain power and control. (There is an analogy between

Nicholas's behavior and that of patients for whom the treatment situation is, to varying degrees, a narcissistic affront. Such patients express an inordinate need to know how therapy works, just what will happen to them in the process, and how they can do it correctly. Again, this is not in the interest of gaining insight, but rather to avoid the experience of confusion, ambiguity, and regression that may ensue, as necessary as these conditions may be for the emergence of fantasy and transference manifestations.)

Nicholas has spent two weekends at Bourani and is thoroughly involved in its psychodrama when Alison writes and asks to meet him in Athens. Nicholas does not want to see Alison; by now Lily has eclipsed her completely. When Conchis questions him about Alison, Nicholas is secretive. When he minimizes her importance, Conchis tells him he is making a mistake preferring Lily to a woman who loves and understands him. Nicholas rejects Conchis's "interpretation" about the difference between fantasy and reality. However, when the visits to Bourani are temporary discontinued by Conchis, Nicholas goes to Athens out of pique, to show Conchis (and himself) that he does not need him.

In Athens, he tries to remain detached from Alison. She compares unfavorably to Lily; nonetheless, Nicholas is still drawn to her. He realizes he loves her, but thinks he cannot give up his wish to possess Lily. He loves them both, and he tells this to Alison, hoping she can understand and accept his dilemma. She cannot; she insists he make a choice. He choses Lily, and Alison leaves Greece, once again badly hurt.

Nicholas resumes his visits to Bourani. The cast of characters in the masque increases. Lily now has a twin sister, Rose (played by her real twin sister), whose presence and attractiveness to Nicholas betray the underlying promiscuity that has characterized his intimate relationships. As the events of the masque become increasingly complex, Nicholas convinces himself (and the reader, at this point) that he is winning Lily/Julie over to his side. She, too, seems to be a victim of Conchis's manipulations. Nicholas wishes to rescue her and secure her love—but he is never sure where truth begins and pretense ends. Suddenly, he receives a letter and a newspaper clipping informing him of Alison's suicide. So deep has been his self-deception that he is shocked at how upset he feels. "To my horror, I began to cry" (p. 405). His pursuit of Lily intensifies; now, even more, he hopes to win her love. Somehow, through Lily, he seeks redemption for having contributed to Alison's misery and death.

But the masque is not yet over. Nicholas succeeds in possessing Lily sexually and in that moment, when he finally believes she loves him, she reveals that this behavior, *too*, is part of the psychodrama. He is suddenly seized, imprisoned, and eventually put on trial before a group of mock psychologists—of whom Lily is now one—where a "case report" on him reveals his problems and shortcomings in humiliatingly accurate detail.

Now the masque is over. Conchis and his retinue disappear. Nicholas returns to England, having lost his teaching job on Phraxos. He is "disintoxicated" of Lily and now comes to realize what Alison meant to him and how deeply he misses her. He ponders the difference between love and sex, love and possession, real relationship and fantasied triumphs. For the first time in his life, he experiences sadness and acknowledges loss.

The final section of *The Magus* involves another plot twist. Once back in England Nicholas discovers that Alison is not dead, that she had been brought into Conchis's Godgame to test Nicholas in some final, crucial manner. The faked suicide ultimately confronts Nicholas with his capacity for guilt and remorse. Can he now, in the face of this further blow to his omnipotence, and his betrayal by the one person he felt he could trust, forgive and relinquish wishes for vengeance? Can he love without winning? Nicholas is made to wait for Alison to be ready to see him. And when she does come to him, it is as herself, no longer part of the masque. She and Nicholas are now left on their own to wrestle with questions of commitment and trust. Whether they will bond or part is not made clear. There is no happy ending to *The Magus*. Rather, there is the sense of Nicholas's transition to adulthood, its realities, ambiguities, and responsibilities. The "happy ending" is psychological, not conventional.

NICHOLAS AS PATIENT

At the mock trial, a parody of a psychiatric case conference is presented with Nicholas as the subject. Despite its dramatic exaggerations and ridiculous hyperbole, we recognize Nicholas as patient. Fowles gives us little biographical information about his protagonist, but there is enough to develop our own less fantastic psychological profile.

In the first chapter, we learn that Nicholas is an only child, disappointed in parents whom he views as limited and insensitive to his nature and needs. He describes his brigadier father as petty, authoritarian, short tempered, and not "really up to his job." His mother is "the very model of a would-be major general's wife" submissive and conventional, although emotionally gentle (p. 17). His attitude toward both of them is essentially contemptuous. Like many adolescents, for whom devaluation is a means of separation, Nicholas wishes for better parents and more glamorous family credentials.

He does not mourn his parents' deaths, but rather defends against his loss by viewing it as a liberation. While his father was alive, Nicholas had to submit to his authority and join the regiment. (Nicholas was a teenager during World War II.) Now, the war over, he is free to identify himself as a poet, a sensitive outsider, as alienated from the establishment as his father was part of it. Nicholas's fear of his father's authority (defended against by disdain) may mask a longing for closeness with his father that the latter's limited personality precluded. Nicholas's later encounters with Conchis arouse both sides of this ambivalence.

Nicholas's descriptions of himself are ironic. He is, in his own words, a cad, an exploiter of women, a snob, and a cynic. But there is something wrong with the ease with which he admits these faults. He seems honest, but is, in fact, self-deceptive. It is as if he needs to see himself as a cad, to treat his defensive shell as his real personality. For instance, he recognizes that he is not a cynic by "nature" but rather by "revolt." "I had got away from what I hated. But I hadn't found where I loved, and so I pretended there was nowhere to love" (p. 19). He also sees the shallowness and dishonesty of his aspirations, but he lacks the motivation to change. His seeming honesty about his own flaws does not produce discomfort. Furthermore, the most damaging aspect of his self-deception is his denial of need and vulnerability. Nicholas's whole personality, which appears narcissistic and self-serving, is an attempt to deny powerful dependent yearnings and the loss and disappointment that would ensue from their frustration.[2] His relationships with women, in particular, embody his problems with need, which he defends against by callous devaluation and promiscuity.

We would expect to find some clues about Nicholas's attitudes toward women from his relationship with his mother. The author only provides us with two. Nicholas wishes for more of her "emotional gentleness," and he clearly resents her loyalty to his father's standards and expectations. "She never argued with him and always behaved as if he were listening in the next room, even when he was thousands of miles away" (p. 17). These few biographical clues suggest a longing for closeness with women (that will, in fact, turn out to be quite intense) and a marked Oedipal rivalry with his father. However, as in therapy, Nicholas's *current* thoughts, feelings, and behaviors are still our main source of evidence about his inner difficulties.

Nicholas knows he cannot love or mourn, that he feels incapable of sadness or remorse, but he does not seem to really care. The encounters with Alison and Conchis will help him care. He will then be able to experience sadness, loss, love, and the compromises that committed adult relationships inevitably entail.

We may summarize the psychological plot of *The Magus* as follows: Nicholas's personality structure, characterized by interpersonal isolation and narcissistic defenses that have protected him from the dangers of pre-Oedipal loss and Oedipal defeat, is greatly modified. He will traverse a path in which massive loss and defeat are unavoidable; he will survive, and he will come to know himself.

THE PROCESS

As in dreams, where there are both manifest and latent meanings, the therapeutic process contained in this novel is also multilayered. The manifest process is the Godgame, the complex psychodrama in which Nicholas willingly participates. It is a deliberately organized and orchestrated series of events developed to confront Nicholas, to expose and challenge his assumptions and defenses in an effort to strip him of a false sense of omnipotence. Nicholas fights to hold onto his power, to maintain knowledge and control. The events of this struggle are so compelling that one may lose sight of an underlying (or latent) process, the unfolding of Nicholas's relationship with Alison. It is this relationship that we believe is the truly mutative one. It is a relationship that would have failed without the assistance of the psychodrama, but the psychodrama would have no real meaning or end point without Alison.

When Nicholas first visits Bourani, he finds a book of English verse on the beach; it has been left for him to see. An underlined passage from T. S. Eliot's poem "Little Gidding" conveys the idea that the end point of all his exploring will be to return to the beginning, "and know the place for the first time" (p. 71).

The quotation tells him what the purpose of his journey is to be, but it is a long time before he understands this. To look at this process in detail, it may help to first separate out Nicholas's relationship with Alison from his relationship to Conchis and his retinue, to examine each of these themes in the novel, and then consider their cumulative effect.

Alison

Elements of class snobbery and avoidance characterize Nicholas's perceptions of Alison and allow him to deny her importance to him. He meets her casually, at a party, and he is immediately attracted to her aura of intense sexuality. Compared to boring English girls, he finds her "crude, but alive." Alison is not interested in his sophisticated poses; she is interested in him. "Gradually . . . she made me talk about myself. She did it by asking blunt questions, and by brushing aside empty answers. I began to talk about being a brigadier's son, about loneliness, and for once mostly not to glamorize myself but simply to explain" (p. 29).

For Nicholas this self-revelation is unusually intimate. His immediate sexual involvement with Alison is a reflection of a shared tendency toward defensive promiscuity, which both use to avoid intimacy. However, despite a shaky beginning, characterized by shame on Alison's part and contempt on Nicholas's, their affair flourishes. Although Nicholas cannot recognize that he loves Alison, he knows she is important to him in some way. He conceals from himself what he knows unconsciously.

> I remember one day when we were standing in one of the rooms at the Tate. Alison was leaning slightly against me, holding my hand, looking in her childish sweet-sucking way at a Renoir. I suddenly had a feeling that we were one body, one person, even there; that if she had disappeared it would have been as if I had lost half of myself. A terrible deathlike feeling, which anyone less cerebral and self-absorbed than I was then would have realized was simply love. I thought it was desire. I drove her straight home and tore her clothes off. (p. 37)

Nicholas feels he cannot love Alison because she is inferior to him. Her status as a colonial, her relative ignorance—she has not graduated from Oxford or any other university, though in fact, she is far from ignorant—are continually emphasized. And Alison knows this. She feels she can never please him. Nevertheless, she—like Muriel in *The Accidental Tourist*—does not give up. Nicholas leaves for Greece feeling "that she loved me more than I loved her, and that consequently I had in some indefinable way won" (p. 50). She is grieved; he is triumphant.

Because he denies his feelings toward Alison, Nicholas is puzzled at his reactions to certain events. He does not connect the intense depression that precedes his first meeting with Conchis with the letter Alison has written breaking off their affair. He knows dimly that he is insulted at losing to a rival, not that he has lost someone he needs. "I thought little about Alison, but I felt about her; that is, I tried to erase her and failed" (p. 59). Repeatedly, he imagines talking with her, sharing his strange experiences on Bourani with someone who understands him and shares a common worldview. He misses her, but he is obtuse to the meaning of his feelings. Cobweb-like, he brushes away recurrent intrusive thoughts.

> I had an acute sense of the absence of Alison, of the probably permanent loss of her; I could imagine her beside me, her hand in mine; and she was warmth, normality, standard to go by. I had always seen myself as potentially a sort of protector of her; and for the first time, that evening at Bourani I saw that perhaps she had been, or could have been, a protector of me. (p. 113)

These thoughts do not draw Nicholas closer to Alison. Rather, they seem to frighten him. He flees her for the fantasy of Lily, who appears in the novel soon after the passage quoted above. Lily has meaning to Nicholas in terms of his Oedipally tinged rivalry with Conchis, but in terms of his relationship with Alison, she is the sought-after and safely unattainable princess to Alison's everyday availability.

When Nicholas meets Alison in Athens, they climb Mount Parnassus together; they have an ordinary adventure replete with blisters, lost pathways, exhaustion, and eventual exhilaration. Nicholas realizes Alison is the only person he knows who could have shared this adventure with him. Up to this point he has been keeping her at arm's length—he keeps his distance sexually by telling her he has syphilis—but as they drive to the mountain he finds himself once again talking frankly and comfortably with her.

> All the way in the car . . . prompted by Alison, I talked about my own father, and perhaps for the first time in my life without bitterness or blame; rather in the way that Conchis talked about his life. And then as I glanced at Alison, who was against the door, half turned towards me, it came to me that she was the only person in the world that I could have been talking like that to; that without noticing it I had slipped back into something of our old relationship . . . too close to need each other's names. (pp. 259–60)

Later, they make love by a waterfall. His feelings of love for Alison flood him once again, and once again he pushes them away. Nicholas is not ready.

His reaction to Alison's "suicide" surprises him, as if the experience on Parnassus had never happened. It is, in fact, only after his final disillusionment with Lily, that Nicholas is overwhelmed with the grief and loss that he has been avoiding. Somehow, Nicholas's passion for Lily does not sufficiently explain his avoidance of Alison. One could as well say that one of his unconscious motives in becoming absorbed in Lily is that her very unattainability, the quality of the fantastic that hovers around her, protects him from a relationship that is accessible and all too real. Of what is Nicholas afraid? As with a patient in treatment, where resistance serves to hide underlying feeling, impulse, or motive, Nicholas lets us see his process of avoidance, of which he *is* aware, but not that which he avoids, of which he is *not* aware. In the culminating scene of The Magus, Nicholas, pleading with Alison not to abandon him, tells her, "You can't hate someone who's really on his knees. Who'll never be more than half a human being without you" (p. 667). Perhaps this passage speaks to Nicholas's fear. There are earlier references to Nicholas's feeling that he and Alison are like one person, that without her he will never be complete. There is the quote previously cited on the way to Parnassus—"too close to need each other's names"; there is the early scene in the Tate Museum; but most crucial of all is an insight Nicholas has about himself late in the novel.

> I was like some freakish parasitic species that could establish itself only in one rare kind of situation, by one precarious symbiosis. They had been wrong, at the trial. It was not that I preyed on girls; but the fact that my only access to normal humanity, to social decency, to any openness of heart, lay through girls, preyed on me. It was in that that I was the real victim. (p. 619)

In describing himself as a parasite Nicholas is too self-critical. Underneath, he fears the regressive feelings that intimacy may unleash. His narcissistic persona is a protection against such need and the possibility of loss.

We might say that Nicholas suffers from an exaggerated version of a central male fear connected with intimacy; that involvement with a woman stirs up the spectre of engulfment by the pre-Oedipal mother. The fear of such regression would make a person like Nicholas a difficult patient to treat in a clinical setting. He would not want to become attached to the therapist or influenced by him or her. Involvement would be tantamount to submission and change would involve the shedding of a central protective fantasy of omnipotence. This, then, brings us to the manifest part of the therapeutic process, Nicholas's involvement with Conchis and the Godgame.

Conchis

Until the very end of the novel, we never know who Maurice Conchis really is. Even when we do, his "true" story remains puzzling. Lily de Seitas (the mother of the two young actresses, Lily and Rose, who are involved with Conchis in his theater) tells Nicholas that Conchis is interested in emotional honesty and human relatedness and that he uses his "theater without walls" to influence certain chosen subjects. The subjects are teachers at the Lord Byron School on Phraxos, and the psychodrama in which they become involved, if they *wish* to, is guided, in large measure, by their own actions and reactions. In a sense, Conchis is *there* and they may use him or not as they like. However controlled and manipulated Nicholas may feel during his visits to Bourani, he is never forced to come or to continue. He continues because he is involved in the unfolding of a drama that he mistakenly believes to be taking place outside of himself. It is, in much larger part, internal. In the way that a therapist's motives are often obscure to the patient (and are, in fact, the subject of much transference-based fantasy) Conchis's motives remain unclear to both Nicholas and the reader.

Conchis presents himself to Nicholas as a psychiatrist, although not as Nicholas's psychiatrist. His relationship with Nicholas, as patient, is always ambiguous. However, in many ways, he behaves like a therapist. Times for visits are set by him and their length controlled. He asks many questions and answers few. He tells Nicholas stories, when he chooses; these seem to be essentially interpretive. He remains objective and relatively unemotional; when he is emotional, it turns out to be a controlled and purposeful display on his part. Nicholas feels Conchis's interest in him is in "some syndrome I exhibited, some category I filled" (p. 94).

As we have already noted, Nicholas begins his visits to Bourani in a state of readiness for a new experience. He has survived a period of severe depression and, unconsciously at least, he may be looking for something from Conchis.

The truth is that I was full of the sort of green stir. Conchis was not more than the chance agent, the event that had come at the right time; just as in the old days I might, after a celibate term at Oxford, have met a girl and begun an affair with her, I had begun something exciting with him. It seemed linked in a way with my wanting to see Alison again. I wanted to live again. (p. 105)

His hopes for change and transformation are revealed in a later intro-spective passage that takes place during his second visit to Bourani:

It was an awareness of a new kind of potentiality, one very different from my old sense of the word, which had been based on the illusions of ambition. The mess of my life, the selfishnesses and false turnings and the treacheries, all these things *could* fall into place, they *could* become a source of construction rather than a source of chaos, and precisely because I had no other choice. (pp. 167–68)

As we have seen in previous chapters, the wish for change, con-scious or unconscious, does not lead to its immediate accomplishment. A difficult process of engagement, struggle, and working through must ensue. Nicholas develops intense feelings toward Conchis almost imme-diately. He admires Conchis and wishes to be admired in turn, but he is also envious, competitive, disbelieving, and suspicious. The immediacy and intensity of these feelings speak to their transferential origins. Indeed, much of what Conchis tells Nicholas about his own life (Conchis's stories) could be understood to be the equivalent of fantasies Nicholas has about Conchis. These "fantasies" alternately reflect Nicholas's awe of Conchis and his wish to belittle him and triumph over him. For instance, Nicholas's infatuation with Lily begins once he hears Conchis's story about her—that Lily was a girlhood sweetheart Conchis lost because of his lack of courage. Conchis deserted the army in World War I, and Lily then rejected him. Nicholas's behavior from that point on reflects a determination to win the present Lily (whom he fantasies at one point to be Conchis's mistress) away from Conchis's influence, and by possessing her, to be more of a man than Conchis.

Nicholas wishes to be like Conchis, as he sees him—powerful, rich, one of the elect—but his character is such that he cannot do this by becoming a pupil and thus, ultimately, a colleague. He feels he must unmask and defeat Conchis, and he tries to do so by winning Lily's alle-giance. Later in the story he attempts to reveal Conchis by researching his true identity and credentials. But the most powerful manifestation of Nicholas's negative transference feelings toward Conchis lies not in his triumphant fantasies and investigative actions, but in his resis-tance to the process in which he has agreed to participate. Even when the psychodrama seems manipulative and cruel and Conchis seems a cross between a Svengali-like charlatan and a Ghandi-like guru, we are aware that Nicholas chooses to be there. He eagerly seeks out fur-ther visits and involvement, but he will not suspend disbelief nor reveal himself straightforwardly. He plays to win, not to be influenced.

Toward the end of the novel, Lily de Seitas explains to Nicholas that in the masque "the subject guides the game" (p. 487). Each scene, or intervention, is staged in response to Nicholas's reactions. The increased intensity, and even violence, of later scenes may be viewed, metaphorically, as more dramatic levels of confrontation and interpretation necessary to address Nicholas's resistance, which, as in psychoanalytic therapy, intensifies as his transference feelings toward Conchis develop and elaborate.

In response to the psychodrama, Nicholas has two fantasies that express opposite sides of his central conflict. He is awed and exhilarated that this is all being staged for him—"as if the world had been reinvented and for me alone" (p. 160). He is also humiliated that he is excluded from a secret that all the others share. Is he powerful and central or weak and excluded? Here we see, reflected in Nicholas, the crucial childhood duality with which Nicholas (and all of us) must come to terms: the highly gratifying fantasy that one is the center of the universe and the painfully disappointing experience of exclusion from the privileges and excitements of the adult world.

The first indication of a break in Nicholas's defenses vis-à-vis Conchis comes at the end of the trial. Here, after Nicholas is blatantly humiliated by being physically restrained, exposed, and forced to hear himself described in an unflattering case history, he is given an opportunity for revenge. He may beat Lily with a cat-o'-nine-tails, but he cannot bring himself to do it. It is not fear or abstract morality that prevent him, but some deeper feeling—compassion, a sense of his, and Lily's, human frailty, perhaps the realization that revenge will not reinstate power or ease pain. Later, he realizes that he does not beat Lily because he accepts his responsibility for Alison's death. The choice of not taking revenge is not a submission to Conchis, but an acceptance of his "lessons" and values.

Following the trial Nicholas does not stop fighting; after all, resistance follows treatment to the end. But his fighting is now modulated. He no longer wants *only* to win—this is symbolized by his relinquishing of Lily—now, he also wants to understand. Nicholas's researches into Conchis's true identity may also be viewed as a metaphor for his acceptance of reality and his exploration of its dimensions. It is a kind of dissolving of the transference.

The inner shifts in Nicholas's character now allow him to grieve Alison in earnest. But he faces another and harder step in his working through. Nicholas feels Alison was the one person he could trust to never betray him. "I knew she was a mirror that did not lie; whose interest in me was real; whose love was real. That had been her supreme virtue: a constant reality" (p. 548). When he discovers that Alison has participated in the Godgame and is, in fact, alive, he can become totally disillusioned and "disintoxicated" with her as he became with Lily. He can become preoccupied with taking revenge, but this does not happen. Though hurt and angry, his revengeful thoughts are overshadowed by his longings to be back together with Alison. A relationship with a loved other has gained dominance over narcissistic aims.

DISCUSSION OF THE PROCESS

Why does Conchis succeed where Alison fails? Alison loves Nicholas but she cannot influence him, while Conchis influences Nicholas, but he does not love him. Apparently it is not enough for Alison to love Nicholas; she does not expect him to be able to change and develop. She says in a letter to him at one point: "I know what you are. So be what you are" (p. 55). The message is not "I know what you are and I want you to be different." Perhaps it is her own lack of self-respect that keeps her from demanding better treatment. Alison is confused herself. She lacks conviction about what she deserves. After her first night with Nicholas, she expresses considerable self-hatred about her promiscuous and masochistic relationships with men. She accepts Nicholas's devaluation of her as a colonial—crude and lower class. Rather than inspiring him with better values (as Rose Vassiliou does with Simon Camish), she is intimidated by his cynical and elitist worldview. She lacks that sense of rightness about herself (and her aims) that characterizes the other literary figures of influence we have studied.

Conchis, on the other hand, is all self-confidence and righteousness. It is never completely clear to the reader *what* his aims are for the outcome of Nicholas's "treatment," but there seems little doubt that he *has* aims. Furthermore, these aims seem to be directed at breaking down Nicholas's arrogance and directing his attention to the reality of his feelings for Alison. The text of the novel is peppered with hints, from the start, that Conchis knows about Alison and her central role in Nicholas's life. He attempts some early and direct advice to this effect, which Nicholas disregards. Go "towards the girl" Conchis tells Nicholas. "She sees through you, you say, she understands you. That is good" (p. 149). When this maneuver fails, Conchis tries others, eventually involving Alison in the Godgame itself.

Unlike Alison, Conchis does influence Nicholas, but it is not a mutual process. Conchis may not remain untouched. He must have powerful motives of his own—Nicholas's conversations with Lily de Seitas suggest that Conchis, too, is working something out. Rather, he does not *seem* to wish to be involved with Nicholas; his role is more that of a catalyst. Throughout the novel, like a leitmotif, Alison appears and reappears. As Conchis's catalytic action is successful, he retreats from the scene leaving Nicholas and Alison as the key players. She becomes the central focus of Nicholas's aims, and the figures of the

Godgame lie like discarded masks all about him.

In terms of our therapeutic narrative—engagement, mutual influence, and directionality—we may summarize the process in *The Magus* as follows: Nicholas's engagement with Alison occurs around the central issue of their search for heterosexual intimacy. This process of engagement remains stalled by Nicholas's defenses against involvement, which keep him immune from influence by Alison. Therefore, he must first become engaged with Conchis where these defenses will be vigorously addressed in an ongoing drama of great emotional significance to Nicholas. Nicholas's initial motivation in engaging with Conchis is based on his fantasy of achieving the special status he attributes to Conchis—by defeating the latter. The process of influence between Nicholas and Conchis involves a struggle. Nicholas's fantasies of specialness are repeatedly stimulated and subsequently deflated by Conchis. Each experience of hope and failure leads to an intensified wish to win, and thus undo the injury. But while this struggle seems to be about triumph and defeat, it actually derives its emotional intensity from Nicholas's disavowed wishes to love and be loved by Conchis. Nicholas needs a father he can admire, and the need to be involved with Conchis fuels his ongoing struggle more than his need for power. In each of their interactions, the tension between self-aggrandisement and admiration for Conchis is present in Nicholas's feelings. Furthermore, Nicholas's greatest fear about the Godgame is not that he will be humiliated—although that fear is very intense—but that the psychodrama will stop, that Conchis will go away. The transition from a narcissistic position (that has its roots in Nicholas's disappointment in and defensive superiority toward his own father) to an involvement with Conchis is the crucial shift that awakens in Nicholas his need for others and makes a return to Alison possible. This is an excellent example of the phenomenon we discussed in our chapter on the accidental therapist; the working out of conflicts with a therapist allows for improved relationships outside of therapy.

The directionality of this process is provided by Conchis, but embodied in Alison. Nicholas's devaluation of Alison begins to change when Conchis extends special status to her by making her a participant in the Godgame. As Conchis and the Godgame fade in importance, Nicholas comes to value Alison more genuinely—in her own right. She embodies ego ideal elements—honesty, a sense of reality, the capacity for intimacy—toward which Nicholas *now* strives. This is the directionality of the process.

Since influence between characters tends to be mutual, what happens to Alison in her interactions with both Nicholas and Conchis? A less fully realized character in the novel, we know her mostly through Nicholas's eyes. She increases in value from this vantage point but not because of Nicholas's direct support and interaction. From the beginning Nicholas represents the status, sophistication, and personal sensitivity that Alison desires. To some degree he becomes her mentor, but his defensive contempt toward her keeps Alison from using her new knowledge and skills to improve her self-esteem. It is Alison's involvement with Conchis that gives her the sense of worth that allows her to refuse to accept a devalued and masochistic position vis-à-vis Nicholas any longer. Conchis respects Alison (Lily de Seitas later tells Nicholas) as a "person whose emotional honesty" does not need to be "put to the test" (p. 639). Respect from Conchis is not easily won. Moreover, by bringing Alison into the psychodrama, Conchis gives her a sense of superiority over Nicholas. However temporary this position may be, she *now* has the experience of being a respected insider to his confused and excluded outsider position. For the moment they have changed roles. Perhaps her temporarily elevated status undoes the narcissistic wound she has suffered at Nicholas's hands. Since she now does not have to look to Nicholas for the acceptance that would heal this injury, she can choose whether or not the terms of the relationship Nicholas offers her are adequate. The mystery of the novel's end leaves us without a clear answer as to the lovers' fate, but Alison, no longer a "slave" to love, can now make choices.

SOME SPECULATIONS ON THE MEANING OF THE "GODGAME"

The psychodrama portion of *The Magus* may be understood from three different, but ultimately complementary perspectives: as reality events, as transference fantasies, or as dreams. In these three views the actual outcome is the same, but the mode of therapeutic influence differs.

In the first instance, we assume these improbable events happened to this protagonist, as described. Therapeutic influence is mediated by reality events working on Nicholas's psyche, much as the outside influences in *The Secret Garden* worked on Mary Lennox and Colin Craven, a sort of therapeutic milieu effect. New values and behaviors are reinforced by modeling and social manipulation.

In the second view of the psychodrama we assume that there is some reality in Nicholas's story, but that it is highly embellished by fantasy. The analogy here is to a transference neurosis, or prolonged transference state.[3] The process of change involves a working through of these fantasies on both conscious and unconscious levels. In this reading, Nicholas's struggles with Conchis are permeated by transference feelings, and his later researches into Conchis's real identity are seen as a dissolving of this transference. Again, as in *The Secret Garden*, the transference relationship reinforces the influence of the environment, and vice versa.

In a third perspective we can view the entire panoply of experiences on Phraxos as a dream or series of dreams. This meshes with our idea that the process in this novel has both manifest and latent levels of meaning. Interestingly, *The Magus*, as a novel, is divided into three sections, which take place in geographically different locales: London, Greece, and again, London. The intrapsychic positions that correspond with these locales are conscious reality, dream state, and again, conscious reality—awakening. In part 1 Nicholas, in reality, falls in love. This poses him with the painful dilemma we have already discussed. He needs Alison, and he cannot tolerate that need. He pushes awareness of his feelings out of his consciousness.

An unconscious wish, striving for gratification, may lead to a dream, a disguised expression of that wish, and a disguised solution to the dilemma that gave rise to it.[4] Trying to solve his problem, Nicholas escapes to Greece. He is now in the world of dreams. The episodes on Bourani, viewed as dream, involve Nicholas's struggles with the problem of loving and his characterological defenses against love. The entire second section of *The Magus* is more comfortable to read when we view it as a series of dreams. We do not expect dreams to be orderly or rational. The confusion and unexpectedness of the events that take place—the frequent switches of identity of the characters; the use of symbols and pictorial images; the condensation of meanings in one image (e.g., Lily/Julie in her many past and present guises); and the displacements of meanings (e.g., Conchis as De Deukans)—are typical dream features. The events of the mock trial are so bizarre and symbolically loaded, with the characters appearing as mythic figures from Tarot cards, that the dreamlike quality of this passage is hard to escape even if one is not attributing this particular interpretation to the novel.

In the third section of *The Magus*, back in London, Nicholas is "awake" again. He is disintoxicated of Lily, his fantasy woman, and he longs to be reunited with Alison, his real woman. In this reading of the novel, Nicholas's investigations of the events and personae of the Godgame may be viewed as his decoding of the dream, his attempts to understand its disguised meanings. These three "readings" of the therapeutic process need not be mutually exclusive. Rather, they work better when integrated. The process is powerful *because* it involves elements of reality influence, the working through of transference, and the particularly forceful sense of conviction that can emerge following a successful understanding of one's own dreams.

In all three readings of this novel—as reality, as transference, and as dream—the events in Greece represent a fantastic series of adventures that work on Nicholas through a kind of shock tactic—the production of emotional disequilibrium created by surprise turnings and events. There is an undercurrent of violence in *The Magus*, particularly in the psychodrama episodes, that we have not encountered in our other literary cases. Conchis, metaphorically, beats Nicholas up. Images of interrogation, brainwashing, and torture permeate some of Conchis's stories, particularly the World War II episodes that culminate

Nicholas's last visit to Bourani, and precede the trial. This "violence" has meanings in all three of our readings. Reality often disturbs and surprises us: it throws us curve balls that will not yield to our need for control and mastery. Coming to terms with the limitations of reality is integral to all successful development; Nicholas's is no exception.

Transference, that ubiquitous human tendency to read the realistic present in terms of the fantastical past, disturbs us endlessly, leading to tensions in treatment that can produce profound change or panicked flight. It is a phenomenon laden with violent feelings that must be modulated and integrated for either treatment situations or human relationships to work.

Dreams *certainly* disturb and confuse us with their powerful imagery and enigmatic meanings, particularly because they come from within us. Disturbing ideas that give rise to violent imagery inside us cannot be evaded by projection or rationalization. "It's only a dream" is a weak attempt to disqualify what shocks and frightens. Therefore, viewing the Godgame as Nicholas's dream leads to a therapeutically profound result. Nicholas must come to understand that this conflict and violence is *his*—that, for instance, Alison's death is his wish, and that to achieve this wish is to lose more than he will gain. In this reading, Nicholas's ambivalent relationship with Conchis may be seen as an inner struggle between infantile entitlement and omnipotence (his need to "know") and realistic compromises. The therapeutic process in this reading of the novel is one of Nicholas's inner shifts and insights, the giving up of his personal Godgame. The violence of the psychodrama scenes, then, symbolizes Nicholas's coming to terms with reality limits, the power of his transference feelings, and the destructive impulses inside him that he acknowledges through his understanding of the dream.

The Magus does not have a clear or happy ending. It has an ambiguous ending, but a therapeutic outcome for the protagonist. Its outcome, in fact, is closer to true therapeutic outcomes than any of our other examples. Nicholas attains maturity, self-knowledge, and a sense of his realistic limitations. Neither he nor the reader have the sense of gratification that accompanies the usual happy ending where boy gets girl. Like Simon in *The Needle's Eye* (Chapter 4), Nicholas compromises. Simon relinquishes the actual possession of Rose but not her idealized meanings to him. Nicholas relinquishes the sense that he can always have what he wants, including Alison, but the realization that, with or without possession, she remains a crucial and meaningful person to him is the legacy of his struggle.

THE HOUSE OF MIRTH (EDITH WHARTON): TRAGEDY—THE FAILURE OF A RELATIONSHIP TO TRANSFORM

The heart of the wise is in the house of mourning, but the heart of fools is in the house of mirth. (Eccles. 7:4)

We feel it will be of interest to look at a "failed case" in literature: if successful literary outcomes parallel successful psychotherapeutic ones, perhaps a failed literary case will reveal some commonalities with failed psychotherapeutic cases. Further, we can study what factors are absent, or present in inadequate degree, to see whether these correspond to what we have found in positive instances. A novel with a negative or destructive outcome is not sufficient for demonstrating a failed case. *Madame Bovary, Anna Karenina*, and Christina Stead's *The Man Who Loved Children* have powerful, tragic outcomes; they end in profound moral and psychological failure—in death, in fact. While they offer stunning examples of the repetition compulsion in its more negative manifestations, these examples do not serve our purpose.[1] We need a novel in which it can be demonstrated that engagement and mutual influence are present between characters, but are not strong enough, or are not accompanied by directionality with a positive vector. Analysis of the factors that lead to such a failure of positive directionality should provide a contrast to those narratives that embody successful intrapsychic change.

Edith Wharton's *The House of Mirth* is a novel well suited to this purpose. Written in 1905, *The House of Mirth* was Wharton's first impoetant novel. Many critics consider it one of her finest, particularly for her depiction of the heroine, Lily Bart. It is a novel about fashionable New York, a novel of manners, and Wharton's passionate condemnation of a society that, in its emphasis on money and power, destroys beauty and moral sensibility. Unlike the other novels we have examined, *The House of Mirth* is a tragedy. Lily Bart ends a suicide, as do Emma Bovary, Anna Karenina, and Henrietta Pollitt[2]: but unlike these heroines, who seem to rush headlong to their fate, Lily struggles to extricate herself from her own fatal craving for luxury and wealth, through the influence of another character, Lawrence Selden. Her struggle is not a successful one.

Louis Auchincloss, in his discussion of Wharton's novel, points out that any number of small, almost insignificant, plot changes would have rescued Lily from the downward spiral that leads to her tragic end.[3] He feels that Wharton's intent is to depict the spiritual bankruptcy of a world that hounds or disregards those without money, and that envies true beauty and refinement. Auchincloss's analysis of Lily's situation is the one most familiar to readers of this novel. His point is that Lily has no choice; she is the victim of a society in which money is the dominant system of exchange. Failure to adhere to the social conventions that derive from this emphasis on financial status ultimately lead to her downfall. A reading of Lily's fate that does not contradict Auchincloss's interpretation is that Lily is embarked on an unconsciously self-destructive course from which Selden, out of his own crippling ambivalence, cannot rescue her. But he does try and she does respond, and it is this engagement and attempt at influence that makes Wharton's novel useful as an example of a failed mutative encounter.

THE STORY

Lily Bart, the orphaned daughter of socially prominent parents, has been a glittering addition to wealthy New York's social scene since her "coming out" at eighteen. Lily is stunningly beautiful, with a sense of taste and a quality of moral refinement that separate her from the members of her own social circle. She also has a serious problem. Without money, she must ultimately marry to maintain her social position; but despite numerous opportunities, she cannot quite bring herself to a mercenary or even practical, prudent match. Lily wants something better—love, really—although she thinks of this in terms of "romance." This is what she tells herself when she attempts to understand and explain her own puzzling behavior.

As the novel begins, Lily's situation is precarious. Although still very beautiful, she is now twenty-nine, and we read of the "purity of tint that she was beginning to lose after eleven years of late hours and indefatigable dancing" (p. 6). Lily lives with an elderly aunt, who keeps her on a tight budget and offers neither emotional support nor practical guidance. Lily has no other resources and is in debt from bridge losses. She cannot control her spending or her need for luxurious living. Wealthier friends exploit her dependence, using her as a sort of informal social secretary, a beauty for their dinner tables and bridge parties, and a charming distraction for their boring husbands as they carry on flirtations with other, more interesting men. Despite her usefulness, the women in Lily's most immediate circle would be very happy to see her married; her beauty and charm are still a threat to them.

Lily is fully aware of how desperate her situation will become if she does not marry soon. Nevertheless, she ruins an opportunity to make a secure match with a stuffy and unimaginative young man, Percy Gryce. She confesses her financial difficulty to Gus Trenor, the husband of her closest friend. He offers to "invest" her small income for her. Lily does not understand that he really means to give her money in exchange for special attentions, even sexual favors. The other women in Lily's world would have understood very well the terms of Gus's offer, but Lily's naivete, a product of denial and idealism, leads her into an error for which she will suffer tragically. When she discovers the source of her newly acquired wealth, honor will not permit her to accept the gift, nor will her scruples let her meet the expected terms. She can only absolve herself by paying the money back, and she has not the means to do so. Hearing of her gambling debts, her aunt disinherits her. Lily is left with only a small legacy, which she feels she must use to discharge her debt to Gus. This will leave her penniless.

As she struggles to manage, she moves step by step down the social ladder, first to the company of the Wellington Brys, a newly wealthy couple, who are flattered at the distinction Lily's presence imparts to their social endeavors; next to a very dubious and dangerous arrangement with Bertha Dorset, a woman of her own immediate social circle—Lily agrees to travel in the Mediterranean with the Dorsets in order to distract George Dorset from his wife's affair with another man; then to a "job" as social consultant and arbiter of taste to the Gormers, another "arriviste" couple, even further down the social ladder; and finally, to a position as social secretary to wealthy Norma Hatch, a young woman whose relationship to proper society is at best marginal. This final step within society's bounds precedes Lily's end as a milliner's assistant. Unable to do even this simple work very well, Lily ends up alone and ostracized, finally a suicide.

LILY AND LAWRENCE SELDEN

This brief plot summary does not capture what is most tragic about Lily's situation. Her refinement and sense of morality leave her weaponless to deal with a society that values only money and has no place for those without it. Lily participates in the flirtation and superficiality of her world, but not its underlying corruptness. We see this in her behavior around her possession of Bertha Dorset's love letters to Lawrence Selden. Lily could use these letters to keep Bertha from exploiting her and, later, to reestablish herself in society—but she does not. Only some powerful inner, unconscious motive can explain this self-defeating pattern.

Most crucial in Lily's confused dealings with her own fate is her relationship with Lawrence Selden. Selden appears at crucial decision points in Lily's life, influencing her in powerful ways, yet not in a direction of cure. It is this relationship that comes closest to being the mutative one we have described in previous chapters. Although it fails, Lily's relationship with Selden indicates clearly an alternative course of action. We will present the encounters between Lily and Selden in detail. A discussion of the intrapsychic situation of both protagonists helps us understand who these people are, leads to elucidation of the process between them, and suggests why it fails.

The psychoanalyst Bennett Simon maintains that plot in tragedy is driven by a series of missed or only partially correct "interpretations" that occur between the characters in the form of commentaries on each other's affects, motivations, and actions.[4] Simon maintains that even in psychoanalytic work interpretations are rarely exact, but that an atmosphere exists in which errors can be addressed and gradually corrected. In tragedy the correct interpretation comes too late, if at all, and the tragic hero or heroine is driven further and further into a subjective, distorted view of reality, with unfortunate results. This perspective on the tragic process is particularly useful in understanding the relationship between Lily Bart and Lawrence Selden.

Selden and Lily are both young, attractive, and single. They have been part of the same social milieu for many years. Although they have always liked one another, they have never been candidates for a marriage. Lily, being poor, must marry money. Selden also comes from a background characterized by good taste and genteel poverty. He works for his living as a lawyer; unlike the other men in this novel, he is not an investor of inherited wealth. Lily and Selden are alike in their shared ambivalence toward a society that neither can wholeheartedly espouse; nor can either of them settle for less. While Lily feels she cannot do without the wealth and luxury to which she feels addicted, some part of her holds it in contempt. Selden, on the other hand, consciously despises society, but, unconsciously, he is unable to resist its claims and gratifications. They become powerfully attracted to each other as they discover a similarity of ideals and longings, but both are unable to step across some boundary—emotional, moral, and social—that would allow them to make a life together. Their encounters are a study in ambivalence and missed opportunities.

Selden's Apartment

Lily's story begins in a meeting with Selden. The first sentences of the novel are "Selden paused in surprise. In the afternoon rush of the Grand Central Station his eyes had been refreshed by the sight of Miss

Lily Bart" (p. 5). Lily has missed her train to the country; she asks Selden to keep her company for a few hours until she can catch the next one. They have tea at his apartment. As an unchaperoned single woman, Lily takes a risk in doing this, and Selden admires her for her spontaneity.

Lily is immediately attracted to Selden's small bachelor apartment with its "pleasantly faded Turkey rug," comfortable armchairs, and shelves of old leather-bound books. Intrigued by the idea of having a place of one's own and attracted to Selden's good taste and refinement, in the face of his limited resources, Lily is drawn to confide in him. As Simon Camish was deeply moved by his first visit to Rose Vassiliou's home (because of "transference" feelings evoked in him) so Lily is emotionally touched. Her own father was a shadowy figure to her, but she knew of his interest in poetry. She may make an unconscious connection between her father and Selden as Simon did between Rose and his mother. The possibility for intimacy—for engagement—is established.

Lily asks Selden why he comes so infrequently to visit her at her aunt's home, especially since they "get on" so well. Teasingly, he tells her that perhaps it is because they get on so well that he avoids her. Lily wonders why he bothers to avoid seeing her since he cannot possibly think she is trying to marry him. They both know she must marry someone with wealth. Meant as a reassurance, Lily's comments may be a slight to Selden's vanity. Selden replies, in a light tone of voice, that perhaps the fact that she does not want to marry him interferes with his inducement to go see her. Lily suddenly becomes serious.

"Dear Mr. Selden, that wasn't worthy of you. It's stupid of you to make love to me and it isn't like you to be stupid. . . . Don't you see . . . that there are men enough to say pleasant things to me and that what I want is a friend who won't be afraid to say disagreeable ones when I need them! Sometimes I have fancied you might be that friend—I don't know why, except that you are neither a prig nor a bounder and that I shouldn't have to pretend with you or be on my guard against you. . . . You don't know how much I need such a friend . . . I've been about too long—people are getting tired of me; they are beginning to say I ought to marry." (p. 11)

"Well, why don't you?" Selden asks. Lily is caught off guard by the very frankness for which she has just pleaded. She becomes evasive at this point and changes the subject; she is moving away from more intimate involvement. However, later in the visit she returns to the subject of marriage and is more forthcoming about her ambivalence. A girl must marry, she tells him, while a man may if he chooses.

"Your coat's a little shabby—but who cares? It doesn't keep people from asking you to dine. If I were shabby no one would have me: a woman is asked out as much for her clothes as for herself. . . . We are expected to be pretty and well-dressed till we drop—and if we can't keep it up alone, we have to go into partnership." (p. 14)

Their conversation is a fascinating mix of an honesty unusual in their ordinary social intercourse, and of missed connections. Whenever they get too close, one or the other withdraws through teasing, ironic banter, or socially correct platitudes. When Lily leaves Selden's apartment, she is aware that she has had an unusual experience; she is involved with Selden, but cannot allow herself to process the significance of this experience. She is still determined to carry out her plan to induce Percy Gryce to marry her.

Bellomont

Lily and Selden next meet that same weekend at Bellomont, country home of Lily's best friends, the Trenors. This is her most fateful encounter with Selden. Consciously, Lily intends to let nothing interfere with her plan to marry Percy Gryce; to this end she pleads with her hostess not to invite Selden for the weekend. She does not trust her own feelings in the comparison between Gryce and Selden. When Selden does show up, ostensibly to pacify Bertha Dorset, a married woman with whom he has just ended an affair, Lily knows he has come to see her. At dinner that night she observes his detachment from the opulence that surrounds them, and she is drawn to him once again.

Her careful plans for the weekend include a trip to church to impress Percy Gryce. On the walk home from church, also carefully planned, she knows Gryce will propose to her. She has set her traps well: "Her intentions, in short, had never been more definite; but poor Lily, for all the hard glaze of her exterior, was inwardly as malleable as wax" (p. 57). Pleading a headache, she sacrifices both church and an afternoon motor excursion with Gryce to go walking with Selden. These actions antagonize the jealous Bertha Dorset, who plays on Gryce's already timid resolve and turns him away from Lily to a safer marital choice.

Lily and Selden spend the afternoon walking in the hills. They are attracted to each other, but each explains these feelings away. Selden tells himself he enjoys watching Lily as a beautiful and masterful manipulator, an operator par excellence. Lily tells herself it is Selden's refinement and discerning intellect, in contrast to the crude materialism of her other friends, that draws her to him; she is not in love with him. Selden talks to her about his "philosophy of life," which is to live in a "republic of the spirit" where material considerations do not matter. Lily seems genuinely excited by this idea in a way that Selden cannot dismiss as flirtation or social manipulation. He has a sudden glimpse of Lily as a woman who hungers for a spirituality quite apart from, and in opposition to, the fulfillment of her social aims. Selden muses:

It was the danger-point of their intercourse that he could not doubt the spontaneity of her liking. From whatever angle he viewed their dawning intimacy, he could not see it as part of her scheme of life; and to be the unforeseen element in a career so accurately planned was stimulating even to a man who had renounced sentimental experiments. (p. 73)

Their conversation turns to Lily's ambitions and how they interfere with her becoming a member of Selden's select "republic of the spirit." She says to him concerning these very ambitions:

"Then the best you can say for me is that after struggling to get them, I probably shan't like them?" She drew a deep breath. "What a miserable future you foresee for me!"

"Well, have you never foreseen it for yourself?"

The slow colour rose to her cheek, not a blush of excitement but drawn from the deep wells of feeling; it was as if the effort of her spirit had produced it.

"Often and often," she said. "But it looks so much darker when you show it to me!"

He made no answer to this exclamation, and for a while they sat silent while something throbbed between them in the wide quiet of the air. (p. 76)

Selden's words carry weight. Lily sees something differently. She has known for a long time that she is shackled to ambitions whose very fulfillment may make her unhappy, but to realize this in his presence has the impact of insight: this is the quality of "surprise and self-consciousness" that Meredith Skura identifies as the hallmark of the psychoanalytic process, and the locus of shifts in a literary work that further the plot toward resolution.[5] In the plot of this novel, however, this moment of insight (the correct interpretation) is not sustained. Rather, it is disqualified. Lily asks Selden why he tortures her with his visions of her unhappiness when he has nothing to offer her instead. They are drawn "across unsounded depths of feeling" to talk of marriage, and now it is Lily who withdraws. She becomes frightened. She wants to be convinced, to have her fears of poverty assuaged, whereas Selden wants her to be willing to sacrifice for him. He fails to recognize the pliancy of her personality and her need for his belief in her *despite* her weakness. He does not understand—nor does Lily—that her frantic need for money relates to early deprivations of love and security. Money is, for Lily, a substitute gratification. Selden, missing this, sees her as more mercenary and determined than she really is. She, in turn, sees him as more committed to his ideals than he really is. These moments between them do not engender understanding and the development of their relationship. Rather, they lead to panic and withdrawal. Lily becomes worried, with good reason, that her indiscreet afternoon with Selden will ruin her chances with Gryce. Seeing her withdraw in fear, Selden becomes disillusioned with her. Unlike figures in other novels we have studied—Muriel in relationship to Macon, Darcy in relationship to Elizabeth—Selden does not see Lily's potential for change or his own potential for influence. His ambivalence is too readily evoked by her fears and indecisiveness.

The Brys Tableau Vivant

Some months have passed. Lily and Selden see each other again at a "tableau vivant" organized by Lily's new friends, the Wellington Brys. Lily's feelings toward Selden now are mixed. She blames him for the loss of a marital opportunity, her "most costly error," but she also longs for his recognition of "this real self of hers, which he had the faculty of drawing out of the depths" and that "was so little accustomed to go alone!" (p. 100). Lily is poised on the edge of social disaster. She is taking money from Gus Trenor thinking it an honest investment of her own funds. Sensing defeat, her old friends have begun to desert her. She now travels, by necessity, in the circle of the Wellington Brys, who are attempting to buy their way into society by staging events like the lavish tableau vivant. Selden sees Lily as a breathtakingly beautiful participant in this gala display. He notes the "touch of poetry in her beauty" that he "always felt in her presence yet lost the sense of when he was not with her" (p. 142). Despite the coolness of their last parting, he is overwhelmed with feeling for her.

In the long moment before the curtain fell, he had time to feel the whole tragedy of her life. It was as though her beauty, thus detached from all that cheapened and vulgarized it, had held out suppliant hands to him from the world in which he and she had once met for a moment, and where he felt an overmastering longing to be with her again. (p. 142)

After the tableau they meet in the conservatory. It is a highly romantic moment, but one marred by cross-purposes. Lily wants Selden to believe in her and to help her rise above her material concerns. He is in love with her.

"You never speak to me; you think hard things of me," she murmured.

"I think of you at any rate, God knows!" he said.

"Then why do we never see each other? Why can't we be friends? You promised once to help me," she continued in the same tone, as though the words were drawn from her unwillingly.

"The only way I can help you is by loving you," Selden said in a low voice. . . . Suddenly she caught his hand and pressed it a moment against her cheek.

"Ah, love me, love me—but don't tell me so!" she sighed with her eyes in his; and before he could speak she had turned and slipped through the arch of boughs, disappearing in the brightness of the room beyond. (p. 145)

Like most of his emotional dimensions, Selden's love is tentative. On her side, Lily cannot take the step that would allow for mutual commitment. Fear and confusion lead to an ambiguous message: love me (don't stop your feelings), but don't tell me so (lest I have to consider seriously my own feelings). Lily prefers to dream. Selden has more resolution now than he ever will again. He follows his declaration with a note asking to see Lily the next day. But before this meeting can take place, disruptive events ensue.

Gus Trenor now reveals to Lily that he has been giving her *his* money rather than investing *hers* and that he expects something from her in return. Lily becomes distraught; she is filled with shame and self-loathing at her own naiveté and moral laxity. She feels dishonored. Whatever it takes, she will pay Gus back; but in the meantime how can she live with her humiliation? "All she looked on was the same and yet changed. There was a great gulf fixed between today and yesterday. Everything in the past seemed simple, natural, full of daylight—and she was alone in a place of darkness and pollution" (p. 156).

Lily is now in a state of desperation and crisis that allows her to consider new alternatives. She remembers that Selden predicted she would come to hate herself. A craving for his love and forgiveness overcomes her: "If I told him everything, would he loathe me? Or would he pity me, and understand me, and save me from loathing myself?" (p. 175). Previous hesitations toward Selden vanish in the wake of her need.

For his part, Selden, aware of the rumors about Lily and Gus Trenor, tries to maintain his belief in Lily's integrity. He feels he understands her weakness, and he imagines carrying her "beyond" her current prison. But Selden knows himself well, for in the next moment he reflects that:

> It was pitiable that he, who knew the mixed motives on which social judgments depend, should still feel himself so swayed by them. How could he lift Lily to a freer vision of life if his own view of her was to be coloured by any mind in which he saw her reflected? (p. 167)

Selden's introspection is prophetic. He accidentally catches a glimpse of Lily leaving the Trenor home late at night. Jealous and disillusioned, he abandons her without giving her an opportunity to defend herself. This misunderstanding certainly has the impact of a missed or incorrect interpretation. Lily has not done what Selden suspects—"sold" herself to Gus sexually—and she could easily have restored his faith in her by telling him so. His appraisal of Lily's behavior is the misinterpretation that does not get corrected until, as in all tragic narrative, it is too late.

Monte Carlo and Norma Hatch

Selden's disillusionment and Lily's wounded pride drive them further apart as they withdraw more deeply into their own characterologically determined behaviors. We might note at this point that engagement is still strong, but mutual influence has floundered. Rather than drawing each other into a series of interactions that would help overcome inhibition, they both regress into old patterns. Selden becomes more than ever a detached spectator of life. No longer in love with Lily, he tells himself that it is her continued pursuit of shallow aims in the face of finer sensibilities that continues to alienate him from her. Lily, increasingly desperate, takes refuge in proud, reckless actions that deny the seriousness of her situation. These actions alternate with moments of painfully conflicted awareness of an inability to act in her own behalf—an inability that is, at heart, both guilty and masochistic.

Although Selden and Lily are now as far apart as they will ever be, they are far from indifferent to each other. In Monte Carlo, where Lily is sailing with the Dorsets, and some months later, when she becomes a social secretary to the wealthy but socially unacceptable Norma Hatch, Selden tries to warn her and rescue her from further social disaster; but his lack of belief in her disqualifies him as both friend and advisor, in her eyes. Feeling both misunderstood and abandoned, Lily's course becomes more fixed and solitary than ever. Bennett Simon describes as an integral part of tragedy the

process of people not being able to back down because they do not feel understood! The tragedy is that the other understands you just enough to lead to frustration and disappointment that he does not fully understand you, a state that further isolates and generates new missed understandings. (Simon, p. 431)

This is the situation between Lily and Selden in the later, painful months of her life as she drifts from the demimonde of Norma Hatch to the millinery establishment and then to unemployment, social isolation, and suicide.

Lily's Suicide

The last time Lily sees Lawrence Selden is on the night she dies. She has come to a morally difficult decision: she will confront Bertha Dorset with the letters Bertha has written Selden and use these as a means of rehabilitating herself in society. Lily has acquired these letters through an interesting set of circumstances. After the opening encounter of the novel, she is seen leaving Selden's apartment by Selden's charlady, who thinks Lily is the author of the letters. This woman has retrieved the letters from Selden's wastebasket; out of economic necessity she attempts to blackmail Lily with them. Lily purchases the letters to protect Selden but is unable to dispose of them. She does not consciously plan ever to use them. She keeps them, perhaps, as a talisman—a way of staying in contact with Selden. But, unconsciously they serve as a reminder that he is not the noble spirit she admires. They are a symbol of his corruptibility. Lily could use the threat of disclosing Bertha's affair with Selden to force her to clear Lily's name and stop her unscrupulous abuse. It has been difficult for Lily to consider this move because it involves an invasion of Selden's privacy, but she also realizes that the consequences for a man (in that society at that time) of an adulterous liaison are negligible compared to those for a woman. He will emerge intact. Furthermore, she finally reasons, her intent is not to blackmail, but to clear her name: "Call it blackmail and it becomes unthinkable; but explain that it injures no one and that the rights regained by it were unjustly forfeited, and he must be a formalist indeed who can find no pleas in its defence" (p. 311).

Lily leaves home, the letters in the bosom of her dress, determined to see Bertha, but once again a fatal ambivalence trips her up. She passes Selden's apartment on the way, and she remembers the tea they had together two years before: "The recollection loosened a throng of benumbed sensations, longings, regrets, imaginings, the throbbing brood of the only spring her heart had ever known." She is suddenly chilled with shame that "to attain her end, she must trade on his name and profit by a secret of his past" (p. 314). She has failed him, she feels, but nevertheless she must see him one more time. She goes up to his apartment.

Lily is now past considerations of propriety or the maintainence of a social facade. She must tell Selden what he has meant to her, that it is his influence that has kept her from becoming what people have thought her to be. Selden is sympathetic, but uncomfortable; he cannot meet Lily's passionate honesty halfway. "Such a situation can be saved only by an immediate outrush of feeling and on Selden's side the determining impulse was still lacking" (p. 318). Lily hardly notices this for she is caught up in her realization that she loves him, and that she wishes him to finally understand "that she had saved herself whole from the seeming ruin of her life" by knowing him. Now Lily realizes, in a flash of self-knowledge, that she cannot betray her values. She throws the letters into his fire, and takes her leave.

The sense of missed connections is strong in this meeting. Having found the strength to make the necessary sacrifices, Lily is now ready to meet Selden on his own terms, but his hesitancy dooms them. His is the dilemma of the obsessional; he does not know what he feels, and he cannot move spontaneously in response to another's needs and signals. When, by the next morning, he has found the courage to go to her, it is too late.

Lily has set her affairs in order. She has recently received her aunt's legacy and is able to pay Gus Trenor the money she owes him. Her debts discharged, she is now penniless. Lily does not consciously plan suicide. Unable to sleep, she has been using chloral hydrate for months; it has begun to lose its effect. She chances an increase in dosage, against which she has been warned, because of her desperate need for relief. Her thoughts that final night reveal a degree of self-knowledge that seems to come out of nowhere, but that has been developing gradually. It is no longer material poverty that she dreads. It is the clutch of solitude at her heart, the sense of being swept like a stray uprooted growth down the heedless current of the years. . . . And as she looked back she saw that there had never been a time when she had had any real relation to life. Her parents too had been rootless, blown hither and thither on every wind of fashion, without any personal existence to shelter them from its shifting gusts. She herself had grown up without any one spot of earth being dearer to her than another; there was no centre of early pieties, of grave endearing traditions, to which her heart could revert and from which it could draw strength for itself and tenderness for others. (p. 331)

Furthermore, Lily sees clearly that Selden has not had the strength either to see them through. Although that awareness does not ruin her love for him, it is the death of any hope for herself. She has achieved a tragic understanding; she cannot go back to her old values, and she sees no way into a better future.

THE PAST

Early in *The House of Mirth* Lily ponders her situation and wonders if it is "her own fault or that of destiny" that she has not achieved the security she craves. In a series of associations, Lily thinks about her childhood. A glimpse of her early family life allows us to develop a psychological picture of Lily—one which attempts to understand her actions as the function of unconscious conflicts and fantasies. This reading of the text is in no way an attempt to contradict Wharton's view of the social and economic forces that shape Lily's fate. Rather, it is an attempt to add the intrapsychic dimension. The material that leads to the development of this viewpoint is drawn from Wharton's own narrative. If we are to understand what goes wrong between Lily and Selden, we must first understand them individually.

Lily is the only child of ill-matched parents, an ambitious and greedy mother and a barely present father whose sole function in the family seems to be to provide the money that is so essential and that always seems to be in such short supply. Lily remembers her father as kindly, but always tired, returning home late from work, a shadowy figure whose early interest in poetry and whose aesthetic aspirations have been totally submerged by the need for financial prosperity. Her home environment is turbulent, her life an unsettling series of trips abroad and domestic social engagements, punctuated by the departure of disgruntled servants and the importunate demands of tradespeople and dressmakers.

Lily's mother is a self-centered and determined woman who lives for society and dreads more than anything the specter of dinginess and poverty. When Lily is nineteen, her father is financially ruined; he dies soon afterward. The cause of his death is left so vague we almost assume he has died because he has ceased to be of any interest to anyone now that he can no longer fulfill his function as provider. While Mrs.

Bart seems quite indifferent to her husband's fate, Lily is filled with pity and sadness. She and her mother are reduced to the genteel poverty her mother finds so unbearable. Mrs. Bart's only consolation is Lily's beauty: in the same maniacal and revengeful way that Miss Havisham brooded over Estella in *Great Expectations,* Mrs. Bart repeatedly tells Lily, "You'll get it all back, with your face!" Lily's beauty becomes an obsession to her mother:

> She studied it with a kind of passion, as though it were some weapon she had slowly fashioned for her vengeance. It was the last asset in their fortunes, the nucleus around which their life was to be rebuilt. She watched it jealously, as though it were her own property and Lily its mere custodian; and she tried to instil into the latter a sense of the responsibility that such a charge involved. (p. 37–38)

After two years of living in this impoverished way, Mrs. Bart dies "of a deep disgust," and Lily is adopted as a companion by her father's sister, Mrs. Peniston. When we first meet her, ten years later, she has not succeeded in using her beauty to "get it all back." As the plot develops, Lily, on the brink of success, undermines herself repeatedly. Even before Selden becomes an influence in her life, we learn how she has let every opportunity slip away. There are too many puzzling instances of her failure to behave in self-protective ways for "fate" alone to be a sufficient explanation.

Lily's inner situation involves a conflict of identifications. Whose daughter is she? While her father is described as a shadowy figure, Lily's unconscious attachment to him may be much stronger than she knows. She is quite interested in his poetic inclinations despite her mother's mockery of this side of his character. She wonders if in some way she takes after him. This more sensitive side of Lily, associated with her capacity to idealize and imagine, has been poorly nourished by those around her, but it survives to find its first recognition by Lawrence Selden. We may speculate that some of Lily's uneasiness with Selden stems from his "transference" meanings. Like her father, he is intellectual; there is a parallel between the leather-bound books in his study and the books in her father's bedroom that are packed off to auction after his death. And, like her father, Selden is only present episodically in her life. She never "sees enough of him," she feels he "avoids" her. To whom is this reproach really directed?

If one of Selden's central meanings to Lily is that of a forbidden Oedipal figure, this might account both for her romanticization of him and her tendency to dismiss him as a marital prospect. It would also explain her need to protect him, at great cost to herself, as a kind of belated expiation to a father she feels she has selfishly exploited and ultimately failed. Finally, to the degree that Selden is father-in-disguise, Lily longs for his approval, but does not really expect him to have the strength of character to rescue her. Her own father was helpless, in the face of her mother's possessiveness, to claim any substantial part of Lily's loyalties, or to introduce alternative values. Lily knows there is something better, but she does not really believe she can get to it. This unconscious belief represents both her identification with her father and a repetition of her relationship with him. He, like Selden, has failed her.

Consciously, Lily is identified with her mother; she thinks of herself as her mother's daughter. Why, then, can't she have that which her mother values and wishes her to have? Perhaps the answer lies partially in Lily's powerful unconscious sense of guilt toward her father. If Lily is successful in her quest for the money and position that are the only values that matter, at least to her mother, she does so, in a sense, over her father's dead body. She also betrays the inner values that she imagines he had, and in that way inflicts further suffering on him.

Lily's ambivalence about success, like most entrenched behaviors, is multiply determined. Besides her feelings about what success means vis-à-vis her father, it means a triumph over her mother, also. Lily would have what her mother did not have, and despite Mrs. Bart's explicit wishes that this come to pass, Lily may be deeply concerned about the envy and hatred that such a success would entail. Certainly in her contemporary relationships with women, she inspires considerable envy and malice. This may represent an unconsciously evoked repetition. For instance, Bertha Dorset has more than one feature in common with Lily's mother, and Bertha's husband, George, is, in Lily's eyes, badly exploited by a wife who uses him for money and position but is fundamentally callous about his welfare.

Lily's conflict is complex. If she were to realize her mother's wishes for her, she would be living out her life as mother's possession. Whatever deeply buried resentment Lily feels toward her mother, it has its outlet, in part, in Lily's refusal to allow herself to be an extension of her mother's ambitions. On the other hand, to die in poverty is an identification, in action, with her mother's fate.

Oedipal triumphs evoke guilt and fear as well as gratification, and for Lily a successful and happy marriage would certainly represent such a triumph. Given what she sees all around her, Lily has little reason to believe in happy marriages, but her failure to provide herself with the protection of *any* marriage is a function of her sense of guilt and of her conflicted identifications and loyalties.

Lily's self-images are also conflicted. There is a strong narcissistic component to her nature. She sees herself as better—more refined and sensitive—than those around her, as indeed she is in some ways. At the same time she feels weak, dependent, insecure, and lacking in moral fiber. Both these views of herself are the functional outcome of a deprived and essentially loveless childhood. For, while her father cared for her, he was unavailable to her. Her unconscious quest for his love may contribute to her dependence on and involvement with another older man, Gus Trenor.

Lily's mother, as we have previously noted, treats Lily like a possession, an extension of herself and her own needs. She pets and spoils her, enhancing Lily's sense of specialness. Mrs. Bart contributes substantially to Lily's feeling that money and the power it bestows are all that *really* matters. Lily's ideals are in conflict with this belief. While she longs to belong to Selden's "republic of the spirit," she is frightened and clings to money as the only security she understands. (In this sense, Selden's doubts about her have some basis in reality.) Lily's moving introspection, on the night of her suicide, about solitude and rootlessness, reveals her ultimate insight into the substitutive nature of her craving for wealth.

We know much less about Lawrence Selden, but Wharton gives us some biographical material. Selden does not plan to marry. "He had meant to keep from permanent ties, not from any poverty of feeling but because, in a different way, he was as much as Lily the victim of his environment" (p. 160). By environment, in this instance, Wharton must be including his intrapsychic situation. Selden is not interested in a "nice" girl; for him this means boredom. It "had been Selden's fate to have a charming mother." No woman can quite live up to her standard. His parents never let financial pressures interfere with their discriminating tastes. Rather than sacrifice standards, they did without. Their style was that of "abstinence . . . combined with elegance in a way exemplified by Mrs. Selden's knack of wearing her old velvet as if it were new" (p. 161). In a passage that gives us an exact reading of where Selden stands in relation to sentimental attachments, the author tells us

his views of womankind in especial were tinged by the remembrance of the one woman who had given him his sense of "values." It was from her that he inherited his detachment from the sumptuary side of life: the stoic's carelessness of material things, combined with the epicurean's pleasure in them. Life shorn of either feeling appeared in him a diminished thing and nowhere was the blending of the two ingredients so essential as in the character of a pretty woman. (p. 161)

For Lily, Selden's comparison of every woman with his mother creates two difficulties. She cannot live up to his demand that she be both elegant and poor; she has not had his early training in this difficult balancing act. But more crucially, since Lily is, like Selden's mother, charming and refined, these qualities both attract and frighten him. If Selden is an Oedipally charged figure for Lily, she is certainly such a figure for him. He dances around her like a moth near a flame. He cannot leave her alone, yet he cannot claim her. He uses a lot of internal energy obsessing over her worth. His concern with vague and unsubstantiated rumors of her sexual transgressions with a married man may be understood as a way of processing Oedipal anxiety about a forbidden object. When, late at night, from the shadows of a Fifth Avenue street corner, Selden sees Lily leave Trenor's house, with Gus looming in the background, the unconscious meanings of this scene are powerful to him. Lily's actual innocence has little chance in the face of so graphic a "primal scene" image.[6]

However, the fact that relationships have Oedipal meanings does not necessarily stop their progress—quite the contrary, sometimes. Elizabeth Bennet and Macon Leary are both highly ambivalent about potential marital attachments; Fitzwilliam Darcy and Muriel Pritchett are strongly tinged with Oedipal significance for their respective partners, but this does not lead to stalemate in their relationships. The difference here is that Selden and Lily cannot get *beyond* their Oedipal meanings to each other. They never come to see each other in the more realistic and pedestrian way that would allow them to be partners in dealing with the difficulties and compromises of life.

As Selden watches Lily in the tableau vivant, he idealizes her beauty as he did his mother's; he admires her as one would a valued possession. As he muses on losing his sense of "the touch of poetry in her beauty" when he is not with her, he reveals that she remains a romanticized and unreal figure to him. And when Lily says to Selden, "love me, but don't tell me so," she does more than avoid her own feelings. She may be conveying another crucial message: "Don't admire me as a beautiful object; show me that you love and understand *me*." However, while Lily wants to be real to Selden, she does not want to relinquish her romanticization of him, or of the larger "grown-up" world of wealth, which she sees from a child's-eye view as dazzling and desirable. Unconsciously, she still wants a rich Prince Charming, the idealized and powerful father of childhood.

THE FAILED CASE

Explanation of the "failed case" necessitates a look beyond individual psyches to the interpersonal level of process. In previous chapters we have seen that both participants in a relationship are potentially changed as the relationship develops. More often, one fits the role of sufferer from conflict, or "patient," and the other the role of "therapist," one less or no longer as conflicted, one who is in a position to help. Simon Camish, Macon Leary, and Mary Lennox could be identified as "patients," while their counterparts, Rose Vassiliou, Muriel Pritchett, and Dickon Sowerby could be seen as therapists. In *Jane Eyre* and *Pride and Prejudice* the influence seems more mutual, although one character is more central to the narrative. In *The House of Mirth* both characters affect each other deeply, but it is Lily who looks to Selden for understanding and help as a patient would to a therapist.

Selden, as a therapeutic figure, fails Lily. He does not believe in her: he does not think her sincere nor does he trust her integrity. Furthermore, he is not convinced she can change. He cannot say of Lily (as Muriel can of Macon) that no matter how paralyzed and anxious she seems, she has the potential to work through her conflicts and move on to new behaviors and solutions. Selden develops a tenuous confidence in Lily, only to relinquish it time after time. In each of their encounters he reaches out a lukewarm hand and pulls it back quickly when it is not eagerly grasped.

We might explain his behavior, in part, as a failure to overcome his "countertransference." He believes untrue rumors. He sees Lily, preconsciously and sometimes consciously, as a sexually amoral woman who gives to others favors he would like for himself. Selden is a man of the world, neither naive nor lacking in the capacity for subtle distinctions. The fact that he so easily believes of Lily what his personal knowledge of her tells him is unlikely to be true points to other origins for his fantasies about her. These fantasies may stem from Selden's internal relationship with his mother. Underneath his admiration and attachment to this "charming" woman, there is, perhaps, a sense of rage and betrayal at having to give her up. Why else is he so fascinated with Lily's social maneuvers and so obsessed with rumors about her that involve successful older men, like Gus Trenor and Sim Rosedale? He is always watching her, and he interprets what he sees out of his own unconscious expectations.

For Lily, Selden's lack of belief makes a positive outcome impossible. Throughout the novel, in the form of comments by Lily's friend, Gerty Farish, and in Lily's own musings, her need for someone who believes her able to become a better person is emphasized. After all, Lily has few inner alternatives of her own, only the thread of a weak paternal identification to carry her through. An encounter late in the novel with Nellie Struthers—a working class woman who has "fallen" and through the love of a good man has been able to put her life together—highlights Lily's realization that if Selden had believed in her, she too might have been able to save herself.

As a mentor Selden has another serious flaw: he is not really true to his own principles. He talks of the "republic of the spirit" but is continually seduced by "la dolce vita." He haunts a society he pretends to despise, and he pursues a very different standard of sexual behavior from the one he expects of Lily. While his behavior is part of the double standard acceptable at that time, not every young man of his set has affairs with married women. If Selden cannot rise above the average standard of integrity expected in his class, how can he expect this of Lily, and how can she really trust him? He lacks that sense of conviction of what is right that is so important to Simon Camish in *Rose*, or to Mary Lennox in *Dickon*.

Furthermore, Selden does not want to change who he is. He values his own position as cool, amused spectator. He may long for passion, but he does little in the pursuit of it. He stands apart, fastidious, and ultimately judgmental. Darcy was also snobbish and fastidious, but able through his love for Elizabeth to modify his pride. At the very end of the novel Selden can look honestly at his own weakness and excessive concern with propriety, at his essential narrow-mindedness, but for Lily his insight has come too late.

Lily's contribution to the failure of their relationship is driven by guilt and her unconscious need for punishment. She is driven by these dynamics long before she meets Selden. Despite them, she is powerfully motivated to seek her salvation through him. In fact, her very fascination with him is double edged. He represents a potential agent of growth and change, but her intercourse with him is ultimately imprudent, the original source of Bertha Dorset's vendetta against her.

One of the most puzzling aspects of Lily's behavior is her failure to clear her name with Selden. Despite social customs that prohibit frank discourse between men and women. Lily and Selden reach a degree of intimacy, particularly in the final scenes, where she might have said to him, "I have committed an indiscretion, unwittingly, but I will make it right. I am worthy of your trust." Her own fear that she lacks moral conviction may be a factor in Lily's reticence. She does not believe in herself. Fearing that when she receives her aunt's legacy, she will put off paying Trenor, she writes the check immediately, leaving herself destitute. Why couldn't she have paid Trenor part of what she owed him, as an act of good faith? This kind of question—why can't Lily do something just a little bit different, since it would take so little for her to save herself—points to Lily's unconscious guilt. Something about her situation suggests an analogy with the "negative therapeutic reaction"—patients who get worse, rather than better, after each step of effective therapeutic work.[7] Unconscious guilt makes Lily undo or ruin opportunities. She destroys her chances to marry Gryce by walking with Selden at Bellomont, and she destroys her chances to marry Selden by becoming anxious about being with him. She holds off Selden's ardor after the tableau vivant, and then she "lets" him see her with Gus Trenor.

It is the consistency and the unremitting quality of Lily's self-defeat that suggest underlying guilt and allow comparisons with a process as powerful as the negative therapeutic reaction. Many therapists view the latter as an impossible barrier to therapeutic progress. If we couple Lily's unconscious self-punishment with Selden's anxious ambivalence, we have a process that is undermined, albeit unconsciously, by both parties. Their urge to engage is present; powerful transferences are in place, but unconscious conflict leads to misunderstandings (incorrect interpretations) that drive both protagonists to take refuge in characterological positions that are ultimately unyielding.

The analogy with the negative therapeutic reaction bears a closer look in terms of Selden's role. Lily's unconscious guilt may be a powerful barrier to change, but she never withdraws from Selden in any final sense. The night of her suicide she is open to him and to the love that he might offer. We might say that this is because she has already unconsciously decided on suicide and has nothing to lose, but she is, in fact, still hopeful and available. Selden "knows," at least unconsciously, what she needs, and he denies her repeatedly. His failure is motivated by something more powerful than anxiety and obsessive ambivalence. No matter how well he rationalizes his witholding from Lily, it is essentially aggressive, even sadistic, at its core. We may speculate that Selden is driven by unconscious fantasies of revenge against a beautiful and charming mother, who has chained him to her in a fantasy attachment, a bond that denies him the possibility of satisfaction with any other woman. His relationship with Lily, then, is not merely the result of flight and missed connections, but an active reenactment of seduction and revenge. In this sense it must be gratifying to Selden, and because of this gratification, his more libidinal and altruistic strivings cannot prevail.

The negative therapeutic reaction, seen clinically, is usually explained on the basis of intrapsychic factors—unconscious guilt and masochism in the patient. However, patients often evoke the latent sadism of the therapist through their repeated frustrations of helpful efforts. When this happens, the patient's sadism interacts with that of the therapist leading to repetitive sadomasochistic enactments that end in deadlock. In the core ambivalence that characterizes all human relationships, libido must neutralize aggression to allow a positive outcome. When this does not happen, we have a failed case in therapy and a tragedy in literature.

We return now to our earlier question concerning the conditions in successful "literary cases" that are missing in our "failed case." This issue will be addressed more thoroughly in Chapter 11, but, in a preliminary way, we may anticipate certain observations. In several of our successful cases (*Pride and Prejudice; Jane Eyre; The Needle's Eye;* and *The Accidental Tourist*) the "therapist" figure's belief in the "patient" figure's capacity for development and transformation is central. This belief is usually unconscious; it is, at any rate, never specifically articulated in the text, but it is reflected in the behavior of the believing character. Darcy, Rochester, Muriel Pritchett, and Rose Vassiliou are not discouraged or driven away by vacillation, regression, or ambivalence in their counterparts. Moreover, they show great persistence in their willingness to maintain the relationship in the face of outright rejection. They never counter with withdrawal or revenge. Contrast this to Selden's tentative approaches and rapid departures in response to Lily's anxious uncertainty. Finally, note that the integrity of the therapist figure's belief in who they are and what they are doing is unshakeable (cf. Dickon in *The Secret Garden* and Rose in *The Needle's Eye*) and this provides the other with an idealized identificatory model and a positive direction in which to move. Lily badly needs Selden's integrity and belief in her and on both counts he cannot maintain a consistent presence.

The relationship between Lily Bart and Lawrence Selden is not a failure because the novel does not have a happy ending. Several of our successful cases—*The Magus* and *The Needle's Eye*, for instance—do not have conventional happy endings. Lily and Selden represent a "failed case" because they do not enable each other to make different choices or to implement the compromises these choices would entail. It is not that they lack alternative courses of action, but that these alternatives do not really appeal. In this chapter we have attempted to explain the intrapsychic situations within the characters that prevent such alternatives from being viable, as well as the interpersonal factors that prevent them from helping each other past their intrapsychic difficulties.

11

CONCLUSION:
WE READ, WE
WRITE, WE TALK TO HEAL

The premise of this book is that we are fascinated by the possibilities of personal growth and transformation, by the possibility of being healed. As therapists, we are interested in psychological change that takes place through relationships with others, and this interest has led us to examine a type of novel in which this is a central theme. Our discovery that some of the most enduring novels in our culture contain such themes suggests that readers find these ideas appealing. People read, in part, because of their interest in how others, including fictional characters, solve problems and get better.

In the sense that reading expands our emotional and intellectual horizons, it is both a healing and a creative experience. Since we read a novel over time, we can control the pace of our reading and the emotional processing of its contents. We can stop, if the material is too exciting; we can re-read, ponder, skip ahead. By writing to Elizabeth, rather than speaking to her in person, Darcy allowed her to process the emotional impact of his revelations over time, as we do when we read. The novel, unlike drama, is under our control—much like the comforting teddy bear or "blanky" of early childhood. Reading takes place in a space somewhere between inner and outer reality, a transitional space, in which, as we identify with characters, we dream, we fantasize, and we problem-solve.[1]

In psychotherapy and psychoanalysis *we talk* to heal. An aspect of the therapeutic experience that connects it with reading and writing is its creative potential. For many patients, treatment may be the most creative enterprise they have ever undertaken, and this experience may further open them up to creativity. The ability to become more creative in treatment (and outside of it) is usually attributed to a variety of overlapping factors: an increased capacity for sublimation due to decreased conflict; modified superego pressures; increased ego strength; identification with the analyst's willingness to question and explore new territory; and insight into the nature of exhibitionistic tensions. In treatment, a patient gradually learns to understand the factors that lead to concealment and inhibition. As these tensions become modified, the patient produces a more honest and revealing story with the therapist. This creative endeavor may lead to others, as a patient discovers and explores capacities that were previously inhibited out of shame or guilt.

A professional woman in her forties entered analysis depressed and in conflict about her work. Analytic work led to a recognition of intense ambitious strivings (which had been partially inhibited and warded off from full conscious recognition) and considerable unconscious envy of those less conflicted and therefore more successful. In particular, the patient denied her own creative wishes and potential, especially in the area of writing. In the transference she envied and feared the analyst, as she had her own father. She was worried that any writing on her part would threaten the analyst, and invoke his criticism and scorn. Her father (also a writer) had encouraged her professional ambitions, but was also a master of subtle but devastating devaluations of her accomplishments. The whole area was so loaded with the potential for humiliation that the patient avoided all reference to the analyst's writings—of which she was well aware— and continued to protest that she, herself, had no wish to write. Finally, the analyst, in an uncharacteristic deviation from analytic technique, gave the patient a copy of a book he had written. He refused to elaborate on why he had done so, and withstood with admirable fortitude the patient's retaliative scorn and criticism about his "breaking the analytic frame." The patient did not understand the analyst's action, but she was soon able to begin writing, with enjoyment and success. Only later did she come to understand the analyst's gift of the book as a highly facilitative gesture, one in which he took the risk of exposing his narcissism to her, through exposing his writing, and at the same time he invited her to join the inner sanctum of writers, which, to this patient, had previously felt forbidden and dangerous. Wisely, this analyst refused to comment on those pieces of her writing that the patient showed him (although he did accept and read them). The patient was able to understand and tolerate his refusal to enter into a reenactment with her (by offering criticism as her father would have done), and she came to feel that her writing was hers alone, not dependent on either analysis or the analyst's approval for its survival.

We read in search of healing, we talk to heal ourselves, and some people write as a healing endeavor. Many people use diaries and personal journals, which may never be seen by anyone else's eyes, to unburden themselves and explore their inner lives, but professional writers, too, seem to be working something out. For instance, the works of Charles Dickens, almost without exception, contain the theme of child abuse, of the innocent young and their sufferings at the hands of the adult world. Dickens himself suffered a severe narcissistic wound in early adolescence when his father and the rest of his family went to debtor's prison and he was sent to work in a blacking factory.[2] He was torn away from his academic studies and from a beloved schoolmaster who had recognized and encouraged his considerable gifts. What, apparently, was most galling to young Dickens was that even after his father was able to leave the debtor's prison, his mother showed no interest in Charles resuming his studies, but was content to have him continue contributing to the family income in this menial way. Dickens gets his revenge by writing over and over about social institutions that exploit children and about silly, unfeeling women. As is often the case with an aggressive solution to a past injury, Dickens's revenge is only temporarily satisfying. He uses his writing to ventilate, and, while the writing gets better and better, his need for ventilation continues.

On the other hand, Margaret Drabble is a writer who seems to have worked something out in her novels. Her early works deal with young, relatively undeveloped women struggling with sexuality, marriage, and motherhood. Her middle novels, of which *The Needle's Eye* is one, deal with more complex heroines and their attempts to lead more self-expressive lives. These women become increasingly less masochistic and more fully actualized as her work continues. Rose Vassiliou is still caught in the toils of guilt and self-deprivation, but Frances Wingate and Kate Armstrong (the heroines of *The Realms of Gold* and *The Middle Ground*, Drabble's next two novels) are women with enviable capacities for self-assertion and personal satisfaction. Drabble then moves on to write a different kind of novel, one more concerned with social patterns and institutions than with individual development. In a letter to us on this question,[3] Drabble writes:

> Yes, I certainly do see the writing of novels as part of a process of discovery and self discovery which may well be (one hopes will be) therapeutic. And once that self is discovered, or accommodated, or accepted, then that particular search can be considered completed. And I do think this is what happened in my own work. I am more interested in making connections, perceiving general patterns, observing larger shapes.

That is, having written a series of novels with a progression of solutions to certain psychological problems, Drabble was ready to move on to another style, one which is more panoramic and describes the interweaving of many characters and social issues.

Storytelling and listening to stories are compelling activities from childhood onward. In telling our experiences, and in hearing those of others, we have opportunities to broaden the range of inner possibilities. In novels about change the reader can experience, through one or more characters, the way in which a relationship can enable these new directions.

THE PROCESS OF CHANGE

Our particular interest is in how people reach new levels of integration through the agency of an important new relationship. We have explored eight novels where there has been a successful transformative process and one where this process has failed. In each case we have reviewed the plot of the novel, discussed unique features of the process of cure it depicts, compared this process to certain aspects of the psychotherapeutic or psychoanalytic experience, and reframed the process along the lines of our therapeutic narrative.

We would now like to review this framework and reemphasize its value in comparing material from different sources. This narrative describes what we feel to be the therapeutic "plot" of many novels and many situations of psychological change that involve more than one person. We will discuss how the narrative works in different novels, with particular emphasis on common features. Finally, we will review and discuss some emotional factors that we feel are the central underpinnings of the ability to change and discuss some of the fantasies with which these emotional factors connect.

In Chapter 1 we proposed our therapeutic narrative, containing three critical elements as a scaffolding for examining the process of psychological change: *engagement, mutual influence,* and *directionality.* The advantage of such a general model is that it does not depend on any particular clinical theory (although it contains clear analogs to clinical elements) and therefore it can be used to examine the process of change in many different kinds of situations—life, literature, and therapy. We have confined ourselves to the last two of these. *Engagement* requires that the participants to change have powerful internal motivations that become activated by the agent of change. This *implies* some sort of readiness and the capacity to become involved with another person. In a clinical setting we would call this the capacity to develop the kind of relatedness necessary to form an alliance between therapist and patient. *Mutual influence* requires that the two parties develop patterns of interaction that propel a continuing sequence of events with emotional significance to both, although the impact is probably greater on the one who is the sufferer or "patient." The clinical analogy here would be the process of working through of conflict based on an understanding—leading to insight—of transferences and resistances. *Directionality* specifies that the nature of influence is such that the "patient's" experience will facilitate internal shifts in a constructive direction. We have postulated that the positive direction of change occurs because the "patient" experiences the "therapist" to a considerable extent as representing and enacting qualities of the patient's ego ideal. That is, the sufferer moves from attraction to *qualities* of the helper that are idealized and desired, to an internalization of more abstract qualities—from the wish to be close to a good person to the desire to be good oneself.

Engagement

If we apply this therapeutic narrative to the process of change in these nine novels, what common elements and what unique features do we find? An overview of the engagement part of the change process could be summarized as follows: A problem exists, a disequilibrium occurs, a meeting takes place, unconscious transferences are activated, and involvement results. In every one of our literary cases, this series of events occurs.

The kind of problems our protagonists face fall into four overlapping categories: developmental, characterological, neurotic, and traumatic. For example, Elizabeth Bennet, Jane Eyre, Mary Lennox, Nicholas Urfe, and Lily Bart are stalled in their development—in the undertaking of life's next task, latency, marriage, or heterosexual intimacy. Part of their difficulty, however, is characterological and neurotic. Elizabeth, Nicholas, and Mary have well-developed narcissistic defenses that promote isolation and prevent intimacy. Jane Eyre's vigilant superego and need for autonomy keep her apart from Rochester when circumstances become problematic. Macon Leary and Silas Marner suffer from the trauma of loss and disappointment in others, but their maladaptive solutions are created by obsessional defenses that in themselves block recovery. Simon Camish suffers primarily from neurotic guilt. So does Lily Bart, although her guilt is much more crippling. In other words, all the problems our characters face fall into these four categories, but not in simple, clear-cut ways. As with formal diagnostic categories in clinical work, the label never describes the whole patient, the real person behind the label.

The existence of a problem does not lead to change. Something must happen to throw the sufferer off balance. If his gold had not been stolen, Silas Marner would have been gazing at it still. If Darcy had not appeared at the Netherfield ball to insult Elizabeth, her sardonic wit might have allowed her to live a life of protected spinsterhood. In some way, a problematic behavior or defense must become less viable as a solution. In our literary examples, one or more things happen to produce this situation. Either the sufferer comes to the end of his or her rope, as do Simon Camish and Macon Leary, or a traumatic event occurs that throws a previous adaptation off balance, e.g., the cholera epidemic in The Secret Garden. Then the disequilibrium must be followed by or coupled with a meeting with the new person who will function therapeutically for the sufferer. The theft of his gold throws Silas's adaptation by withdrawal into disarray, and the entrance of Eppie into his life provides the opportunity for a relationship that will be the means of his recovery. Simon's meeting with Rose, at a time of emotional desperation, starts a process going inside of him. Macon's old separation wounds from childhood are reopened by the loss of his son, but his characterological rigidities preclude his having the emotional wherewithal to work this out until he becomes involved with Muriel.

Disequilibrium and a meeting are interwoven events.

These literary meetings, seemingly so different from novel to novel, all contain three elements. First, there must be a "fit" between the characters that draws them together. The fit may be one of similarity, a having-in-common that gives people a sense of immediate recognition, or it may be a complementarity—seeing in the other a feature one would like in oneself. In the best drawn cases—Elizabeth and Darcy, for example—both are present. Elizabeth and Darcy share the love of a sister, and certain standards of intellectual, social, and moral worthiness. But Darcy admires Elizabeth's outspokenness, which contrasts with his reticence. Rose and Simon share similar self-depriving but highly moral ideals and the experience of having hated their childhood homes. Lily Bart and Lawrence Selden are alike in their uneasy ambivalence toward high society. On the other hand, Nicholas is drawn by Alison's Australian down-to-earth qualities because they are different from his English upper-middle-class ways, just as Macon is intrigued by Muriel's adventurousness and her imperviousness to the niceties of middle-class propriety.

Secondly, the appeal of the therapist-figure is enhanced by some kind of valued status, sometimes based on the sufferer's admiration of the therapist's ideals and behavior, sometimes on the therapist's perceived power. The most striking example of the latter is Conchis's power, as perceived by Nicholas. Such power appears in other novels, too. Simon Camish, Jane Eyre, and Elizabeth Bennet are all aware of the high social status of their counterparts. In part, sufferers engage with therapeutic figures because the latter have something they want, something they hope to achieve for themselves through possession, emulation, or identification. While this status is represented in some novels as social position or power, what is compelling for the sufferer is that these are evidences of desired psychological capacities.

A third and most important factor in engagement is its transference meaning. Two people who are to have such a powerful influence on one another must have, or develop rapidly, meanings that have to do with important persons, wishes, or motives from the past. We know this is so in all kinds of clinical therapeutic situations, and we find it unfailingly in our literary examples. The objection could be raised that we assume it will be there (again based on a priori theory), and narratives, being open to many readings, then yield up transference meanings. This is in some sense true—transference is such a ubiquitous phenomenon it is bound to be found anywhere we look—but it is also worth noting how frequently authors include specific biographical material, often immaterial to the plot, but enriching to an understanding of the "origin" of these transferences. Authorial intent may be shrouded in mystery, but these novelists make the discovery of therapeutic encounters very accessible by their understanding of the connections between past experience and present motivations.

Another way of conceptualizing the inevitability of transference meanings in human interactions is to point out that transference is our way of *remembering* our relational past. The transference meanings of one person to another have much to do with having things in common and with perceived status, so once again all three factors overlap. The result is a situation of intense involvement, loaded with transference perceptions and wishes on both sides. It has to go somewhere, and this brings us to *mutual influence.*

Mutual Influence

The parties to change become involved in a series of meetings and encounters that have several consistent characteristics: they take place over some time; they occur within some mutually acceptable framework, with its own rules about procedure and the management of certain issues—status, expression of affection, and resolution of conflict; they proceed by way of progressive destabilizations and new equilibriums that move in the direction of permanent change. The progressive and incremental quality of these shifts provides much of the drama of the novels.

All our literary case studies take place over time. We are not dealing with "road to Damascus" transformations. The time frame in these novels falls between six months (*The Secret Garden*), where the action takes place from winter through the following spring—to two years (*The House of Mirth*). The action of the other stories takes place within the space of about one year. More crucial than the *actual* time is the sense of significant and repetitive events occurring over time. Our characters interact, introspect, progress, and regress, as patients do in therapy.

In the therapeutic setting, the expectation of continued meetings is built into the treatment contract; the nature of the interactions that will take place is gradually established as well. Patients learn that in this setting things can (and should) be said that cannot (and should not) be said elsewhere. The "rules" of therapy set up a strange and disquieting imbalance, but one that gradually makes sense to both patient and therapist. Our literary couples must establish their own set of rules. This usually involves a rationalization for continued meetings and an unspoken set of agreements about the sort of behavior that is appropriate, including what will be talked about. Naturally, these agreements must revolve around issues of importance to both parties. In *The Needle's Eye*, initial meetings between Simon and Rose are justified for Simon to advise Rose about her custody suit. This is how they rationalize their desire to be together and to talk about what is most on their minds. Macon Leary and Muriel Pritchett meet, at least initially, to train Edward, an excuse that will lead to the later retraining of Macon. The meetings of Darcy and Elizabeth, and of Lily

Bart and Lawrence Selden are facilitated by the rules of etiquette and courtship in their particular social milieus. Mary and Dickon meet to play—the permitted social intercourse of childhood—and Jane Eyre and Rochester meet as employer and governess, the only way they *can* meet, at first.

The initial reason for meeting gradually changes and opens up. Rose and Simon become central figures in each other's inner lives; Muriel and Macon become lovers; Jane and Rochester cross the boundaries and restrictions dictated by their social roles. Gradually, they all transcend the rationalized excuses of their continued meetings to become enduringly important to each other. In these literary examples, characters begin with certain rules of what can and cannot be said and gradually expand their areas of discourse to achieve greater intimacy, sometimes by saying the previously unsayable, e.g., Nicholas's final declaration of love and need to Alison. The analogy in therapy is that the process becomes sufficiently powerful and meaningful that it impels the patient to break out of his or her internal rules to voice feelings and attitudes that have been suppressed.

The process of mutual influence, then, occurs over time and depends on an initial set of rules and conventions that permit interactions to occur, but the process ultimately involves the development of an understanding that is truer to inner realities. This happens, as we have previously pointed out, through a series of destabilizing encounters (creating, in Meredith Skura's words, "surprise and self-consciousness") during which change and regression alternate. Destabilization may lead to new behaviors, or to the reinforcing of old defensive patterns, or to both.

Let us review how this works in one of our literary case studies— *The Needle's Eye.* Simon is surprised and disquieted at his wish to be seated next to Rose at dinner. To regain psychological balance he reinstitutes old defenses. He becomes critical of Rose, both at the dinner party and, later, at her home. At the same time, he is continuing to have what, for him, is a meaningful and gratifying conversation with her. Rose's withdrawal in reaction to Simon's defensively motivated criticism distresses him, and leads him to move toward her again, more actively. Her reaction serves as an interpretation to Simon of the aggressive, destructive, and isolating effect of his behavior. He is sufficiently desirous of maintaining the new relationship that he changes his external behavior, and begins to question its internal basis.

Simon creates an occasion to see Rose again (by taking her legal papers), while he tells himself that her behavior in giving him those papers was highly imprudent. Wish (to see Rose) and defense (criticism of Rose) lead Simon to a new position, a compromise. He will suspend his general mistrust of women and their motives enough to allow a relationship to develop with Rose, but he will delude himself about the nature of that relationship. He is not attracted to her—he is helping her. As he comes to trust her more and to know himself better, he will become more honest about his feelings toward her. Then he will require a new compromise. Since a sexual relationship with Rose would make Simon too guilty and anxious, he will relinquish that particular wish and settle instead for a friendship that involves the sharing of ideals. This sharing of ideals, in turn, is important to him; he is not settling for second best. To achieve this compromise, Simon must test Rose's goodwill and reliability over and over. As we described in Chapter 4, Simon moves closer and draws away; as he does so, he begins to understand what it is he is doing.

This is an example of what we mean when we talk about a series of destabilizing experiences occurring around central issues of importance to the patient and leading to a new equilibrium, one which involves change. We have focused on this kind of back-and-forth struggle in all of our literary cases and compared it to the process of working through in psychotherapy. There, we talk about the emergence of transference feelings toward the therapist leading to resistance that, when interpreted, or spontaneously seen by the patient, leads to insight and intrapsychic change. Simon's feelings toward Rose are highly colored by her transference meanings to him—Drabble spells this out for us when she has Simon wonder several times why he thinks about his mother and Rose at the same time—and his criticism and withdrawal are his form of resistance to further intimacy with her and insight into himself. In Simon's case, insight is a function of his own emotional reactions and later introspection. Rose never tells him he is mistrustful; he figures this out himself. Because Rose is important to him, he is willing to suspend, and ultimately modify, that mistrust.

A clinical example describes how mutual influence works in psychotherapy.

A patient in his early thirties entered psychotherapy to work on his difficulties with assertion and with achieving his creative goals. He had been raised by parents who were highly controlling and very critical of his every statement and action, but at the same time extremely sensitive to anything they perceived as criticism or negativity directed toward themselves. The patient developed an interpersonal style characterized by compliance and placation of others; beneath this he was chafing with unexpressed impulses, thoughts, and angry feelings. He was used to having his every motive viewed with suspicion and disbelief.

In treatment, a situation gradually developed in which the patient experienced all interventions as critical, even though he frequently reassured the therapist that he knew her comments were not meant this way. His reassurances stemmed from a transference-based perception of the therapist as sensitive and quick to misunderstand. The patient had a hard time trusting that the therapist's motives in establishing the therapeutic contract and doing the interpretive work of treatment were in his, the patient's, interest.

The major work of the therapy revolved around this issue as the patient came gradually to trust the therapist, and to realize how his *own* deep mistrust and anger inhibited his own relationships, particularly with women, and his creativity. This was, in part, facilitated by a change in the therapist who came to realize her usual active and questioning style as particularly upsetting to *this* patient who had so much difficulty crediting his own observations and fantasies. The therapist backed away enough to leave the patient room to explore, but not so much that the patient felt rejected. (Silence also had critical meanings to this patient.)

Adjustments in professional style—style itself is a reflection of the therapist's character—in response to an individual patient's need may be one of the major ways that therapists enact their part of mutual influence. Change in fiction and psychotherapeutic change involve hard work. The initial excitement of engagement—what we sometimes call the "honeymoon period" of psychoanalysis or psychotherapy—is followed by the arduous negotiations of the period of mutual influence.

Directionality

Directionality is where mutual influence is headed. Change must go somewhere; different attitudes, emotions, and behaviors must become manifest. We enter a relationship, including the therapy relationship, with the hope that it will make us more content, and more effective, that its outcome will be positive for us. Do we ever make a major life change without the *hope* that it will be for the better?

Who determines the direction in which a process is to go—the therapist or the patient? Or, are they both involved—in which case the development of directionality may be part of the negotiations of mutual influence? In the actual therapy situation (and in novels) these permutations all occur. The patient may enter therapy with a goal for change on which both therapist and patient essentially agree.

A woman in her mid-twenties entered therapy to understand and modify her difficulties establishing a satisfactory relationship with a man. Although her views of herself, and of men, underwent considerable change in the process, her original goal, to understand and modify, remained the same throughout. The therapist concurred with this goal in the sense that she came to see that the patient's major troubling fantasies and interpersonal difficulties were initially expressed in her relationships with men. These fantasies (of being shamed and emotionally tortured) gradually emerged in the transference where they could be experienced, observed, understood, and modified. Eventually, this led to broader and more salutary changes in all of the patient's relationships.

However, this concurrency of direction is not the usual situation in therapy. More often, patients come to treatment with goals that unconsciously include the perpetuation of some childhood wish or fantasy. The patient wishes to be gratified and supported, even empowered, in the maintainance of certain defenses and the fulfillment of certain wishes. In some cases, the therapist's goals are quite opposite to those of the patient, and the work of therapy may largely involve the patient's coming to see the unrealistic, or even dangerous, nature of his or her goals. This is often the case with court-ordered treatments, and in the treatment of impulsive adolescents, but it also occurs, in more subtle forms, in the treatment of some well-motivated adults.

The most common situation, however, is one in which patients enter treatment with a sense of subjective distress and a need for change, but with their sense of what direction this change should take clouded by unconscious distortions in their views of themselves and others. Here, the directionality of the process gradually emerges, as therapist and patient come to understand more of the patient's history, feelings, and motivations. The therapist recognizes that the patient is in trouble and that there are more as well as less adaptive ways to move out of this trouble, but the therapist does not try to determine the direction the patient will finally choose. Rather, the therapist's goal is to enable the patient to discover and implement his or her own goals. This is, in part, what we mean when we speak of the analytic attitude: the therapist attempts to maintain an interested, nonjudgmental, noninter-fering stance in order to allow the patient's own story, with its own direction, to evolve. The therapist's goal, in a sense, is to maintain the *therapeutic* goal, that of increasing understanding, of analyzing motive and behavior, of not being derailed by attempts to reenact, retaliate, or destroy the therapeutic process.

However, the careful maintenance of an analytic attitude does not prevent therapy from having a certain tilt when it comes to the issue of directionality. For, as we have seen repeatedly in our literary cases, the patient admires the therapist because the latter is seen as a reflection of elements of the patient's ideal self. The therapist repre-sents that which the patient would like to emulate. Put another way, the patient sees the therapist as having attitudes and strengths that he or she would like to have.

A patient whose development had led to her valuing aggression and power over tenderness and closeness initially experienced her therapist's efforts to understand her as attacks. Gradually, by restraining the frequency of his comments, and letting the patient do the bulk of the therapeutic work, the therapist was able to get across his conviction that understanding was valuable in itself. The patient came ruefully to put it, "Well, you would say try to figure out what I'm doing, don't just lash out." The "neutral" position of the therapist became a directional pull for this patient, away from hurting (and inevitable unconscious guilt), towards caring (in the form of understanding and being understood).

In our literary case studies, directionality is established in the same ways as in therapeutic situations: it develops as the process of mutual influence progresses. For instance, in *The Secret Garden*, Mary Lennox has a wish to grow up and to be loved, but her goals are hampered by her wish to retain the gratification of getting her own way. The directionality of the changes she undergoes is provided by her admiration for others—Dickon, in particular. She wishes to be like him, but at first it is a wish for his powers and skills, an extension of having her own way. Gradually, she comes to emulate his considerate treatment of others and his capacity for cooperation. Her goals develop out of the process she undergoes. Simon Camish seems to know what he wants from Rose—to be what she is. He thinks of her as "a vision kindly bestowed"—his way back to the ideals that would make his life meaningful. In this sense, he seems to know the direction he seeks, but it is, as we have seen, a direction that represents a compromise, and that emerges from a process of relinquishment. Rose and Simon influence each other in that both relinquish a kind of specialness: Simon gives up possession of Rose, and Rose gives up a level of enacted fanaticism that is both stubborn and childishly omnipotent at its core.

Our most striking example of the emergence of positive goals through a process of mutual influence occurs in *The Magus*. Nicholas begins with a clear wish to intensify his narcissistic defenses—to not have to need anyone, and to co-opt Conchis's power. The goal he eventually develops of pursuing a committed relationship evolves, after arduous work, as the very opposite of his original wishes. Finally, in our failed case, a positive directionality does *not* evolve from the process that takes place between Lily Bart and Lawrence Selden. We have seen how unconscious guilt and unconscious sadism conspire to undermine the pull toward relatedness even in the presence of engagement.

It may be worth emphasizing at this point that our narrative of change works to describe change that proceeds in a totally negative direction.[4] Pierre Laclos's novel, *Les Liaisons Dangereuses*, exemplifies a destructive relationship. The two central characters, Valmont and the marquise, are involved in a relationship in which the quest for revenge is their shared purpose. Although they were once lovers, they now engage to support the aim of revenge on another couple—former partners who have jilted them and subsequently come together in an affair. Valmont and the marquise are drawn together by a shared narcissistic injury resulting from rejection. Mutual influence is strong in this novel (unlike *The House of Mirth*) as each partner keeps the other committed to spiteful and revengeful motives. In our other novels, the sufferer consistently begins with a narcissistic adaptation that becomes more object related through the influence of another character; in *Les Liaisons Dangereuses*, both characters remain narcissistically preoccupied throughout. In fact, much of the drama of the novel centers around Valmont's weakening commitment to this goal (as he falls in love with the young and beautiful Madame de Tourvel) and the marquise's mocking and coercive use of his loyalty to *her* to interdict this development. When the novel ends, Valmont is dead, and the marquise is left with the fruits of a bitter victory, alone and shunned.

HOPE, TRUST, AND TOLERANCE

The idea of common features in different kinds of healing situations is not a new one. In *Persuasion and Healing* Jerome Frank discusses elements of the healing process that apply to widely different situations of influence—from religious conversion and brainwashing to psychotherapy.[5] Frank feels that in all healing situations the sufferer must be in a state of distress and aroused receptivity. Trust in the healer is based on the latter's social status and is strongly enhanced by the healer's optimism, concern, and dedication. Furthermore, the combination of the healer's status and his or her uncritical acceptance of the sufferer leads to an increase in self-esteem and a decrease in shame on the sufferer's part. Once the sufferer enters the healing (or persuasive) situation, a series of repetitive interactions occurs that leads to enhanced cognition, emotional shifts, and changes in attitude and behavior. Frank also feels that the healer mediates between the sufferer and society and is the standard bearer of the direction in which the sufferer is to go. Because he is discussing situations of forced, as well as voluntary, influence, Frank sees the healer as bringing about change through coercion as well as through emulation.

Frank's work is relevant to our study in two ways. His findings contain, by implication, our ideas of engagement, mutual influence, and directionality. In fact, we are putting his findings into a new language that can be applied to another kind of healing situation—literary healing. Furthermore, Frank foreshadows the subjective factors in the sufferer that we have found to be operating in our successful cases and absent in our novel of failure. We will now describe those features of the sufferer's internal experience that, we believe, explain the emotional impact of the change experience.

At the end of Chapter 10, we cited three qualities in our therapist figures that seemed central to facilitating change in our patient figures. To begin with, the therapist must have a strong wish that the patient will change and a firm belief in the patient's capacity to change. *The Accidental Tourist* illustrates this point. Muriel wants Macon to change (so that he will then be willing to marry her), and she holds firm to the belief that he can do so. He is important to her. All our literary therapists have personal agendas, as we have seen, but this does not change the impact of their beliefs on their literary patients. The impact is to arouse, or rearouse, *hope* that change is possible. If the therapist either gives up conviction or never develops belief in the patient's capacities, as is the case in *The House of Mirth*, the process is a failure.

We have seen that admiration for the therapist (or for certain qualities he or she embodies) is a factor enabling engagement to occur and influence to proceed. Of particular importance is the therapist's integrity and adherence to ideals and purpose. Our literary therapists do not compromise their integrity even when they are in danger of losing what they most want. One way or another they "do what is right." Rose's longing for Simon's approbation and friendship never leads to seduction or manipulation on her part. Our literary therapists are not, in themselves, paragons of mental health—witness Rose's violent temper, Muriel's neurotic relationship with her son, Darcy's pride, and Alison's insecurity—but they function reliably in those relationships that are the substance of the process we are exploring. Their behavior enables *trust* to develop.

A third, and crucial quality distinguishes our literary therapists—their ability to withstand tests of their commitment and integrity. These therapist figures show a remarkable ability to tolerate a range of difficult behaviors and enactments from their emotional counterparts, behaviors that are often rejecting, wounding, and sadistic.

They tolerate these behaviors without withdrawal or retaliation, without seeking revenge. They are neither uninvolved nor neutral but somehow their loving or altruistic feelings prevail. We could put this even more strongly and say that our patient figures are allowed to bring their most problematic behaviors into the relationship. In an actual clinical situation, we would be talking about the emergence of the transference neurosis, particularly of negative (hostile) transference elements. Every therapist knows that a therapy that is too friendly and supportive, that is, where negative elements do not emerge, is likely to be of limited value to the patient. Perhaps it is hard to believe in a love that has only been exposed to good behavior; love that has survived hatred and aggression seems more solid.

Our literary therapists know the worst! Let us return to our opening example, from *Pride and Prejudice*, Darcy has been subjected to Elizabeth's sarcasm, wrath, and rejection. He is painfully wounded, but he never turns his back on Elizabeth. Rather, not unlike a therapist, he does two things. He admits an element of justification in her accusations—he has ruined Jane's chances with Bingley—but he also interprets, in effect, through his explanatory letter, Elizabeth's distortions that have allowed her to reverse and misunderstand the Darcy-Wickham situation.

If hope is the outcome of the therapist's belief in the patient's capacity to change, and trust is the outcome of the therapist's integrity and ability not to retaliate, then one of the outcomes of the therapist's tolerance is an inner permission to have insight. One can admit the most problematic parts of oneself because it is safe. Elizabeth has not been paid back in kind; Darcy's response to her outburst is a demonstration of his confidence in her intelligence and honesty. Perhaps, this is what allows her to begin a process of self-examination—"Til this moment I never knew myself." It is precisely Darcy's demonstration of belief in her inherent goodwill, in the face of a demonstration on her part of the very opposite, that is so powerful.

The clinical analog lies in the way therapists tolerate and use their countertransference to deepen understanding. Recent views of countertransference see it as inevitable in the drama that is played out between patient and therapist. Therapists are unconsciously drawn into enactments with their patients that they later are able to process and convey. Like our literary therapists, they get deeply involved, and like these literary figures, they try not to respond in kind. In the case of professional therapists, it is a deliberately cultivated and necessary part of the analytic attitude that keeps the therapist striving toward neutrality and away from hostile actions toward the patient. Literary therapists are motivated more personally—by love, admiration, and need. However, regardless of motive, it is the steadfast belief and reliable behavior of therapists, both real and literary, that is meaningful.

THE HEALING FANTASY

In *The Dynamics of Literary Response* Norman Holland refers to core unconscious fantasies that, when made manageable through literary disguise, explain what appeals to us in literature.[6] He feels each reader discovers and processes personally meaningful fantasies in different texts. In Chapter 7, we discussed the appeal of a children's novel—*The Secret Garden*—in terms of a subtext involving fantasies about growth and development (the approach of puberty). We would like to expand that discussion to the other novels we have examined. Since reader preference seems to have something to do with the underlying fantasies readers discover in texts, our choice of these particular novels is related to our interest in psychological change and how it comes about.

The overarching fantasy suggested by these texts is that relating to others can heal us. This fantasy has, we believe, origins in the wishes and feelings of early childhood. It relates, in part, to our wish to recapture the unquestioning love and acceptance of the early mother-child relationship and, in part, to the wishes for strength and empowerment that relate to both the father-child and mother-child relationship. However, to divide up the fantasy of healing along the lines of specific early relationships is to narrow its scope unnecessarily. Fantasies of being healed cover a broad spectrum of wishes to love and to be loved, to empower and to be empowered. Implicit in these fantasies is the wish to be loved despite one's worst failings. A more technical way of describing this fantasy would be to say that it refers to the development and modification of ego and superego functions. When we speak of ego functions, we are talking about the ability to be effective—in thought, feeling, and action. When we refer to superego functions, we are talking about the area of beliefs and values, how each person "does what is right" in living his or her life.

In one way or another, our literary patients undergo some measure of development or modification in both these broad areas of function. Mary Lennox, being a child, has more to develop than to modify. She lacks both the knowledge and abilities she needs at her age (ego functions), and she needs to develop a better sense of what is right in negotiating with the world (superego guidelines). Simon Camish, on the other hand, has a superego, a punitive and self-depriving one, but he feels himself to be lacking an inner sense of rightness. In modifying both these superego qualities, he becomes less self-depriving and critical and more content with who he is and how he lives. At the same time, the alteration of his narcissistic defenses (part of his ego) enhances his ability to work and relate to others with enjoyment. Jane Eyre and Rochester influence each other in a way that can be described as superego modification. Jane becomes less moralistic and withholding; Rochester learns he cannot always have what he wants and that some things are worth waiting for. Under the combined influence of trauma and a new opportunity, Silas Marner modifies a limiting defensive adaptation to life. Nicholas Urfe is healed in his ability to love; this is a complex change that involves both ego and superego elements. To get to the ability to love, Nicholas must modify defenses and develop a belief in the value of loving another person. In most of our literary examples and in clinical psychotherapeutic work, all parts of the personality are impacted in the process of change.

In Chapter 1 we spoke of our interest in the literary conception of the therapeutic. We wondered if these novels would yield a unitary theory of how people change, some universal process writers tap into in developing their stories. In fact, these nine novels depict a rather broad spectrum of therapeutic experiences. The question is how to classify them in a way that allows for useful comparison with clinical therapeutic theories. *Silas Marner* and *Heidi* provide examples of healing through unquestioning love and acceptance; they suggest comparison to a totally supportive process where defenses are shored up rather than interpreted. *The Accidental Tourist* and *The Secret Garden* provide convincing examples of the "corrective emotional experience" where an expected negative response does not occur, allowing for new behaviors. *The Secret Garden* and *The Magus* illustrate the power of multiple therapeutic modalities; a transference-laden relationship combined with a therapeutic milieu in the former case, and with psychodrama in the latter. *Pride and Prejudice, Jane Eyre, The Needle's Eye,* and *The Magus* depict healing relationships that are intensely interactive and interpretive, lending themselves to closer comparison with the psychoanalytic process.

A useful way of integrating these disparate modalities is to conceptualize them along a spectrum of passivity and activity in the patient's relationship to the therapist. On the passive end would be Silas Marner, who experiences what is happening to him with relatively little insight. His experiences have considerable impact, but he is receptive and acted upon for the most part. In the intermediate part of the spectrum would be the children in *The Secret Garden* and a relatively passive protagonist like Macon Leary. Although insight is part of the picture in these novels, most of the action comes from the therapeutic agents. In contrast, all our other patient figures are actively involved in a process of struggle and self-examination. In fact, literary depictions of change occur along the same spectrum of passivity to activity that we see in the psychotherapies.

Whether active or passive, the core experience of an effective change process has certain recurring elements. There must be readiness, often created by the disruption of an only partially successful adaptation developed early in life. A new person appears, one who is willing to become involved emotionally with the sufferer. The two engage emotionally, with the sense of a new experience, a new start. A pattern of relating develops out of the engagement in which old, negative assumptions are put to the test, and proven wrong. In particular, the helping figure is able to tolerate anger and frustration, and offers a more hopeful point of view. Together, the two develop a direction in their relationship that is positive, and that results in stable internal changes. This is, in effect, our proposal for a model of how gradual intrapsychic change comes about in relationships, whether in therapy, in life, or in fiction.

In conclusion, we have tried to accomplish two things in this book. Drawing on our human fascination with personal growth and transformation, we have tried to draw a parallel between processes of change in literature and in treatment and to show how their similarities can be understood by reference to a common plot or therapeutic narrative for change. Furthermore, we believe that the novels we have chosen for this study appeal to readers because of the themes of transformation through relating that are contained in their stories. Change is difficult; reading about successful change is heartening. Just as novelists describe many of the phenomena of psychotherapy, so, too, a successful psychotherapy is a creative and productive experience of narration.

NOTES

CHAPTER 1

1. A parallel situation in life and literature: We are fully aware of the fact that a fictional character is not comparable to a real person. Our interest is in *processes;* we feel that authors must draw on real or possible patterns of interaction in their plots. The fact that we can find parallels strongly suggests that fiction and reality are drawn from the same base of human experience, and thus that literature can tell us about such interactions.

2. One current school of clinical theory: We refer to the work of Schafer (1983) and Spence (1982), who have developed the metaphor of narrative for discussion of psychoanalytic process.

3. Actual relating based on romantic love: The emergence of romantic love and the concept of childhood in Western culture are described in de Rougemont's *Love in the Western World* (1954) and Aries' *Centuries of Childhood* (1962).

4. Free association: Freud describes the rationale and technique in his 1915 paper, "On Beginning the Treatment," *Standard Edition,* Vol. 12, p. 134.

5. In the 1920s and 1930s: The central works in this later phase of Freud's thinking were *The Ego and the Id* (1923) and *Inhibitions, Symptoms and Anxiety* (1926). The enumeration and dynamics of defenses are described in Anna Freud's *The Ego and the Mechanisms of Defense* (1936). Modern American ego psychology is exemplified by Brenner's *The Mind in Conflict* (1982).

6. The therapeutic dyad: The point of view reflected here is found in a wide variety of psychoanalytic writing: Racker (1957), Jacobs (1991), Hoffman (1992), Renik (1993b).

7. Read a novel in many ways: See footnote 1, this chapter. For a deeper discussion of multiple readings of a text see Eagleton's *Literary Theory* (1983), the chapter on post-structuralism.

8. "The fundamental difference": E. M. Forster, *Aspects of the Novel* (1927), pp. 46-47.

9. "What is interesting": Skura (1981), *The Literary Use of the Psychoanalytic Process,* p. 201.

10. "If I knew what the meanings of my books were": Margaret Drabble, quoted in *Harper's Magazine*, February 1990, p. 38.

CHAPTER 2

1. She cannot, after all, replace Mrs. Bennet: A significant aspect of the resolution of the Oedipal conflict is a positive identification with the parent of the same sex. To make such an identification, the child must be able to love and admire that parent. When the relationship is difficult, the child is left with an unaltered wish to possess the opposite sex parent, with the attendant anxiety and guilt.

2. "Transference neurosis": Freud believed that under the conditions of analysis the patient construes aspects of the analytic relationship in a way that corresponds to the "infantile neurosis," i.e., the conclusions that the child drew about the central relationships in the family. It is the remobilization of these issues in the transference neurosis that enables analytic change. A contemporary view modifies Freud's by suggesting that the analytic relationship is not so much a replay as a new experience constantly being tested against old assumptions.

3. Current models of analytic and therapeutic change: Both clinical and research models now emphasize the mutual and interactive qualities of process. Clinical models include those of Kohut (1984), Hoffman (1992), Renik (1993b), and many others. Research models are exemplified by Jones (1993) and Weiss and Sampson (1987).

4. Narcissistic defenses . . . . hysterical defenses: Narcissistic defenses protect against awareness of distressing feelings by attempting to deny involvement with others who might evoke such feelings. Hysterical defenses repress the feelings, so that, for example, sexual attraction might be replaced by revulsion.

5. Like the good mother: The observation that the parents "pull" the child along developmentally through specific interactional cues is described by Mahler, Pine, and Bergman (1975).

CHAPTER 3

1. Asceticism: Anna Freud (1936) first pointed out this phenomenon of adolescence, a massive defense against the psychic danger of the sexual wishes and arousal that follow the onset of puberty. Asceticism may be carried into action in such socially acceptable ways as entering training for religious orders, or espousing altruistic social causes. It may also appear in a more individual, symptomatic form such as anorexia.

2. Maternal overtones: These observations are drawn from Williams (1989).

3. Aggressiveness of her own superego pressures: In Freud's structural theory, the superego derives its force from the drives. The earlier or more primitive aspects of superego are heavily weighted with aggression (rather than libido) and hence may appear as a particulary harsh conscience.

4. Masochistic: In masochism aggression is turned against the self as a defense against the dangers consequent to hating or attacking the love object. Jane is angry with Rochester for his prior marriage. With St. John she is drawn to a psychological solution in which she merges attachment and hatred turned against the self.

5.   Dreams or extra-therapeutic enactments: In psychoanalysis the impact of events in the treatment may be reflected in the patient's dream life or in his or her actions outside therapy.

6.   "Corrective emotional experience": This is a term introduced by Alexander et al. (1946). In a modification of psychoanalytic technique Alexander proposed that the analyst deliberately react in ways designed to "correct" the problematic tendencies of the patient. This approach has been criticized for its manipulativeness and presumption about what the patient needs. Recently, with a greater recognition of the interactive nature of process, the term has been revived (Renik, 1993a).

CHAPTER 4

1.   The novels of Henry James: See J. V. Creighton's 1985 critical study of Margaret Drabble.

2.   A transference experience: See the chapter on transference in Greenson (1967) for a full elaboration of the phenomenon of transference as it appears in clinical situations.

3.   "Termination" phase: The technical meaning of this term refers to the final stages of a psychoanalytic treatment in which idealizations based on transference wishes are relinquished in favor of a more realistic and limited relationship. Another hallmark of the termination phase is the internalization of some of the therapist's ego capacities and values.

4.   The missing maternal object and her functions: See Kohut, (1971), *The Analysis of the Self.* Kohut elaborates several important concepts having to do with the development of a cohesive sense of self through the use of "self-objects." Kohut's theory postulates two crucial developmental needs, the need to idealize important others and the need for adequate mirroring, in order to develop a sense of worth and meaningful personal values. It is the "idealized self-object" that Rose represents to Simon.

CHAPTER 5

1.   A panic attack: Panic attacks are massive discharges of anxiety characterized by severe physiological symptoms: rapid heartbeat, trembling, sweating, shortness of breath and fear of suffocating or dying. These attacks are triggered in phobic situations or by forbidden unconscious thoughts or wishes. Although there are biochemical factors that predispose certain people to suffer such attacks, from a psychoanalytic point of view they represent a failure of the ego to use anxiety as a *signal* of danger. Defenses cannot be mobilized, and the ego is overwhelmed. See also Freud, (1926), *Inhibitions, Symptoms and Anxiety.*

2.   Parts of Macon's psyche: In this schematic understanding of Macon's psychological situation, we are drawing on Freud's 1923 theory of the tripartite structure of the mind (*The Ego and the Id*). Freud viewed the ego as developing gradually out of the id (the site of unconscious impulses and wishes) to mediate the demands of reality. The superego develops later in life and is the repository of moral values and societal demands. The ego now has to mediate between the id, the superego, and external reality. Also see notes, Chapter 6.

3. Pass certain crucial tests: See Weiss and Sampson (1987) for a discussion of control-mastery theory. In this theory of psychoanalytic process, the patient attempts to assess the safety of the analytic situation through a series of unconscious tests of the analyst's motives and understanding.

4. Lucia Tower: See her 1956 paper on countertransference for one of the earliest and most brilliant discussions of this phenomenon and its necessary role in the analytic process.

CHAPTER 6

1. Psychoanalytic libido theory: Freud's libido theory emphasized the drives. Initially libido, or sexual energy in the widest sense, was the only drive; later, Freud added aggression as a second drive. His ego psychology gave a significant role to the ego, the executive part of the psyche, responsible for mediating between the drives, the outside world, and the superego. Self psychology, developed by Heinz Kohut in the 1970s de-emphasized drives and ego in favor of a psychology that spoke of the subjective experience of self.

2. Object relations: This refers to the internal, subjective representation of relationships. The term derives from Freud's original usage: relatedness was motivated by drive energy. The drive is directed toward an object.

3. Turned away from human objects: Freud's observation of the linkage between anality and the focus on money is well known. An excellent discussion of the syndrome in modern psychoanalytic terms is provided by Shengold (1985).

4. Eliot gives us not only an accessible, "manifest" story: "Manifest" and "latent" refer to levels of awareness in Freud's interpretive approach to the dream. The manifest dream is what the dreamer recalls. The latent dream is the set of meanings that are disguised within the manifest dream. Also see notes, Chapter 9.

5. The chance to "start over": This idea is implicit in Freud's recognition of transference, i.e., that patients project old relationship patterns on the analyst. An elaboration of this idea in terms that emphasize the newness of the analytic relationship is given by Loewald (1960).

6. The world is killed off and protected: Again, the ideas about the protective, defensive function of isolation from involvement are drawn from Shengold (1985).

CHAPTER 7

1. Central metaphors: See Kate Friedlander (1942) and Lily Peller (1958; 1959) for further discussion of the meanings of reading during the latency period.

2. Classification of Sarnoff: See *Latency* (1976) for a definitive discussion of this developmental period.

3. Paralyzing hypochondriacal fears: Colin's illness is hysteria; he suffers from a conversion symptom (hysterical paralysis). This novel was written about fifteen years after Freud published *Studies in Hysteria*. (We doubt that Burnett's use of the illness had anything to do with awareness of Freud's work, but rather represents a description of a common kind of affliction in the late nineteenth century.) In Freud's view, Colin's symptoms would represent a compromise between forbidden unconscious impulses and defenses against their expression. We could hypothesize that Colin cannot directly express the rage he feels at his

abandonment by both his parents. His paralysis expresses that inability, but he certainly takes out his rage on those around him (his father included) through the role of demanding invalid.

4. Drives and drive derivatives: These terms are drawn from Freudian metapsychology. In his final version of the dual instinct theory (*Beyond the Pleasure Principle,* 1920), Freud postulated sexual and aggressive drives as primary unconscious motivators of the psyche. The drives, however, never appear in pure form, but rather in their derivatives, e.g., the wish for closeness, affection, and sexual satisfaction, the wish for separation, power, and achievement.

5. Pathological grief: See Freud's, (1917), "Mourning and Melancholia." Archibald Craven suffers from melancholia—pathological, unresolved grief. His depression, at heart, represents rage at his wife for abandoning him, and at his son for killing her. This rage is turned inward against himself in the form of severe depression.

6. Therapeutic milieu: The term "therapeutic milieu" (also referred to as "therapeutic community") refers to a deliberately developed form of social organization in psychiatric hospitals and other treatment settings for the mentally ill. Milieu treatment is characterized by values and norms of behavior that emphasize group cohesion, patient participation, and treatment of one patient by another. Patients, or members, are immersed in activities and rituals whose goal is to disrupt old maladaptive patterns and establish new modes of behavior that are eventually integrated into healthier ("nonpatient") roles.

CHAPTER 8

1. A symptom that makes her passive and helpless: See Palmer (1988) for a more thorough discussion of Heidi's appeal to latency-aged girls.

CHAPTER 9

1. Preface to the revised version: See John Fowles, (1978), *The Magus.* Although Fowles's 1978 revision of his 1965 novel does not differ substantially from the original, its ending reveals a maturity and self-knowledge on the part of the protagonist that is lacking in the previous version. It is this revised ending that makes *The Magus* suitable for our purposes as a novel with a therapeutic narrative.

2. Nicholas's whole personality: In a clinical setting Nicholas would be described as someone with narcissistic defenses against affect and attachment. He uses illusions of omnipotent power and control to defend against need and loss. A therapeutic relationship would be characterized by powerful resistances that might take the form of remoteness, devaluation of the therapist, and extreme sensitivity to criticism and withdrawal in others.

3. Transference neurosis: See notes, Chapter 2.

4. A dream, a disguised expression of that wish: See Freud (1900), *The Interpretation of Dreams.* Our analysis of Nicholas's experience on Phraxos as a dream is based on Freud's ideas about the meaning and interpretation of dreams. Briefly, Freud hypothesized that all dreams are disguised expressions of infantile wishes, released by the relaxing of the repression barrier during sleep. The latent meaning of the dream may be decoded from its manifest content by the dreamer's

associations. The dreamer uses various forms of disguise—condensation, displacement, and symbolization—to keep the true meaning of the dream hidden from consciousness.

CHAPTER 10

1. The repetition compulsion: This is a term first used by Freud in "Remembering, Repeating and Working Through," which appeared in *Papers on Technique* (1911-1915). Freud is referring to a tendency (based on the persistence of wishes in the unconscious) to repeat behaviors, even maladaptive ones, despite insight and conscious motivation to change. Unresolved conflict is *remembered* in the form of actions that repeat experiences of the past.

2. Henrietta Pollitt: She is the heroine of Christina Stead's 1940 novel, *The Man Who Loved Children.*

3. Louis Auchincloss: See the excellent afterword in Wharton (1905), *The House of Mirth.*

4. That plot in tragedy: See Bennett Simon's 1984 paper for further discussion of the similarities between plot development in tragedy and certain kinds of psychoanalytic developments.

5. "Surprise and self-consciousness": See Skura, (1981), *The Literary Use of the Psychoanalytic Process,* p. 200.

6. "Primal scene" image: This is a psychoanalytic concept that encapsulates the young child's intense curiosity and powerful fantasies about the parent's sexual activities, from which he or she is excluded. Whether or not children are exposed to this activity, they develop fantastical ideas about the aggressive and sexual nature of the parental physical relationship.

7. "Negative therapeutic reaction": This is a term originally coined by Freud in *The Ego and the Id* (1923) to describe patients who get *worse* whenever they seem to be getting better in psychoanalysis. Freud attributed this phenomenon to unconscious guilt and the need for punishment. Contemporary psychoanalytic writers have developed additional explanations including the wish to stay ill in order to hold onto dependent gratifications and the wish, stemming from unconscious envy, to destroy the treatment.

CHAPTER 11

1. A transitional space: See Winnicott, (1951), "Transitional Objects and Transitional Phenomena." The concept of transitional space is related to Winnicott's ideas about the transitional object. Just as the child's teddy bear is neither part of himself nor part of the mother it represents, transitional space is located neither in intrapsychic nor outside reality, but rather somewhere in between. It is where fantasy and creativity take place, the arena of illusion and cultural experience.

2. A severe narcissistic wound: See Forster, (1928), *The Life of Charles Dickens,* for a more complete discussion of this seminal event in Dickens' life.

3. In a letter to us on this question: Letter dated April 21, 1991, from Margaret Drabble to one of the authors (BA).

4. Totally negative direction: See Laclos, (1989), *Les Liaisons Dangereuses.*

5.   Elements of the healing process: See Frank, (1981), *Persuasion and Healing*, for a scholarly discussion of the healing process as it occurs across a wide spectrum of social phenomena.

6.   Core unconscious fantasies: Holland, (1968), *The Dynamics of Literary Response*, uses this concept to elucidate an important feature of reader response, the unconscious elements in the emotional response to texts.

SELECTED BIBLIOGRAPHY

Abend, S. (Ed.). (1990). Issue on psychoanalytic process. *Psychoanalytic Quarterly, 59*.

Abrams, S. (1987). The psychoanalytic process. *International Journal of Psychoanalysis, 68*, 441–452.

Alexander, F., French, T. M., et al. (1946). *Psychoanalytic therapy.* New York: Ronald Press.

Almond, B. (1989). The secret garden: A therapeutic metaphor. *Psychoanalytic Study of the Child, 45*, 477–494.

———. (1990). A healing relationship in Margaret Drabble's novel *The needle's eye. Annual of Psychoanalysis, 19*, 91–106.

———. (1992). The accidental therapist: Intrapsychic change in a novel. *Literature and Psychology, 38*, 84–104.

Almond, R. (1974). *The healing community: Dynamics of the therapeutic milieu.* New York: Jason Aronson, Inc.

———. (1989). Psychological change in Jane Austen's *Pride and prejudice. Psychoanalytic Study of the Child, 44*, 307–324.

———. (1992). *Silas Marner:* Psychological change in fiction, *Annual of Psychoanalysis, 20*, 171–190.

———. (1995). The analytic role: A mediating influence in the interplay of transference and countertransference, *Journal of the American Psychoanalytic Association, 43*, 469–494.

Aries, P. (1962). *Centuries of childhood: A social history of family life.* New York: Alfred A. Knopf.

Austen, J. (1982). *Pride and prejudice.* New York: Washington Square Press. (Original work published 1813)

Benedek, T. (1959). Parenthood as a developmental phase. *Journal of the American Psychoanalytic Association, 78*, 389–417.

Bettelheim, B. (1976). *The uses of enchantment.* New York: Alfred A. Knopf.

Bird, B. (1972). Notes on transference: Universal phenomenon and hardest part of analysis. *Journal of the American Psychoanalytic Association, 20,* 267–301.

Boesky, D. (1990). The psychoanalytic process and its components. *Psychoanalytic Quarterly , 59,* 550–584.

Bornstein, B. (1951). On latency. *Psychoanalytic Study of the Child, 5,* 279–285.

Brenner, C. (1982). *The mind in conflict.* New York: International Universities Press.

Breuer, J., & Freud, S. (1893–1895). Studies on hysteria. *Standard Edition, 2,* 3–309.

Brontë, C. (1988). *Jane Eyre.* Toronto: Bantam Books. (Original work published 1847)

Burnett, F. H. (1984). *The secret garden.* New York: Dell. (Original work published 1911)

Calev, V. (1987). The process in psychoanalysis. *Dialogue, 7,* 13–21.

Creighton, J. V. (1985). *Margaret Drabble.* London and New York: Methuen.

de Rougemont, D. (1954). *Love in the western world.* Boston: Beacon Press.

Dickens, C. (1850). *David Copperfield.* Chilton, MA: The Colonial Press.

———. (1861). *Great Expectations.* Chilton, MA: The Colonial Press.

Drabble, M. (1972). *The needle's eye.* New York: Alfred A. Knopf.

Eagleton, T. (1983). *Literary theory.* Minneapolis: University of Minnesota Press.

Eliot, G. (1981). *Silas Marner.* New York: Signet Classics Edition. (Original work published 1861)

Erikson, E. (1959). Identity and the life cycle. *Psychological Issues Monograph 1.* New York: International Universities Press.

Forster, E. M. (1927). *Aspects of the novel.* New York: Harcourt, Brace and Company.

Forster, J. (1928). *The life of Charles Dickens.* New York: Doubleday, Doran and Co. Inc. (Original work published 1871–74)

Fowles, J. (1978). *The magus.* New York: Dell. (Original work published 1965)

Frank, J. (1981). *Persuasion and healing* (3rd ed.). Baltimore: Johns Hopkins Univ. Press.

Fraser, R. (1988). *The Brontës: Charlotte Brontë and her family.* New York: Fawcett Columbine.

Freud, A. (1936). Instinctual anxiety during puberty. *Collected Works* (Vol. 2, pp. 152–172).

———. (1936). *The ego and the mechanisms of defense.* New York: International Universities Press.

Freud, S. (1900). *The interpretation of dreams. Standard Edition,* 4 & 5.

———. (1905). Fragment of an analysis of a case of hysteria. *Standard Edition, 7,* 3–122.

———. (1908). Creative writers and day–dreaming. *Standard Edition, 9,* 141–153.

———. (1911–15). *Papers on technique. Standard Edition, 12,* 89–171.

———. (1912). The dynamics of transference. *Standard Edition, 12,* 97–108.

———. (1917). Mourning and melancholia. *Standard Edition, 14,* 243–258.

———. (1920). *Beyond the pleasure principle. Standard Edition, 18,* 7–64.

———. (1921). *Group psychology and the analysis of the ego. Standard Edition, 18,* 69–143.

———. (1923). *The ego and the id. Standard Edition, 19,* 3–59.

———. (1926). *Inhibitions, symptoms and anxiety. Standard Edition, 20,* 87–184.

Friedlander, K. (1942). Children's books and their function in latency and prepuberty. *American Imago, 3,* 129–148.

Garis, R. (1968). Learning experiences and change. In B. Southam (Ed.), *Critical essays on Jane Austen.* London: Routledge & Kegan Paul.

Gill, M. M. (1982). *The analysis of transference.* New York: International Universities Press.

Goldberg, A. (1988). Changing psychic structure through treatment: From empathy to self–reflection, *Journal of the American Psychoanalytic Association, 36,* 211–224.

Gray, P. (1990). The nature of therapeutic action in psychoanalysis. *Journal of the American Psychoanalytic Association, 38,* 1083–1098.

Greenacre, P. (1954). The role of transference. *Journal of the American Psychoanalytic Association, 2,* 671–684.

Greenberg, J., & Mitchell, J. (1983). *Object relations in psychoanalytic theory.* Cambridge: Harvard University Press.

Greenson, R. (1967). *The technique and practice of psychoanalysis.* New York: International Universities Press.

Hannay, J. (1986). *The intertextuality of fate: A study of Margaret Drabble.* Columbia: University of Missouri Press.

Hardy, J. (1985). *Jane Austen's heroines.* Boston: Methuen.

Harley, M. (1971). Some reflections on identity problems in prepuberty. In J. McDevitt & C. Settlage (Eds.), *Separation-Individuation* (pp. 385–403). New York: International Universities Press. (Original work published 1962)

Hartmann, H. (1958). *The ego and the problem of adaptation.* New York: International Universities Press. (Original work published 1939)

Hoffman, I. Z. (1992). Expressive participation and psychoanalytic discipline. *Contemporary Psychoanalysis, 28,* 1–14.

Holland, N. (1968). *The dynamics of literary response.* New York: Columbia University Press.

Jacobs, T. J. (1991). *The use of the self.* Madison, CT: International Universities Press.

James, W. (1902). *The varieties of religious experience.* New Hyde Park: University Books.

Jones, E. E., et al. (1993). A paradigm for single case research: The time-series study of a long-term psychotherapy for depression. *Journal of Consulting and Clinical Psychology, 61,* 381–394.

Kohut, H. (1971). *The analysis of the self.* New York: International Universities Press.

———. (1977). *The restoration of the self.* New York: International Universities Press.

———. (1984). *How does analysis cure?* Chicago: University of Chicago Press.

Laclos, C. (1989). *Les liaisons dangereuses.* New York: Bantam Books. (Original work published 1782)

Levinson, D. (1978). *The seasons of a man's life.* New York: Alfred A. Knopf.

Lewis, R. W. B. (1975). *Edith Wharton.* New York: Harper and Row.

Lindemann, E. (1979). *Beyond grief.* New York: Jason Aronson.

Loewald, H. W. (1960). On the therapeutic action of psychoanalysis. *International Journal of Psychoanalysis, 41*, 16–33.

Mahler, M., Pine, F., & Bergman, A. (1975). *The psychological birth of the human infant*. New York: Basic Books.

Mayer, E. L. (1985). Everybody must be just like me: Female castration anxiety. *International Journal of Psychoanalysis, 66*, 331–348.

Palmer, A. (1988). Heidi's metaphoric appeal to latency. *Psychoanalytic Study of the Child, 43*, 387–397.

Paris, B. (1978). *Character and conflict in Jane Austen's novels*. Detroit: Wayne State University Press.

Peller, L. E. (1958). Reading and daydreams in latency. *Journal of the American Psychoanalytic Association, 6*, 57–70.

―――. (1959). Daydreams and children's favorite books. *Psychoanalytic Study of the Child, 14*, 414–433.

Poovey, M. (1988). The anathematized race: *The governess and Jane Eyre*. In *Uneven developments: The ideological work of gender in mid-Victorian England*. Chicago: University of Chicago Press.

Racker, H. (1957). The meanings and uses of countertransference. *Psychoanalytic Quarterly, 26*, 303–357.

Renik, O. (1993a). Analytic interaction: Conceptualizing technique in light of the analyst's irreducible subjectivity. *Psychoanalytic Quarterly, 62*, 553–571.

―――. (1993b). Countertransference enactment and the psychoanalytic process. In M. J. Horowitz, O. F. Kernberg, & E. M. Weinshel (Eds.), *Psychic structure and psychic change. Essays in honor of Robert Wallerstein, M.D.* Madison, CT: International Universities Press.

Rich, A. (1982). *Jane Eyre*, a tale. In *On lies, secrets, and silence*. New York: W. W. Norton.

Rinaker, C. (1936). A psychoanalytic note on Jane Austen. *Psychoanalytic Quarterly, 5*, 108–115.

Rothenberg, A. (1988). *The creative process of psychotherapy*. New York: Norton.

Sarnoff, C. (1976). *Latency*. New York: Jason Aronson

Schafer, R. (1983). *The analytic attitude*. New York: Basic Books.

Scharfman, M. (1979). Conceptualizing the nature of therapeutic action of psychoanalysis. *Journal of the American Psychoanalytic Association, 27*, 627–642.

Settlage, C. (1985). Adult development and therapeutic process. Paper presented at the Edward G. Billings' Lectureship on Clinical Implications of Adult Development, Denver, CO.

Shapiro, T. & Perry, R. (1976). Latency revisited. *Psychoanalytic Study of the Child, 31*, 79–105.

Shengold, L. (1985). Defensive anality and anal narcissism. *International Journal of Psychoanalysis, 66*, 47–73.

Simon, B. (1984). "With cunning delays and evermounting excitement": Or what thickens the plot in tragedy and in psychoanalysis. In Chicago Psychoanalytic Society and the Chicago Institute for Psychoanalysis Conference, *Psychoanalysis: Emotions and behavior monographs* (Vol. 3, pp. 387–435).

Skura, M. (1981). *The literary use of the psychoanalytic process.* New Haven: Yale University Press.

Spence, D. (1982). *Narrative truth and historical truth.* New York: Norton.

Spyri, J. (1956). *Heidi.* Harmondsworth: Penguin Books. (Original work published 1880)

Stead, C. (1940). *The man who loved children.* New York: Avon Press.

Tower, L. (1956). Countertransference. *Journal of the American Psychoanalytic Association, 4,* 224–255.

Tyler, A. (1985). *The acccidental tourist.* New York: Alfred A. Knopf.

Wallerstein, R. (1988). Assessment of structural change in psychoanalytic therapy and research. *Journal of the American Psychoanalytic Association, 36,* 241–262.

Watt, I. (1957). *The rise of the novel.* Berkeley: University of California Press.

Weinshel, E. (1984). Some observations on the psychoanalytic process. *Psychoanalytic Quarterly, 53,* 63–92.

Weiss, J. & Sampson, H. (1987). *The psychoanalytic process.* New York: Guilford Press.

Wharton, E. (1905). *The house of mirth.* New York: New American Library.

Williams, C. (1989). Closing the book: The intertextual end of *Jane Eyre.* In Jerome McGann (Ed.), *Victorian connections.* Charlottesville: University of Virginia Press.

Winnicott, D. W. (1971). Transitional objects and transitional phenomena. In *Playing and reality.* London: Tavistock. (Original work published 1951)

INDEX

About the Authors

BARBARA ALMOND is a Clinical Assistant Professor in the Department of Psychiatry at Stanford University Medical Center. She received her M.D. from Yale University and did her psychiatric training at Georgetown and Stanford. Dr. Almond is an advanced candidate at the San Francisco Psychoanalytic Institute and has a private practice in Palo Alto, CA.

RICHARD ALMOND is a member of the faculty at the San Francisco Psychoanalytic Institute and is Clincial Professor of Psychiatry at the Stanford University School of Medicine. Dr. Almond received his M.D. from Yale University and did his psychiatric training at Yale. He is the author of *The Healing Community* (1974) and is currently in private practice in Palo Alto, CA.

ISBN 0-275-95362-9

90000>

9 780275 953621

HARDCOVER BAR CODE